MOVIE-MADE LOS ANGELES

Contemporary Approaches to Film and Media Series

A complete listing of the books in this series can
be found online at wsupress.wayne.edu.

GENERAL EDITOR

Barry Keith Grant
Brock University

MOVIE-MADE
LOS ANGELES

JOHN TRAFTON

WAYNE STATE UNIVERSITY PRESS
DETROIT

ISBN 9780814347768 (paperback)
ISBN 9780814347775 (hardcover)
ISBN 9780814347782 (e-book)

Library of Congress Control Number: 2022951625

Cover photo by John Trafton. Cover design by Chelsea Hunter.

Grateful acknowledgment is made to the Leonard and Harriette Simons Endowed Family Fund and the Thelma Gray James Fund for the generous support of the publication of this volume.

Wayne State University Press rests on Waawiyaataanong, also referred to as Detroit, the ancestral and contemporary homeland of the Three Fires Confederacy. These sovereign lands were granted by the Ojibwe, Odawa, Potawatomi, and Wyandot Nations, in 1807, through the Treaty of Detroit. Wayne State University Press affirms Indigenous sovereignty and honors all tribes with a connection to Detroit. With our Native neighbors, the press works to advance educational equity and promote a better future for the earth and all people.

Wayne State University Press
Leonard N. Simons Building
4809 Woodward Avenue
Detroit, Michigan 48201-1309

Visit us online at wsupress.wayne.edu.

Contents

Acknowledgments

This journey began while I was visiting Los Angeles during the summer of 2010. For "beach reading," I brought my worn-out copy of Mike Davis's *City of Quartz: Excavating the Future in Los Angeles*, and a secret history of L.A. unfolded everywhere I ventured. Thus, my first thank-you goes to the late Mike Davis for planting the seed of this project. I enjoyed our correspondence over the years, and his work has supplied valuable frameworks for reading Los Angeles's history and interpreting the lasting influence of its visual culture. He will be greatly missed.

For years, I had heard about Thom Andersen's legendary video essay *Los Angeles Plays Itself* but never had the chance to see it until its release to the public in 2014. I watched it while on a plane to Los Angeles, and I was instantly hooked—I would watch it several more times that week alone. A big thank-you to Andersen for his film, which propelled this project from thought to reality and has inspired both my research and teaching.

Having grown up in Los Angeles, I know firsthand how cinema infiltrates and shapes various aspects of L.A. life. It was no surprise that I found film noir parallels in the research phase of this project, driving from archive to archive in L.A. in pursuit of the truth, like Mike Hammer in *Kiss Me Deadly* or Phillip Marlowe in *The Big Sleep* or *The Long Goodbye*. Some key characters in this hard-boiled mystery: John Cahoon from the Natural History Museum of Los Angeles's Seaver Center for Western History; Maya Montañez Smukler from the UCLA Film and Television Archive; Jean Stern and Dora James from the Irvine Art Museum; and Mark Hilbert from the Hilbert Museum at Chapman University. Thank

you all for your help with this project. Other archives and research librar-
ies that provided crucial resources: the Huntington Research Library, the
Margaret Herrick Library, Claremont Colleges Library, and the Cal Arts
Valencia Special Collections.

I have been privileged to meet and learn from so many brilliant
scholars during this project. My thanks to Gordon McClelland for guidance while researching Southern California scene painting and the
movement's influence on cinematic practices. Meeting with David E.
James at USC film school one sunny afternoon helped propel the project in exciting and refreshing directions, as did his book *The Most Typical Avant-Garde: History and Geography of Minor Cinemas in Los Angeles*.
James Tweedie's influence on this project cannot be overstated, as I write
these acknowledgments a few minutes from his University of Washington office. Tweedie's work on modern architecture and cinematic design
played a significant role in my approach to key aspects of this book, so
my most sincere thanks to him. My thanks to Brian Jacobson and Rene
Bruckner for their influential work on early Hollywood and for their
support of the project. I am grateful as well to Barbara Lamprecht, Elliot
Simon, and Raymond Neutra for support, encouragement, and providing
a unique look into the Richard and Dion Neutra papers. Additionally,
my thanks to Eileen Rositzka for being an early supporter of the project,
whose work on cinematic cartography and poetics echoes throughout
this book. Rest in peace, Eileen.

What a pleasure it has been to work with Wayne State University
Press. I would like to thank Marie Sweetman for her support, encouragement, and thoughtfulness at every stage of this journey. Thanks as well
to Barry Grant for believing in the project and for his invaluable feedback
and support throughout the process.

I have had the good fortune to work with inspiring and supportive
colleagues. First, I would like to thank my mentor and friend Robert
Burgoyne—for his wisdom, guidance, and encouragement. At Seattle
University, a warm thank-you to Kirsten Thompson, Alex Johnston,
and Benjamin Schultz-Figueroa for their support and thoughtful sug-
gestions. What an honor it is to call them my friends and colleagues.
From the Seattle International Film Festival, I would like to thank Megan
Garbayo-Lopez, Dustin Kaspar, Beth Barrett, and all the amazing SIFF

movie lovers who approached me after each talk with ideas and suggestions in cinephile friendship.

Last, 1 would like to thank my friends and family. Thank you to Mom, Dad, Roland, and Katherine. Love and gratitude to Urmi, Devang, Navnit, and Gita. And much love and thanks to Pari for believing in me every step of the way.

Introduction

"300 Days of Sunshine"

The world dreamed of cinema throughout the nineteenth century. Large-scale panorama paintings of great battles and cityscapes anticipated the IMAX experience. Magic lantern shows brought the spirits of the dead to life, literally with smoke and mirrors. An American landscape, scorched by a horrific civil war, was documented through photography. Photo development technology expanded alongside studio networks, putting these images in rapid circulation with increased accessibility. Portable painting equipment, such as collapsible easels and paint tubes, enabled the artist to paint outside, chasing the sunlight in ways that foreshadowed outdoor cinematography. These art forms cemented narrative strategies for engaging the sensoria that were readily adopted by film pioneers, who, by the 1910s, took these techniques westward from the production houses of New York, New Jersey, and Chicago. Their destination was a city at the heart of a thriving agricultural economy that was experiencing a rapid population boom and a flourishing real estate market. At this time, Los Angeles was quickly becoming the largest city on the West Coast, up from being the 187th largest city in the nation nearly thirty years earlier.[1] But why was Los Angeles chosen as the place where cinema would flower as an art form? It is because Los Angeles was a cinematic city before the movies arrived.

Traditional narratives about why the movies came to Los Angeles tend to center on two factors. First, the city's proximity to the Mexican border, as legend has it, provided an easy escape route to evade patent agents. This story ties in with the allegation that the term *movie* originated as a pejorative. The residents of a community known as Hollywood Ranch at the dawn of the twentieth century used the word to describe the motion picture showmen who had formed "movie camps" operating in the nearby canyons. This dry community founded by Kansas prohibitionists took a hostile view of the "movies" as a threat to the decency of their churchgoing community, lending credence to these early filmmakers being ranked as "outlaws."[2] While this story "makes for a good legend," as Carey McWilliams has noted, it has been debunked as a fantastical creation myth that Hollywood loves to tell about itself.[3] The filmmakers who set up movie camps and eventually studios in Los Angeles were hardly outlaws, as most had already formed an alliance under the Motion Picture Patent Company agreement of 1908, which largely exempted their films from patent restrictions.[4] It is also worth noting that at the time of these so-called outlaw filmmakers, Mexico was only accessible by train or by 130 miles of dirt road inhospitable to motor vehicles carrying hundreds of pounds of film equipment.[5]

The second factor, the promise of ideal outdoor shooting locations, is partly true, though it provides an incomplete picture. Southern California is a Mediterranean environmental system. This is the rarest of the Earth's major ecosystems, covering between 3 percent to 5 percent of the planet's surface. Elsewhere, it is found in the classic Mediterranean (Spain, France, Italy, and Greece), Central Chile, the coastal portions of Western and South Australia, and South Africa's Cape Province.[6] As a result, the phrase "300 Days of Sunshine" became a popular marketing slogan aimed at enticing filmmakers to relocate to Southern California.[7] While the region's climate certainly did provide filmmakers with ideal conditions for outdoor shooting, this explanation is largely the product of regional booster rhetoric aimed at real estate sales, internalized by an emerging Los Angeles–based film industry eager to write its own history. As Brian Jacobson asks, "If the region's fabled natural lighting was so desirable," why then did early L.A. studios use East Coast studio styles of light-regulating glass and electrical alternatives to sunlight?[8] Furthermore, the 300 Days of Sunshine slogan was often accompanied by "Edenic iconography," visuals that "emphasized the Mediterranean climate and pastoral fertility of the city" in stark contrast to the "over-populated, ugly, polluted and dangerous urban-industrial cities of the Midwest and East Coast."⁹ This "Edenic iconography" included photographic albums of Santa Monica beach camps, travel brochures inviting visitors to take part in scenes from popular novels set in Old California, and the vibrantly colored labels on boxes of oranges shipped back east, visible evidence of what a naturalistic California lifestyle had to offer. The trope of 300 Days of Sunshine, therefore, needs to be reread within a broader discussion of visual culture and an industry of mythmaking.

At the dawn of the twentieth century, Los Angeles was home to an industry of image production and image circulation for public consumption, geared directly toward growing the region's population. Through their visual language and distribution practices, these images positioned California as a land of place substitution and transformative experience. Photography distinguished itself from popular painted spectacles through widely distributed photography albums (still and stereoscopic) and by directly aiding the Southern Pacific Railroad Company in opening the region to the rest of nation. By contrast, California painters would give art traditions that were fading in Europe a new lease on life in the California sun. These California impressionists (dismissively referred to by critics as the Eucalyptus School) would advance a popular mythology of the region in partnership with prominent California real estate promoters who, in turn, gave these artists nationwide exposure. The signature colors of these outdoor painters were also used in the visual marketing of real estate, agribusiness, and health retreats, industries that often partnered with the Los Angeles Chamber of Commerce to stimulate migration. Though California impressionism would decline in popularity by the 1920s, the movement supplied film artisans with techniques for animation, special effects, scenic design, and film promotion. California tourism drew on the iconography and signature styles of both photography and painting to create immersive experiences that cast participants as conquerors of the Wild West. Additionally, California tourism was infused with a cultural mythology of the state's Spanish and Mexican colonial past, offering proto-cinematic experiences to those who ventured to the land of sunshine. A different story of both Los Angeles and American film emerges when one considers how pre-cinema visual culture was practiced in Southern California in a way that provided filmmakers with a template for patterning the imaginations of spectators and building a mythmaking business.

Los Angeles is not unique when it comes to cities projecting popular images of themselves through visual culture and narrative art. The same can be said about London, Paris, Venice, and other major European cultural centers throughout the nineteenth century. Nor would Los Angeles be the only city to accomplish this feat during the twentieth century, as Seoul, Tokyo, Mumbai, and Mexico City readily come to mind. What makes Los Angeles an interesting case study, however, is that its exponential growth from 1880 to 1920 came on the heels of crucial technological advances in the visual and narrative arts: mammoth glass plate technology for producing panoramic photography; the invention of the metal paint tube in 1841 by John Goffe Rand, which allowed for painting to take place outside of a studio setting; stereoscopic viewing devices that added depth and theatrical staging to still photographs; dioramas and similarly designed exhibition halls for displaying painted panoramas; and, of course, the advent of motion picture technology in a variety of formats, some of which were pioneered in California and the American West (such as Eadweard Muybridge's galloping horse experiment).

The city of Los Angeles also emerged when visual culture demonstrated for movie pioneers new ways of envisioning cinematic spectators. Panoramic and stereoscopic photography of Southern California not only provided a visual cartography of the region for potential investors and migrants, it also offered immersive and participatory experiences of a land known nationwide as "semi-tropical California." Painting, tourism promotions, and real estate marketing were encoded with colors and symbols linked to a state mythology, promising the weary traveler a fantasy life. Immersion, participatory experience, and fantasy life were elements of visual culture forms in L.A. and Southern California that provided a template for moviemakers on how to organize the visual arts into a world-building business network. Thus, the earlier Hollywood studios that emerged in the neighborhoods of Echo Park, Los Feliz, Silver Lake, and Culver City from approximately 1909 to 1920 can be read as multimedia organizations from the outset.

By 1917, motion pictures had superseded other visual culture forms as the primary booster of Southern California life. This is significant for two reasons. First, this is the time that most historians place as the start of the Hollywood studio system. Famous Players–Lasky, which would later become Paramount Pictures, formed in 1916. Metro Pictures, Goldwyn

Pictures, and Louis B. Mayer Pictures, the three cornerstones of MGM, were formed in 1915, 1916, and 1918 respectively. Universal Pictures opened its new studio facility in 1915, relocating from the Hollywood Blondeau Tavern at Sunset and Gower to what is now known as Universal City, nestled against the San Fernando Valley side of the Hollywood Hills. The rise of the studios around this time effectively set the stage for what is considered classic Hollywood cinema and ended what Charlie Keil terms "the transitional period": roughly 1907 to 1915, when motion pictures were characterized by an increased narrative complexity, greater individuation of characters, and more attention to "narratively relevant, spatial relationships" achieved through mise-en-scène.[10]

The second reason is that this is the moment when Los Angeles fully emerged as what Allen J. Scott describes as a "cultural economy": a "group of sectors [or] culture product industries" that produce goods and services whose "subjective meaning is high in comparison to their utilitarian purpose." In a cultural economy (or "dream factory" as Hollywood became known), "every domain of social life, including capitalism itself, [becomes] a legitimate site of cultural production."[11] This book looks at how Hollywood, an industry based on world building and place substitution, was the product of Los Angeles's visual culture: a constellation of cross-pollinated aesthetic forms and attractions that narrativized the region and promised travelers a transformative experience. Photography, painting, tourist attractions, and architecture—as the following chapters show—coded Southern California as an immersive, performative space in which the spectator was invited to participate in a quest for self-actualization.

This book's title, an homage to the work of Robert Sklar, also suggests a reciprocal relationship between film and the city of Los Angeles that continued after Hollywood's ascendancy toward the end of the 1910s. For example, as shown in chapter 6, Southern California eclectic architecture (the comingling of historical styles in home design) was directly inspired by motion picture settings and production design practices, marketed to a rapidly growing population that was becoming increasingly familiar with film's visual language. By contrast, modern homes that had become synonymous with affluent Los Angeles life (largely through the legacies of Richard Neutra and Rudolph Schindler) exhibit cinematic design thinking: taking into consideration how light impacts objects and how procession can be manipulated. Both architecture styles can be read, alongside California photography, tourist attractions, and painting movements, as wedded to broader practices of place substitution. The reputation of the region as a land of transposable otherness was firmly entrenched by the start of the twentieth century, inspiring motion picture industry practices that were utilized and expanded on throughout the rest of the century. The cycle can thus be read: (1) Los Angeles grew from a dusty, backwater town (overshadowed regionally by San Francisco) into an economic powerhouse through a mythmaking industry, (2) the city's most visible industry, moving pictures, assumed control of the mythmaking industry (reorchestrating popular art forms and narrative strategies), (3) the movies projected popular images of the city through cinematic language and practices, and (4) the city absorbed these popular images and projected them back through a variety of multimediascapes. One could argue (as Paul Karlstrom does) that Los Angeles effectively entered the twentieth century as a postmodernist city.[12]

MEMORY RETRIEVAL: LOS ANGELES FILM STUDIES

> Like many adventurous businessmen of the day, [the boosters] claimed to be possessed by the evangelical spirit. But they were selling something even grander than leather-tooled editions of the good book. They were selling the City on the Hill as prime real estate, in its entirety, including the hill itself, which was located near the new train station immediately downtown, near full city lots for sale, along newly paved streets, with a view of good farmland for sale in the valleys surrounding.
> —Norman M. Klein, *The History of Forgetting*

My research for this book was catapulted by two key texts. In *City of Quartz*, Mike Davis identifies several categories of "Los Angeles intellectuals" who contributed to shaping the city's self-image in the first half of the twentieth century. While each of these groups intersect with visual arts in some manner, the first two—the Boosters and the Debunkers—are crucial to understanding the formation of Los Angeles as a cultural economy during the 1910s and 1920s. The Boosters sold California as an American Eden through popular magazines, poetry, painting, and stage plays—a myth industry constructed through a sanitized presentation of the region's Spanish/Mexican colonial past and a romanticization of the area's physical landscape. For example, the first editor of the *Los Angeles Times*, Charles Fletcher "Don Carlos" Lummis (1859–1928), presented Southern California as an *Americana paradiso* in the pages of his magazines *Land of Sunshine* and *Out West*, an endeavor supported by the Los Angeles Chamber of Commerce and intersecting with the desert health movements at the turn of the century. Largely operating out of the Pasadena area, the Boosters (or the Arroyo group, named after the Arroyo Seco dry riverbed that runs through Pasadena) constructed a "comprehensive fiction of Southern California as the promised land of a millenarian Anglo-Saxon racial odyssey," and "imagery, motifs, values, and legends" they promoted were in turn "endlessly reproduced by Hollywood."[13]

The Debunkers, by contrast, were class-conscious writers, journalists, and artists who deconstructed booster mythology by centering "class violence" in the "construction of the city" and skewered the "garden city ethos celebrated by the Arroyans."[14] Davis places the writings of Upton Sinclair and Carey McWilliams as prime literary examples, though he also cites the Group of Independent Artists of Los Angeles's exhibition in 1923 as a strong debunking statement from local cubists, dynamists, and expressionists against the aforementioned impressionist landscape artists who visually perpetrated boosterism. I use this clash between boosterism and anti-boosterism in this book as a framework for understanding the duality of Los Angeles's self-image construction that emerged from the film industry and interconnected sectors of L.A.'s cultural economy. Additionally, as much of Los Angeles's early twentieth-century self-image was orchestrated through a whitewashed story of California's Hispanic and indigenous past, the Booster/Debunker framework borrowed from Davis and used in this book is intended to energize conversations around film history and representation, especially when one considers that present-day Los Angeles is one of the most diverse cities in the world.

The other text is Thom Andersen's documentary/video essay *Los Angeles Plays Itself*, whose wide commercial release in 2014 was partly the genesis for this book. "If we can appreciate documentaries for their fictional qualities, then perhaps we can appreciate fictional films for their documentary revelations," notes Andersen in the film (narrated by Encke King), suggesting that a history of the city can be gleaned from Los Angeles cinema. Beginning with the idea that Los Angeles is the "most photographed city in the world" but at the same time it "is the least photogenic," the film is a symphony about Los Angeles cinema told in three movements: "The City as Subject," "The City as Character, Part I," and "The City as Character, Part II." These movements are followed by a coda that argues for a form of L.A. neorealist cinema: films that depict a "city of walkers" and bus riders. This book is inspired by the way Andersen explores the city's image construction through film, arguing that the region's pre-cinema visual culture played a key role not only in developing Los Angeles into a cultural economy but also in providing the cinema with the visual grammar for creating the city as a subject or character.

Both *Los Angeles Plays Itself* and *City of Quartz* challenge the idea that L.A. is anywhere and nowhere by persuasively asserting that L.A. is a *somewhere*. For Davis and Andersen, that *somewhere* is a "socially polarized" city whose sense of history and public space has been systematically destroyed by neoliberal assaults and globalization. Here, I bring in another text that played an instrumental role in how I frame my research and explore the ways that the early motion picture industry reorchestrated the practices and strategies of pre-cinema visual culture. In Vincent Brook's *Land of Smoke and Mirrors: A Cultural History of Los Angeles*, the *palimpsest* is used as the master metaphor for the cover-up and the "bleeding through" of Los Angeles's history. Literally from the Greek and Latin meaning "scraped clean and used again," palimpsests were ancient and medieval manuscripts designed to be written on, erased (washed over in white paint), and written over again.[15] In writing this book, I found the palimpsest metaphor an incredibly useful framework for exploring how cinema and prior forms of visual culture contributed to the historical and cultural erasure of Los Angeles's past through their positioning of the region as a land of place substitution. The by-product of place substitution, or the creation of Los Angeles as an *anyspace*, is a historical erasure of Los Angeles as a specific place existing in a specific time. In response, this book uses the palimpsest metaphor to frame scholarship on Los Angeles and cinema as performing a recovery of these palimpsest layers, rewriting the city from an *anyspace* (or a "non-space") to a recontextualized space belonging to both its visible and marginalized people.

Norman M. Klein's *The History of Forgetting: Los Angeles and the Erasure of Memory* strengthened this book's analysis of cultural memory construction through visual culture, largely in how Klein applies the concept of "social imaginary" to the context of L.A. history. In this book, I take social imaginary to be a popular memory construct, "a collective memory of an event or place that never occurred but [that] is built [in the imagination] anyway."[16] According the Klein, a social imaginary consists of images—"mental cameos"—that appear in our mind's eye when we hear a certain word or phrase. The pre-cinema visual culture explored in this book—mental cameos created through photography, painting, advertising, theatrical performances, and architectural design—constructed a social imaginary of Los Angeles during the late nineteenth century and into the early twentieth century, capitalized on by the real estate industry and converted into storytelling practices by the ascendant motion picture industry. The word *imaginary* suggests an evacuation or erasure of the real thing, and, with Klein's work as a guiding force, this book seeks to map the erasures created by the social imaginary constructed through Southern California visual culture. Examining Los Angeles cultural history in this way constitutes what Klein describes as "anti-tour," a journey through a locale that seeks to bring into relief that which is no longer there, an antidote for historical erasure and the burying of the real Los Angeles behind palimpsest layers.

Reyner Banham's *Los Angeles: The Architecture of Four Ecologies* was instrumental in shaping this book's exploration of geography and built environments. Films set in Los Angeles invariably engage with at least one of these ecologies in ways that reveal aspects of their social and political assemblage. The first ecology is the "surfburbia" (or "the Beaches"), cities along the edge of the Pacific Ocean stretching from Malibu in the north to the port of Long Beach in the south. The Beaches, according to Banham, "are what other metropolises should envy in Los Angeles, more than any other aspect of the city," noting also that "the culture of the beach is in many ways a symbolic rejection of the values of the consumer society."[17] The second ecology is the foothills, residential neighborhoods built into the metropolitan area's varied hillside territories, notably the Hollywood Hills, the Santa Monica Mountains, the Verdugo

Hills, and the San Gabriel Mountains. These are affluent corners of Los Angeles characterized not only by a mingling of architectural styles but also by "an overwhelming sense of déjà vu."[18] The third ecology is the flatlands (or the "Plains of Id"), which are, for Banham, the world's image of Los Angeles: an "endless plain endlessly griddled with endless streets, peppered endlessly with ticky tacky houses clustered in indistinguishable neighborhoods, slashed across by endless freeways that have destroyed any community spirit that may have existed, and so on . . . endlessly."[19] Last, the fourth ecology is Autotopia, the freeway system that entangles the L.A. landscape like concrete ribbons. This ecology, according to Banham, is more than simply a place—it is also a "state of mind" in which the "automobile as a work of art is almost as specific to the Los Angeles freeways as the surfboard to the Los Angeles Beaches."[20] Additionally, Banham was the first to apply the notion of the palimpsest directly to Los Angeles, specifically to Autotopia, which he described as a "transportation *palimpsest*" that facilitated the transformation of the city from its premodern ancestry to its postmodern aspirations.

In the chapters that follow, I show how California visual culture forms, centered around world building and environments, contributed to the formation of Hollywood as a network of multimedia organizations. Each chapter focuses on one aspect of California visual culture that impacted the development of Los Angeles and its film industry during a period that California historian Kevin Starr refers to as the state's Progressive Era (approximately 1880–1920), a period that saw a phenomenal population boom fueled largely by visual marketing and an industry of folklore.[21] My approach to exploring each visual form draws on the aforementioned texts and critical frameworks in varying degrees, and yet, in discussing the history of each form, I also seek to sketch out what theorist Adrian Ivakhiv describes as the two ecologies of images: "images of ecology" and the "ecology of images."[22] The images of ecology can be understood as the dominant aspects of the natural landscape that are featured in or depicted by these forms, and each chapter considers the ways that geography and built environments fashioned a particular vision of Southern California, contributed to infrastructural development, and spurred population growth. The ecology of images, by contrast, refers to the social, economic, political, ethical, and technological relations that surrounded these forms, especially in terms of their production and consumption. These chapters look at each form's image ecology in terms of (1) the material elements used in its creation, (2) the social process that occurred to "produce, distribute, or make use of the images," and (3) the interactive system of information exchange between the images' material and social elements that generates "affect, perception, and meaning."[23]

Chapter 1 looks at the growth of Los Angeles during the Progressive Era as a product of a crucial relationship between photographers and railroad companies. Scenic photographer Carleton Watkins (1829–1916) utilized mammoth plate technology and drew on the panorama photography techniques of Eadweard Muybridge to aid the Southern Pacific Railroad Company in the creation of the Tehachapi Loop in 1876, effectively opening the Los Angeles basin to the rest of the country by rail travel. Fueled by a desire to compete with popular painted panorama spectacles, panoramic photography flourished in Los Angeles throughout the late nineteenth century, offering new ways of visualizing cityscapes that have a distinct presence in Los Angeles–set cinema. Some of these panorama photographers also produced stereoscopic views of Los Angeles and the greater Southern California area, and companies like H. T. Payne, the Historical Society of California, and the Pan American Publishing Company distributed stereoscopic albums nationwide. This rapid circulation of images gave rise to a cultural imaginary of Los Angeles before motion pictures started to arrive. By the early 1910s, audiences outside of Los Angeles readily responded to moving images of Mack Sennett's Keystone Cops hurtling down the wide streets of Echo Park and Silver Lake, as California photography had already fostered a recognizable Los Angeles look. The relationship between visualization and transportation has been explored extensively in a variety of media studies contexts.[24] What I am interested in exploring in chapter 1 is how Southern California Progressive Era photography, in conjunction with civic planning and engineering, mobilized the formation of Reyner Banham's L.A. ecologies and Los Angeles as a cultural economy.

The concept of *cartographic cinema*—a term used by scholars to describe how a film's formal elements map a physical terrain in the imagination of the spectator—is central to chapter 1's exploration of Southern California Progressive Era photography and its role in setting the stage for the motion picture industry. Filmed space, according to

Giuliana Bruno, is "comprised constantly of moving centers" through which film conventions and narrative strategies "locate and pattern the imagination" of the spectator, who mentally maps the diegetic landscape.[25] Films set in Los Angeles are an ideal site for exploring the phenomenon of cartographic cinema, with noir cinema providing notable case studies, as the city's automobile culture and sprawling layout often play a significant role in these narratives. In this book, I am interested in the ways that pre-cinema visuals forms anticipated the phenomenon of cartographic cinema and provided a template for film's cartographic functions to develop in the streets of Los Angeles during the 1910s and 1920s. Chapter 1 explores how photography in California during the Progressive Era anticipated cinema's cartographic functions in two ways: (1) through partnerships between photographers and railroad companies (foreshadowing motion pictures through "moving pictures") and (2) through photographers competing with the painted image's capacity to replicate natural physicality.

Chapter 2 concerns painting in Southern California from the 1890s to the 1920s, focusing on an outdoor impressionist style commonly referred to as Southern California *plein air* painting. The style used the region's natural beauty to fuel back-to-nature attitudes that contrasted sharply with the rapid urbanization of the downtown Los Angeles area. Painters like William Wendt (1865–1946), Guy Rose (1867–1925), and Richard E. Miller (1875–1943) were steeped in the style of French impressionism and used California's terrain and climate to provide the style with a new lease on life, creating what Michael McManus described as a "beautiful anachronism."[26] These paintings shaped the social imaginary of Southern California by engaging with the region's natural landscapes, foreshadowing early Hollywood's signature practices of place substitution. The grassy hills, sycamore canyons, and groves of eucalyptus trees reinforced that state's emblematic colors and created a nationwide familiarity with the region's flora. Los Angeles's location far from the world's art centers shielded the region from the grim realities found in other art forms, making plein air the dominant style until modern forms began to make inroads into Los Angeles during the late 1910s and early 1920s.

Chapter 2 considers the influence of plein air techniques on film production design, special effects, animation, and art education, part of a broader legacy of California visual culture and its impact on Los

Angeles's development as a cultural economy. By the 1930s, California plein air had faded from the California art scene in the face of modern art forms that rose in opposition to the conservativism and nostalgic sensibilities of impressionism. Added to this, the Great Depression made it increasingly difficult for artists to make a living selling art. As a result, the students of both plein air and modern art entered the motion picture industry and shaped evolving visual practices.

As far as film's painterly heritage is concerned, expressionism is a movement explored more frequently, with the style connected strongly to studio-bound projects of Weimar cinema and later incorporated into film noir and various cycles of Hollywood horror cinema. This book, however, positions regional Southern California painting (plein air and its successors in the 1920s California scene painting movement) as another art style with a strong influence on filmic practices. I consider the ways that plein air shaped cinematographic strategies for harnessing outdoor sunlight, using high key lighting and atmosphere color to create a higher range of storytelling, composing shots outdoors using the rule of thirds, and drawing upon a "feel of life" when creating levels of light and temperature.

Both photography and painting cemented a distinctly California look and feel in the social imaginary that cast the state as not just a place but a state of mind. Southern California was known as the end of the frontier, or the end of the "Wild West," a place that was both wild and tame, primitive and civilized. Taking advantage of California's reputation as a blank slate upon which dreamers could project themselves, a tourism industry arose in Southern California that offered proto-cinematic transformative experiences. In the San Gabriel Mountains or the California Channel Islands, visitors could reenact the taming of the frontier from the comfort and security of enclosed and immersive narrative worlds, supported by attendant visual cultural forms. Chapter 3 looks at turn-of-the-century tourism in California, and the booster ideology that underscored these attractions, as part of a larger California culture that demonstrated to early filmmakers how to envision an ideal spectator and control reception. As the chapter highlights, there is a paradoxical relationship between Tom Gunning's notion of "the cinema of attractions" and turn-of-the-century tourist attractions.[27] For Gunning, the cinema of attractions privileges "theatrical display" over "narrative absorption," whereas "narrative absorption" was a goal of many Southern California tourist attractions. By the time early film-makers were looking to relocate from the Midwest and the East Coast, the Southern California attractions industry had demonstrated to the rest of the country how the region's varied geography and "rich array of settings" provided ideal conditions for immersive and participatory experiences.

While some tourist attractions allowed participants to envision themselves as conquerors of the Wild West and inheritors of the American destiny, there were others that promised an immersion into popular narrative fiction worlds, ones rooted in a mythology of California's Spanish and Mexican colonial past. *Ramona* tourism capitalized on the popularity of Helen Hunt Jackson's novel of the same name, fostering a proto-cinematic industry of pilgrimage by dedicated *Ramona* fans to sites in Ventura County and San Diego County where crucial moments of the novel were believed to have taken place. Chapter 4 continues this book's exploration of California tourism and visual culture through what is commonly referred to as the "Mission Legend": an evocation of Southern California's pre-statehood Spanish colonial/Mexican ranchero past, viewed through rose-tinted nostalgia and understood in mythical terms. Returning to the palimpsest metaphor, this creation myth of California has long obscured the atrocities visited upon California's indigenous population as well as a "real history" of Mexican American Los Angeles that would provide a more complete picture the city's transformation into a cultural economy. The chapter, along with other recent scholarship on Los Angeles's Latin origins, performs a retrieval of these layers to recontextualize this history and bring competing histories into relief.

In dialogue with *Los Angeles Plays Itself* and *City of Quartz*, this book invites the viewer/reader to reenvision L.A. as a "somewhere," in effect dismantling the palimpsest layers of Los Angeles's history and recognizing Los Angeles-as-anywhere and place-substitution practices as part of a history of forgetting. Starting in the Progressive Era with photography, painting, and tourist attractions, the motion picture industry took over and repurposed these practices by the end of the 1910s with great efficacy. In chapter 5, I consider the mechanisms used by L.A.'s film production network during the 1910s and 1920s to maintain its status as the region's chief booster and to control the reception of these place-substitution practices. The chapter explores how the early Hollywood community developed the contours of its self-made image, and crucial to this exploration are the notions of "imagined community" and cinematic "paratext." Developed by theorist and historian Benedict Anderson, the term *imagined community* describes a nation-state as a socially constructed group joined through shared culture and iconography.[28] Here, I am applying this concept to Hollywood as a community that simultaneously inhabited a specific location and came to embody that location in the social imaginary. In film reception studies, paratexts are things exterior to a text that influence how that text is received (for example, marketing material, fan culture, collectables and ephemera). Chapter 5 looks at how film journalism, trade magazines, fan culture, and early film historiography were used to control both the public perception of the industry's newly founded home in Southern California and the industry itself as an imagined community.

Architecture in Southern California has a complex relationship with the development of Los Angeles as the home of American cinema, as two architectural styles have histories that are intertwined with California visual culture and film industry practices. California eclectic, or the random grazing among historical styles in domestic or commercial building design, mirrored Hollywood's practice of place substitution and the creation of fantasy worlds. During the 1920s, this design trend rose in direct response to the motion picture industry and its tendency toward world building and simulated environments, capitalizing on an increasing familiarity with film's visual references and discernable messages. The Spanish Colonial Revival home is one example of a style that falls under this architectural category, linking the burgeoning film industry with the visual grammar of regional boosterism. Modernism, by contrast, is very cinematic in its design thinking, as it is largely concerned with manipulating procession, how light affects the way that objects look, and spatial relations. Yet at the same time, the style was constructed in opposition to the "cheap opulence" of California eclectic and came to embody a growing politically forward-thinking California progressivism.[29] By the late 1920s and early 1930s, the modernist style had become a useful tool for set designers, and at the same time it served as a symbol of affluence. Hollywood executives, stars, and craftspeople adopted modernism into both their personal and professional lives, further entrenching the style into the Los Angeles cultural landscape. Chapter 6 considers how early Hollywood studio practices contributed to the growth of Los Angeles through a variety of architectural trends, culminating at the end of the Progressive Era with modernism.

As all of these visual forms, with their images of ecology and ecology of images, have informed the perception of Southern California as a place and state of mind, the concluding chapter provides an overview of how these forms have been repurposed at varying stages of film history to depict Los Angeles on the silver screen. Los Angeles cinema, the focus of chapter 7, exemplifies the enduring legacy of early Southern California visual culture by drawing on the visual codes and representational methods of these forms, engaging with the competing images of Los Angeles from the Progressive Era (Booster and Debunker perspectives). Taking a cue from the idea that Los Angeles cinema reveals a history of the city, in varying degrees, this final chapter is both an exploration of Progressive Era visual culture's continued impact on how the image of the city is constructed/received and an invitation to other scholars to sketch out more complete or competing histories of L.A. on film through the methodologies and approaches employed by this book. If the movies made Los Angeles, as others have argued, then the final chapter charts a lineage from the movie-made Los Angeles of the present day to the cinematic city that existed before the movies arrived.

1

SEMI-TROPICAL CALIFORNIA

In 1929, the All-Year-Round Club of California, headed by real estate tycoon Harry Chandler, produced the magazine *Southern California through the Camera*.[1] Photographs of leisure life in the "joyous South-land" trumpeted the region as a place of profound inspiration for "art-ists, writers, and moving picture directors." A California impressionist painting, *Lake Pasadena and the Flintridge Biltmore Hotel from Linda Vista Peak* (Orrin A. White, date unknown), graces the cover, promising "a trip abroad in your own America." Images of Death Valley tourism suggest that travelers will be stars in their own Rudy Valentino motion picture romance. Production stills from silent films set in California's colonial past, shot among local historical landmarks, imply that California was always a cinematic setting. I will return to this magazine in later chap-ters, but for now I would like to consider its centerpiece image: a two-page panorama photo of downtown Los Angeles at night. This aerial shot of L.A., supplied by photographer Robert Earl Spence (credited as "Spence Airplane"), pictorially captures Los Angeles as the prototype for a modern American city: multi-centered, dispersed, and less con-cerned with "city" than with "region."[2] The conventional "vertical city" that emerged throughout the United States during the late nineteenth century is rendered horizontal here through panoramic photography, a vision of Los Angeles that would become deeply ingrained in the visual grammar of the films set in the city. Spence's photo, however, is also the culmination of a photographic language that developed decades earlier for the purpose of vividly transcribing the Southland's topography and environments. This was a way of seeing California that was internalized by commerce, civil engineers, and ultimately, the cinematographers who came to L.A. during the early twentieth century.

Scholarship of pre-cinema photography offers a different set of possibilities for understanding how Los Angeles developed into a cultural economy: a constellation of "cultural product industries" whose goods and services carry a "subjective meaning that is high in comparison to their utilitarian purpose."[3] For Allen J. Scott, the formation of a cultural economy is accomplished in three phases: (1) the initial geographical distribution of production over a given landscape, (2) the location's emergence as a "nascent agglomeration," or an early assemblage of culture-producing sectors, and (3) the consolidation of the agglomeration's "market reach," intensifying the cultural economy's competitive advantages over other locations.[4] During California's Progressive Era (approximately 1880–1920), photography aided each of these phases of Los Angeles's formation as a cultural economy, and this chapter explores this process through several key functions of Southern California photography during this historical time frame. First, I explore how photography aided in the cartography of the region, assisting landscape development and transportation industries through visual landscape surveying. Second, this chapter looks at the way that California photography was designed to evoke a style of living that emphasized a freedom from the constraints of traditional urban life. Last, this chapter considers the ways that turn-of-the-century photography in California produced a culture of fine art photography, constructed in stark contrast to the form's industrial role.

Early L.A. films, silent slapstick films especially, set their physical spectacles in spaces that were familiar to audiences through mass-marketed two-dimensional images. Reenvisioning the city through the moving image created a three-dimensional space that beckoned the spectator to navigate through it. Filmed at ground level—the motion picture camera was often mounted to a moving car traveling at high speeds through Echo Park, Silver Lake, and Los Feliz—early L.A. films are an early example of what scholars have come to term *cinematic cartography*: a "conglomeration of . . . different scholarly disciplines (geography, philosophy, and film/media studies)" that offers different perspectives on spatial perception and subjective positions in the world of screen media.[5] As the term suggests, the formal elements of cinema possess the ability to map a physical terrain in the imagination of the spectator, and this has been traditionally accomplished through film's recognizable conventions (establishing shots and montage editing, for example), which "[locate] and [pattern] the imagination of its spectators."[6] This is because, as Giuliana Bruno argues, filmed space as "not quite the homogenous space of a classical unified central perspective." Rather, it is heterogenous and "comprised constantly of moving centers" in which the spectator is also a passenger mapping the diegetic landscape.[7] In short, spectators are invited to project themselves through the visuals and narrative strategies into a mentally mapped cinematic space. In some instances, this is accomplished using actual maps onscreen that are soon followed by wide-angle landscapes or pans across vast terrain. This is a practice commonly associated with World War II combat films and matinee adventure films (repurposed in Spielberg's *Indiana Jones* films for the titular character's globe-trotting scenes).[8] Emphasis on topography through mise-en-scène and composition is a staple of the western genre: cinematic cartography that situates the spectator in the midst of a Sergio Leone gunfight (in anamorphic wide framing, punctuated by rhythmic montage) or that places the viewer alongside Ethan Edwards (John Wayne) in his five-year cross-country journey in John Ford's *The Searchers* (1956).[9] And as is the case with the tracking shots and Steadicam movements in Stanley Kubrick's work, cartographic cinema may also map both a physical space and a descent into a character's psychological breakdown. What I am interested in here, however, is how cinematic cartography (and its attendant practices) was a product of antecedent forms of visualization. Photography in California during the Progressive Era anticipated cinema's cartographic functions in two ways: (1) through partnerships between photographers and railroad companies (foreshadowing motion pictures through "moving pictures"), and (2) through photographers competing with the painted image's capacity to replicate natural physicality.

Nineteenth-century America was a "crowded visual marketplace" in which painted panorama exhibitions, a form that had originated in Europe toward the end of the eighteenth century, dominated through their epic scope and appeal to the senses.[10] Competing with panorama paintings required that photographers mimic the panorama's "expansive topographical scope, narrative structure, and public aspects," and, since 1851, the California landscape had provided the ideal conditions for photographers to attain these panorama qualities. Daguerreotypist Carleton Watkins emerged from the midcentury San Francisco photography community to capture the majestic beauty of Yosemite, Northern California, and the Pacific Northwest through "mammoth plate" technology: cameras designed to capture sweeping vistas using eighteen-inch by twenty-two-inch glass negatives. Watkins's photographic landscapes, alongside the work of other panorama photographers operating in the West at the time, mounted a challenge to the public appeal of the painted panorama while at the same time advancing photography's capacity for tapping into the sublime aspects of nature settings popularized by writers like Thoreau and the painters of the Hudson River School.[11] Watkins's work in Southern California, however, has largely been underexplored, despite its significant contribution to the growth of Los Angeles's infrastructure and population toward the end of the century.[12] In the mountains just south of present-day Bakersfield, Watkins repurposed his skills as a photographic panoramist to provide the Southern Pacific Railroad Company with large-scale visual evidence to persuade investors and Washington officials of the region's viability for land development. Watkins's mammoth plate cameras surveyed the construction of Tehachapi Loop in 1876, effectively opening the Los Angeles basin to the rest of the nation by rail travel and expanding the cartographic possibilities of the photographic image. The transformation of Los Angeles and the greater region of Southern California from a ranchland in decline to a metropolis on the rise, I argue, was made possible through the photographic image, including and especially panoramic photography, which anticipated the visual grammar of Spence Airplane's L.A. views.

Visual marketing of Southern California would be employed by the Southern Pacific long after the construction of the Tehachapi Loop, often wedded to an industry of California mythmaking as much as serving a cartographic purpose. Though photography would be one of several visual forms employed by the Southern Pacific, Southern California visual culture in general advanced a distinct Southern California feeling (or distinctly L.A. feeling) that could be gleaned from the images. Progressive Era photography's second function will be explored in this chapter in relation to the subjective perception of Los Angeles as an urban space, or what is known as *stadtbild* in German. Literally meaning "townscape" or "cityscape," stadtbild implies a feeling that is projected by a city's features, geography, climate, and designed elements. Vincent Brook in an interview for *Notebook on Cities and Culture* remarks that Los Angeles lacks a stadtbild, owing largely to its polynucleated layout and often contradictory nature.[13] When locating common features and patterns in Progressive Era photography, however, it becomes clear that that Los Angeles does in fact have a stadtbild: a sense of freedom augmented by the vastness and openness of its surroundings. The photographic forms explored in this chapter anticipated this stadtbild through their expansive and varied presentation of Southern California landscapes. Panorama photography encoded the environment with the promise of personal transformation and limitless opportunity, whereas still and stereoscopic photo albums captured the development of this L.A. stadtbild through images of a rapidly growing downtown area and wild landscapes on the peripheral edge. I will return to this interplay between the urban and the wild in chapters 3 and 6, but for now I am interested in the way that panorama photography and the photo album industry promoted, on a national level, a "Southern California look": a territory with porous boundaries between the wild and the tame where the familiar and the unfamiliar comingle.

While the "Southern California look" became a reliable tool for regional boosterism, the geography of the Southland also provided a site for photography to develop as an art form, in contrast to the form's marketing and cartographic functions. Mark Shiel notes that from 1900 to 1915, Los Angeles was one of "the most important centers for fine art photography," and that such photographers standardized an iconography of the region that came to be affiliated with the American motion picture industry.[14] This was also a period in which photography, according to Louise Hornby, "sought a discrete identity" and was defined in radical opposition to film through its stillness.[15] This chapter will explore photography's third function through examining the West Coast followers of the Photo-Secession (with Edward Weston as a notable example), who played a crucial role in recognizing still photography as part of a continuum of visual culture. These art photographers found inspiration from the motion picture industry during the 1910s and 1920s in that they tended to favor "heavy dramatic references to art history," displayed a willingness to incorporate professional studio practices and, most important, relied heavily on a "club and salon system," echoing film industry production and exhibition networks.[16]

THE TEHACHAPI LOOP

In 1850, Los Angeles was a "violent encampment" and a "zone of racial conflict" at the end of the frontier, a dusty outpost of only 1,610 residents that showed no real potential to become a city of wealth and culture.[17] The original pueblo was falling into decay among a series of dirt roads lined by mustard trees, bordered on one side by a river that had been reduced to a dirty sanitation system. The region's Mexican, Spanish, and indigenous history was threatened with erasure through neglect and deliberate whitewash, soon to be exacerbated through the 1851 Land Act: the raising of property taxes on grand cattle pastures in places with names like San Pedro, La Brea, Los Feliz, and Santa Monica. San Francisco, by contrast, was the site of rapid growth in the wake of the gold rush, drawing East Coast bankers, international merchants, playwrights, and literary giants. The development of San Francisco into a cosmopolitan city around the mid-nineteenth century attracted all the trappings of East Coast city culture: a bustling theater community, art galleries, and photographers eager to experiment with the form's possibilities in California's varied environments. Some of the earliest photographs of California were daguerreotypes of the San Francisco Bay around 1850–51: notably images of Yerba Buena Cove and views of the Berkeley Hills from what is present-day Pacific Heights. Early photographs of newly constructed cultural landmarks, such as an image of the Bella Union Theater (1851), also document the construction of the city's cultural infrastructure, many of which would be destroyed in the great earthquake of 1906. The earthquake made international news, whereas labor disputes in Los Angeles the same year barely registered nationally. Yet by 1917, Los Angeles overtook San Francisco as the largest city on the West Coast and the region's cultural hub. The story of San Francisco's displacement by Los Angeles as the West Coast's largest economy was facilitated in large part by photography. A crucial starting point for this story is photography's struggle to compete with painted forms on a national level.

Americans during the midcentury, according to Martha A. Sandweiss, "professed to value accuracy in literary and visual reportage," and yet the photograph's "faithfulness to actual appearances seemed at odds with [a] more widespread fascination" with fidelity "to experience."[18] The painted panorama spectacle invariably provided the biggest challenge, as its theatrical qualities foreshadowed innovations in motion picture exhibition and distribution. Great battles, cityscapes, and rugged landscapes were presented in circular rotundas—sometimes in motion, controlled by gear mechanisms under the floor—and occasionally accompanied by live music or a public lecturer. The aim of the moving panorama painting was to create an illusion of a real world in motion with constantly changing perspectives, disrupting the centralized perspective of traditional paintings. International panorama companies formed in the early nineteenth century were prototypes of the multimedia studio networks of the twentieth century: employing artists who could produce a panorama in less than a year; operating out of company-owned workshops built to the shape of the exhibition rotundas where they would eventually be shown; managing a network of exhibition houses in coordination with local businessmen, promotion agents, and financiers.[19] By the 1870s, the center of gravity of panorama production had shifted from Europe to the United States, with moving panoramas largely seen as not only a U.S. innovation but also a popular U.S. export. By Stephan Oettermann's estimation, more than one hundred million spectators visited painted panorama exhibitions worldwide from 1870 to the end of the century.[20]

Los Angeles during the latter half of the nineteenth century was no exception. The Los Angeles Panorama Company, for example, opened in 1887 on South Main, with its debut spectacle *The Siege of Paris* (1870–71), a copy of the Paris original by Henri Felix Emmanuel Philippoteaux.[21] The exhibition site was a circular rotunda reminiscent of the diorama building designed by Louis Daguerre in 1821, and its exhibitions were often accompanied by hourly lectures on the subjects on display. Another panorama exhibition was established in 1887 in Washington Gardens; in anticipation of L.A.'s modern architecture design practices, it was constructed in a partially covered viewing hall that blended artistic spectacle with the park's natural setting.[22] Though the panorama painting waned in popularity throughout the 1890s and 1900s in Los Angeles and elsewhere, it is difficult to deny the popularity of the form and its impact on cinema. Panoramic vision, according to Jan Olsson, with its constant reframing of the landscape and perception of time and space, "offered a veritable education of the eye further elaborated upon by filmmakers."[23]

The photographers of the mid-nineteenth century understood that in order to gain competitive advantage against the painted panorama, it was necessary to develop their technical expertise and audience-building strategies in ways that captured these moving paintings' "expansive topographic scope, narrative structure, and public aspects."[24] Consider first John Banvard's *Mississippi from the Mouth of the Missouri to New Orleans* (1846), a moving painted panorama experience in which photography played a crucial role in bringing Banvard's vision to fruition. *Mississippi* enlists the spectator as a participant in westward expansion—a mode of address that would be replicated by the Southern California tourism industry discussed in chapter 3—taking the viewer on a journey down the mighty river while a public lecturer provides commentary. This spectacular display first appeared in Louisville, Kentucky, in an exhibition hall for which the painting was initially designed, and then toured Boston, New York, and eventually London. The success and popularity of Banvard's panorama inspired John Wesley Jones's *Pantoscope of California, Nebraska, Utah, and the Mormons* (1852) and Robert Vance's *Views of California* (1851), paintings whose promotional literature cited the role of fifteen hundred daguerreotypes (Jones) and three hundred fullplate daguerreotypes (Vance) in their creation. Despite photography's role in the creation of these large-scale re-creations of San Francisco and California gold country, sketch artists and painters remained firmly in control of how Americans saw and understood unfolding historical events and westward expansion. Yet at the same time, these painted works provided a template for photographers to elevate their work to the scope of the panoramic form, emphasizing vastness and the sublime elements of the landscape.

Here I bring Carleton Watkins into the story of how the West was visualized. Known primarily for his majestic photographs of Yosemite, Watkins made a name for himself nationally by producing detailed landscapes captured on large negatives from distant points of view.[25] His panoramic images of San Francisco, however, provide some insight into what Daniel A. Novak characterizes as photography's transformation "from being a visual residue of history" toward "new fictional and narrative possibilities."[26] Watkins started experimenting with the panoramic form as early as 1858, piecing together separate large-plate images to produce one whole image, and by 1864 he had produced his first continuous panorama photograph of San Francisco from Nob Hill—involving five mammoth plate negatives "meticulously contrived to overlap and form an eight-foot-long, one hundred eighty–degree vista."[27] Watkins's custom-built camera was central to the creation of this cityscape, large enough to handle the eighteen-inch by twenty-two-inch glass plate negatives that came to be known as "mammoth plates." According to Tyler Green, Watkins's construction of this new camera during the early 1860s (a testimony to his family's cabinetmaking trade) was part of an effort both to compete with established national photographers (such as the famed Civil War photographer Alexander Gardner) and to declare loud and clear that the images he produced were not "for use as etchings" in a newspaper or magazine, nor to be used to produce photo albums. Rather, Watkins's images were designed with grand exhibition halls in mind, on par with those for displaying panorama paintings.[28]

Watkins would produce several more panoramas of San Francisco, sometimes as single images (such as his 1868 *The Golden Gate from Telegraph Hill* or *San Francisco from Twin Peaks, Looking Northeast*, circa 1869) and others as expanded panoramas from multiple plates.[29] His *Panorama from California and Powell Street, San Francisco* (between 1871 and 1874), for example, was constructed from "stereo halves," images culled from several produced by stereoscopic equipment at strategically placed locations. A distinguishing feature of these city panoramas is their "radical elaboration of the horizon line" with an "expanded field of vision"; Watkins's panoramas mimicked the visual thrust of the horizon line, producing an image "impossible to take in at a single glance."[30] This sense of vastness and expanded field of vision was seen as an innately modern feature of the panoramic form, locating a "feel" exuded by the western landscape.[31]

Through Watkins's panoramas, we can see the early development of photography's cartographic functions, as they demonstrate the medium's capacity to provide the viewer with new patterns for receiving subjects and landscapes.[32] The spectator is given a decentered position through the vastness of the panoramic image, comprised of moving centers in a way that is like motion picture settings. At the same time,

Figure 1.1. Portion of an early *Panorama from California and Powell Street, San Francisco* in stereo halves, by Carleton Watkins, between 1871 and 1874. (J. Paul Getty Research Institute, Photo Archive, Los Angeles, CA.)

the spectator can apprehend the intensity of the images through the panorama's composition and the vantage point offered by its presentation or exhibition. This experience offered by the panoramic form can be understood through what art historian Abraham Moritz "Aby" Warburg (1866–1929) termed "pathos formula": the way that a work of art is aesthetically organized so that the spectator can experience its subject matter and become emotionally involved from a safe vantage point. This formal aesthetic strategy produces what Elisabeth Bronfen describes as art's ability to generate an intense emotion by "tapping into one's imaginative capacity," while at the same time offering a conceptual presentation of the subject being depicted.[33] Consider Watkins's *Panorama from California and Powell Street, San Francisco* (fig. 1.1). Multiple vanishing points bring the spectator's vision to different portions of the overall horizon line as if an invisible editor were present. Starting with a view from down Powell Street, then shifting over to a view out to Yerba Buena Island, and then to a view toward the buildings of Nob Hill, the stereo halves and resulting panorama anticipate, in pictorial form, what Paul Virilio referred to as "panoramic telemetry": an overlap of surveillance technology with moving image technology that throughout the late nineteenth and early twentieth century resulted in wide screen cinema.[34]

Through this strategy, or pathos formula, the panorama degree view of San Francisco essentially maps the city anew even for its residents by defamiliarizing the location; by "subverting our routine perception" of urban space, panoramic photography performs what the formalists describe as a "shock . . . into awareness."[35] In short, photography's cartographic capabilities reside in the manner in which it takes the familiar (the form's promise to show the real and observable world) and makes it strange through the formal strategies of the work's creator, inviting the viewer to experience the photographic subject anew.

Pathos formula and defamiliarization can also be seen in Eadweard Muybridge's San Francisco panoramas, produced a few years after Watkins's and from a similar vantage point. Muybridge's 1877 and 1878 panoramas were created before his famous *The Horse in Motion* (1878) experiment in Palo Alto, and yet what is interesting is that both the panoramas and *Horse in Motion* photographs were created through sequential chrono-photography. His panoramas were shot on massive collodion plates from the top of Nob Hill and produced a 360-degree seamless view of the city, employing "initially eleven and then later thirteen panels."[36] Tom Gunning describes Muybridge's pathos formula, or formal strategy guiding the spectator, as a calculated charting of space and time for the purpose of making "visible a drama that would otherwise remain invisible."[37] Viewers faced with this all-encompassing city view develop a sense that they are traveling through a day in the life of the city that transcends time, achieved through Muybridge's elaboration of the technical and aesthetic stakes involved in bringing movement to still life.[38] While Watkins explicitly created his panoramas for grand exhibition halls, Muybridge departed from this expectation, allowing for his panorama panels to be sold nationwide in a variety of formats, including cabinet display albums, individual frame views, and elephant accordion folios.[39] Both Watkins and Muybridge used large-scale photography to compete with the painted panorama's public appeal, developing a pre-cinematic cityscape language that anticipated city symphony motion pictures, but Muybridge's distribution of his San Francisco vistas was part and parcel of an industry of image circulation that impacted all the visual forms discussed in this book.

While Muybridge worked on his city panoramas in Northern California, Watkins was in Southern California, lending panoramic photography craft to the Southern Pacific Railroad Company on a project that would eventually open Los Angeles to the rest of the nation. Separating Los Angeles County from California's Central Valley, the Tehachapi Mountains had, since 1866, presented a seemingly insurmountable challenge to the Southern Pacific's construction of a line between San Francisco and Los Angeles. The Tehachapi Mountains are of great significance to this story of Los Angeles and its development into a distinctive cultural economy, as this range has traditionally demarcated Southern California from Central California. Carey McWilliams writes that the Tehachapi range has long symbolized the divide between the north and what had come to be known as California del Sur, or "sub-tropical California": not only do the Tehachapis "serve to keep out the heat and dust of the desert, but they are high enough to snatch moisture from the ocean winds and to form clouds."[40] Bridging the Sierra Nevada range to the east with the coastal mountain range, the Tehachapis feature the California shrubland (or chaparral) and oak forests commonly associated with Southern California's Mediterranean ecosystem, but at the same time one can find the coniferous flora native to Northern California. As testimony to the place-substitution potential afforded to the movies by California's varied terrain, the Tehachapi Mountains have stood in for a Montana Badlands dinosaur excavation site in *Jurassic Park* (1993) and as the Tehachapis themselves in *The Grapes of Wrath* (1940); as evidence of the difficulties faced by industrial construction in these mountains, the unscrupulous Daniel Plainview of *There Will Be Blood* (2007) dismisses the idea of building a pipeline "around fifty miles of Tehachapi Mountains" as "thick." At the time of the Southern Pacific's line construction, there was no route directly through the mountain range that provided a manageable gradient for rail travel. Securing the resources required to produce engineering solutions to this problem meant providing investors and regulators with a realistic, visible narrative of this predicament. This was a task for which Watkins's panoramic photography techniques were well suited.

Photography in the service of surveyance projects was not uncommon during the nineteenth century. For example, while working on an 1840 project to determine the boundary between Maine and Canada, architect and engineer James Renwick employed photographer Edward Anthony to assist the surveyors by making daguerreotypes of the landscape as visible documentation.[41] Moreover, using photography to document a rail route was not a new practice at the time of the Tehachapi Loop construction, nor was it a novel idea to employ a panoramist for the job. For example, Albert Hart became the official photographer for the Central Pacific Railroad in 1866, drawing on his expertise as a moving panorama painter to organize the visual story of the route into a "sequential linear narrative."[42] Collis Huntington, industrialist and director of the Southern Pacific's operations, recognized the value of photographic surveyance to the Tehachapi dilemma, realizing that to continue developing in California would require providing Washington regulators and East Coast financiers with visible evidence of the Southern Pacific's progress and ingenuity.[43] Furthermore, the San Francisco to Los Angeles line was to connect with another line from Fort Yuma, Arizona to San Diego, for which the Southern Pacific was involved in a conflict with the rival Texas and Pacific over the building rights. Understanding that he needed his photographic evidence of the Tehachapi construction to be powerful enough to "disincentivize Congress from supporting [Texas and Pacific]," Huntington hired his longtime friend and business partner to document what would become known as the Tehachapi Loop: a system of overlapping loops and tunnels southeast of Keene (a town thirty miles southeast of Bakersfield) that would allow for a train to ascend through the mountains in a manageable way.

For the Tehachapi Loop, Watkins used ten mammoth plate pictures of portions of the loop to produce a two-part panorama of the entire loop. A key element of this panorama was his strategy of composition and spatial arrangement borrowed from his city panoramas and previous nature photography. He selected a site for positioning his camera atop a three-hundred-foot grassy hill from which a "fringe of stone jutted five to ten feet out of the ground at an angle" that made it look like the stone was point toward the loop in the distance.[44] This practice also Watkins repurposed from his previous nature landscape panoramas of Northern California and the Pacific Northwest. It may seem tempting to dismiss these photographs as serving purely commercial and industrial purposes rather than being works of art with a meaningful resonance; Joel Snyder notes that "although often beautiful, these [photographs] were intended primarily as 'disinterested reports' often being made on commission for railroad, mining, and lumber companies as advertisements of the West aimed at investors."[45] It is important to remember, however, how the

Figure 1.2. Portion of Carleton Watkins's *Tehachapi Loop, Southern Pacific Railroad, Kern County, California*, 1877. (J. Paul Getty Research Institute, Photo Archive, Los Angeles, CA.)

concept of pathos formula, an idea originally ascribed to painted forms, is exhibited in Watkins's Tehachapi panorama. The presentation of the landscape invites the viewer to engage with curiosity, evoking elements of the sublime just as his images of San Francisco, the sequoia trees of Calaveras County, or Mt. Hood did in previous years.

This visible evidence resulted in two crucial outcomes. First, Watkins became well versed in Southern California topography and the business of producing visual documentation for the railroad industry. From 1877 to the 1890s, his career would be connected to the Southern Pacific, documenting the company's purchase of two Los Angeles–based railroads: the Los Angeles and San Pedro (running from downtown to Wilmington Harbor) and the Los Angeles and Independence (running from downtown to Santa Monica).[46] Furthermore, photography in the wake of the Watkins's Tehachapi Loop mammoth plates and Muybridge's San Francisco panoramas quite often went hand in hand with the demands of regional land developers and boosters. "Progress on bridge construction and urban development" during the late nineteenth century, according to James H. Rubin, "was monitored by photographers, sometimes working on state commission."[47] Second, the triumph of the Southern Pacific as a result of Watkins's photography, Tyler Green notes, was ultimately the catalyst for "the West's transition from a mining region . . . to a region focused on agribusiness."[48] By the mid-1880s, the impact of this development, accompanied by campaigns of visualization, could be clearly felt through migration and the transfer of wealth to the region. As Robert M. Fogelson observes, the region was so well promoted by visual marketing that by 1885 the Southern Pacific and Santa Fe "reduced their fares from the East by two-thirds," by 1887 the transfer of real estate in Los Angeles County rose to approximately $95 million (up from $28 million the previous year), and the population of Los Angeles increased to 50,395 by 1890, up from 11,183 in 1880 (by 1900 the population reached nearly 102,000).[49] Though Los Angeles may have been founded in 1781, alongside a roaring river flowing into the Pacific Ocean, it was during this period at the end of the nineteenth century that an actual city begin to take shape in a real sense: a young city emerging from a former "violent encampment" at the heart of semi-tropical California.

"THE LAND OF HEART'S DESIRE"

> There is no other land so lovely, so constant, so generous. It lies between the desert and the sea—God's two sanatoriums for weary flesh and weary mind. The Sierra's eternal snows, the desert's clean, hot breath, the Ocean's cool winds and the warmth of the sinuous current of Japan winding through it, all combine to make the climate hopelessly unrivaled by even the most favored shores of the Mediterranean. It is a land of artists' dreams, endless with flower-flamed uplands, swinging lomas, and majestic mountains. It changes with every color of the day and is soft and sweet unspeakably under low-hanging stars and great shining moons.
> — John S. McGroarty, "The Land of Heart's Desire"

California, according to John S. McGroarty, is not just an exemplar of Earth's ideal climates and ecosystems. It is also a place for spiritual transformation as a direct result of the landscape's enchanting power. Booster publications during the late nineteenth century, such as Charles Fletcher Lummis's *Land of Sunshine* and *Out West* magazines, preached the same gospel, but a crucial component of their message was the use of Edenic iconography: visuals that "emphasized the Mediterranean climate and pastoral fertility" of the region in stark contrast to the "overpopulated, ugly, polluted, and dangerous urban-industrial cities of the Midwest and East Coast."[50] Images of Santa Monica beach camps, travel advertisements inviting visitors to take part in scenes from popular novels set in Old California, and vibrantly colored brochures from the citrus industry cemented a Southern California look and feel that would be readily adapted by image makers of the twentieth century. Yet this "look and feel" did not originate with Lummis and other members of the Arroyo group, though their work did provide this California feeling with definition and rework it in the service of industrial and commercial development. This sense of vastness and openness, a Los Angeles stadtbild that became recognizable through films set in the Southland, can be seen in the photographic practices and distribution modes in Southern California from the 1870s through the 1890s.

In 1871, Civil War photographer Timothy O'Sullivan joined an expedition through the American Southwest with the Army Corp of Engineers, led by Lieutenant George M. Wheeler and accompanied by geologist G. K. Gilbert. Years earlier, O'Sullivan has made a name for himself on the national stage by bringing the harsh realities of combat into the public imagination. As a conflict heavily documented by photographers like O'Sullivan, Matthew Brady, and Alexander Gardner, the Civil War had featured several photographic genres, including "scorched earth photography"—images of battlefields strewn with corpses, such as O'Sullivan's *The Harvest of Death* (1863), filmed after the battle of Gettysburg. After the war, O'Sullivan turned toward a new mission: mythologizing the American West by providing it with visual narration. Traveling along the Colorado River, O'Sullivan photographed the jaw-like entrances to canyons, Mojave Indian guides, and valley vistas using stereoscopic equipment. Stereoscopic photography had been around since at least the 1840s, though its popularity increased during the Civil War. By the time of the Wheeler Expedition, O'Sullivan and others recognized a potential for stereoscopic photography beyond its novelty value. Stereoscopic photography could be used to infuse objects and places with ethereal qualities, generating a mythical allure. Additionally, Wheeler recognized the promotional potential of O'Sullivan's images: "a full and characteristic representation of that very grand and peculiar scenery among the cañons of the Colorado."[51] The photographs of this expedition, along with images of previous surveys and a later expedition from 1873, were circulated as a set of stereographs in 1873.[52] Later, in 1876, a more extensive set of 180 photographs were printed for display at the Philadelphia Centennial Exposition and later sold nationwide. Despite the popularity of these stereoscopic sets, the significance of O'Sullivan's work was largely overlooked until reevaluations of his work in the twentieth century, notably with Ansel Adams writing enthusiastically about the Wheeler Expedition photographs and later with John Szarkowski's tenure as the curator of photography at the Metropolitan Museum of Art, starting in 1962. Szarkowski observed that out of "the half-dozen photographers who worked with the Government Surveys . . . O'Sullivan was perhaps the one with the purest, the most consistent, and the most inventive vision."[53]

The Wheeler Expedition photographs set the stage for Southern California as a center for photography, a micro–cultural economy that was a harbinger of the larger cultural economy that was to arrive in Los Angeles during the early twentieth century. These images of canyons, mesas, and expansive valleys foreshadowed one of the primary functions of California photography as visual boosterism: evoking a style of living in which the lines between indoor and outdoor living are blurred and freedom from the constraints imposed by traditional urban life is attainable. Yet there is a conflicting legacy at the heart of Progressive Era photography that became woven into boosterism during the latter half of the nineteenth century. One the one hand, these images demonstrated photography's ability to challenge the appeal and popularity of painted forms, much as the panorama photography of Carleton Watkins had previously. While landscape painting produced a connection between the frontier and notions of the sublime in the American cultural imaginary, the novelty of stereoscopy and its ability to impart a sense of immediacy to the image-spectator relationship contributed heavily to making the West compelling and familiar. On the other hand, the Wheeler photographs are also coded with what Alan Braddock and Karl Kusserow describe as the "visual logic of American imperialism," documenting the expropriation of land that had traditionally been understood by indigenous peoples as land that cannot be owned but rather "belonged to."[54] The photographic mapping of the Southwest by O'Sullivan, as Braddock and Kusserow suggest, presents topography and geography in a manner that runs counter to what philosopher Viola Faye Cordova has termed "bounded space": land determined by "tradition, agreement, and intimate knowledge of topographical features and directionality, where reciprocal obligations stewardship and spirituality prevail."[55] As photographers set their sights on Los Angeles around the late 1870s, a time when the location was about to undergo a rapid transformation in the wake of increased migration through rail travel, both legacies would contribute to a common language of booster aesthetics: mobilizing Anglo American nationalist sentiment through a visualized California mythology.

By 1878, the stereoscope was a commonplace device in middle-class households across America.[56] This way of seeing the world, with its theatrical staging of images, was a forerunner of contemporary 3D cinema spectacles, but the stereoscopic industry can also be read as a precursor to present-day social media image circulation. The Los Angeles stereoscopic photo albums that emerged at the start of the Progressive Era informed Americans' cultural imagination of what lay on the frontier through near-immersive images of a city being constructed in stark contrast to the layout of older East Coast and Midwest cities. Added to this, these albums also presented nature settings, lush gardens, and fertile agricultural terrain as coexisting in close proximity to developing urban centers. American public culture, according to Robert Hariman and John Luis Lucaites, bestowed positive qualities upon these circulated images of California, wedding Southern California life to assertions of citizenship and nationalism.[57] This image and perception of Southern California as an end-of-the-frontier space where the lines between wild and civilized are blurred would play a major role in the promotion of tourist industry attractions and later the development of motion picture studios in the region (an issue I will return to in chapter 3). Starting with the work of H. T. Payne, let us consider first the presentation of Southern California ecology in early L.A. photography, topography and environments that evolved into Progressive Era visual culture's recognizable signposts of Southern California's look and feel.

Figure 1.3. Single stereoscopic *Panorama of Los Angeles* taken from Fort Hill, by H. T. Payne & Company, 1885. (J. Paul Getty Research Institute, Photo Archive, Los Angeles, CA.)

H. T. Payne & Company published two stereoscopic photo albums in 1876, before the completion of the Tehachapi Loop: *Southern California Scenery* and *Semi-Tropical California*. Henry T. Payne, a resident of Southern California at the time, made a name for himself that year presenting both albums as well as previous work (nearly one thousand images) at the Centennial Exposition in Philadelphia. From his gallery and publishing house on North Main Street in present-day downtown, inherited from pioneering California photographer William M. Godfrey, Payne tapped into a growing national mythology about the Golden State's promises of transformation and rejuvenation. The term *semi-tropical*, used in the title of one of his most popular albums, is a nod to the use of this description in the popular travel writings of Charles Nordhoff, who maintained that the "health-restoring land" gave way to "wonderfully and variously productive soil, without tropical malaria."[58] The aim of Payne's images was to provide visual narration to accompany the words of Nordhoff and other boosters. Both albums provided the viewer with scenes around Los Angeles County, Orange County, and San Bernardino County, showing rural settings, historical landmarks, and a growing urban center that was steadily emerging from the city's "violent encampment" period.[59] In these collections, dual images are mounted onto mustard-colored cards, measuring approximately seven inches by four and a half, each with a description and credits on the front. These three-dimensional images presented the illusion of urbanization in motion: women walking among orange groves on the periphery of the developing downtown area, ships departing Wilmington Harbor, a view of "Los Angeles from Fort Hill" (now the Fort Moore Pioneer Memorial on North Hill Street), and views from a bustling Spring Street, for example. With each photo slide viewed through a binocular set, or stereoscope, the spectator experiences Los Angeles and the surrounding area as what *Scientific American* described in its review of the device that same year as "the mind, guided by the experience of many years," receiving the "impression of various distances."[60]

Alongside images of urban life reimagined, these H. T. Payne albums also showcased nature settings in a way that anticipated Mike Davis's description of the "wild" and the "urban" in L.A.: categories and distinctions that are best conceived as variable qualities and processes rather than neatly bound little boxes. Images of the old campground of Santa Monica, the Eaton Canyon waterfall (referred to as "La Belle Cascade" on the slide) near present-day Altadena, and fan-leaf palms adorning residential settings suggest that that difference between indoors and outdoors was never clearly defined in Los Angeles from the outset. Other images of poplar rows in Orange County and cactus fences in Los Angeles also advance a presentation of Southern California life as what booster Charles Dudley Warner would later describe as a land so hospitable that "every sort of tree, shrub, root, grain, and flower can be brought here from any zone and temperature."[61] By capturing these scenes so vividly (and with the sensory stimulation afforded by the stereoscopic format), *Semi-Tropical California* and *Southern California Scenery* offered visible evidence of Southern California as both an environment of varied topography and a potential site for place-substitution practices, cementing this reputation in the imagination of spectators nationwide, including image makers whose innovative photography would eventually lead to the advent of motion pictures.

Acknowledging Southern California's past also played a crucial role in image creation and image consumption. Both albums feature photos of Mission San Fernando Rey de España and Mission San Gabriel

Arcángel.[62] Payne's later albums of the 1880s and 1890s, as well as those from other stereoview producers, also featured missions throughout the greater Southern California area. These remnants of California's colonial past are shown overgrown with tall grass and in disrepair, as if this fading memory of Old California, held in suspended animation, is about to be swallowed up by the land. In documenting California's ghosts of the pre-statehood past, these albums anticipate the role that an appropriated history of California would play in the formation of Los Angeles's cultural economy as a machine for mythmaking in two distinct ways. On the one hand, these haunting images document what journalist Carey McWilliams described as the "last vestiges of Spanish influence . . . submerged . . . but never fully extinguished."[63] The 1851 Land Act, followed by crippling droughts, had a devastating impact on the cattle economy, and by 1876, the once-affluent Spanish-speaking *ranchero* families had fallen into poverty and racial marginalization, with the "Spanish appearance of Southern California towns changed overnight" into "undeniably gringo villages."[64] By the mid-1880s, however, the image of the California Mexican had been transformed into a "picturesque element . . . of the social life and economy of the region," rooted in a mythmaking industry fueled by the popularity of Helen Hunt Jackson's novel *Ramona* (an issue I will return to in chapter 4). Payne's 1876 stereoviews of Spanish mission sites, therefore, record a moment in history between a period of cultural erasure and cultural appropriation, two tendencies that would largely define early Hollywood's treatment of California's history. On the other hand, Payne's mission photography points toward what Nanna Verhoeff describes as the "museal quality" of early films from Biograph and Kalem during the first decade of the twentieth century: nonfiction, short-subject films used as tools for "teaching about history, geography, and ethnography," evoking the spectator's awareness of the "pastness" of the subject and transforming that awareness into a museum effect that generates excitement and satisfies curiosity.[65] In this regard, these remnants of California's Spanish past instructed image makers and image consumers about the value of history and memory as tools for generating an emotional engagement with a visual narrative, an ingredient for producing a California look and feel pictorially.

Stereographs, as Jonathan Crary argues, do not belong to the realm of photographic realism; rather, they have more in common with theatrical staging and illusion.[66] This suggests that the stereoviews in *Semi-Tropical California* and related albums can be read as creating an immersive California that is more in dialogue with the Banvard's *Mississippi* panorama than single-shot photography. The spectator is invited to get lost in the experience, and it is in this sense that Payne's stereographs possess performative qualities: the spectator is situated in Nordhoff's "health-restoring land" through views of the "wild" existing at the edge of an expanding urban space. The viewer is connected to a historical relic that is a site for the colonial gaze (locating the other) and a modern reversal (locating oneself) simultaneously.

Curiously, *Semi-Tropical California* also features two nonstereoscopic panorama photographs spanning two pages each: one of Los Angeles and another of San Bernardino. Payne's panoramas serve as a reminder of the importance of this wide form in photography's competition with popular painted spectacles, much in the way that the work of Watkins and Muybridge illustrates. At the same time, these panorama photos foreshadow the visual language that cinema would use to transcribe the Los Angeles area as a horizonal urban space, tapping into the cartographic qualities of Watkins's survey panoramas and city landscapes. This sense of vastness, emphasis on natural life, and pre-statehood history are all crucial components in the development of California image making up to the release of the H. T. Payne albums—a lingering sense of the region's place on the the frontier that would carry into modernity.

Following the completion of the Southern Pacific's line and the rapid population expansion of the Los Angeles area, H. T. Payne would produce more stereoscopic albums documenting this regional development, and other stereoscopic albums followed suit in infusing the region with a similarly recognizable look. *Views of Southern California* (H. T. Payne, 1881), for example, featured more views of Southern California missions than previous albums (San Juan Capistrano, notably), suggesting a growing interest in a mythological California past. Later, photographers such as Carleton Watkins, I. W. Taber, Benjamin W. Kilburn (founder of the B. W. Kilburn Stereoscopic View Company), J. C. Brewster, and T. W. Ingersoll (founder of the Ingersoll View Company) either created and distributed stereoviews of Southern California or allowed their photography to be converted to stereoviews for mass distribution. Griffith and Griffith, a company founded in Philadelphia in 1896, is also a notable entry in this story of visualizing California; it produced everyday street views in newly constructed and well-manicured Los Angeles neighborhoods around the time when motion pictures started to make inroads into Southern California (approximately 1904–10). This overlap between the rise of the film industry and the decline of the photo album industry is significant because it pinpoints a time and place in which motion pictures assumed control of projecting the Southern California stadtbild and affecting the social imaginary.

Turning away from stereoscopic albums, high-end single-frame photo albums at the turn of the century, also intended for parlor room showcasing, evoke a similar (and marketable) California feeling centered around environment and style of living. Harry Ellington Brooks's *Southern California: The Land of Sunshine* (1893), for example, was sponsored by the Los Angeles Chamber of Commerce for the Chicago World's Columbian Exposition in 1893 and was intended to accompany his book on California's "natural features, resources, and prospects."[67] Lou V. Chapin's box set of photographs, *Artwork in Southern California* (1900), presented Los Angeles as a "sequence of immaculate parks and park-like residential streets," echoing the H. T. Payne images and foreshadowing the Griffith and Griffith views of an idealized place to live.[68] A striking connection between the pioneering photography of the Wheeler Expedition and turn-of-the-century L.A. photography, however, can be found in the Historical Society of Southern California's *Los Angeles and Southern California Photo Album*, published in 1903. Coming on the heels of the city's first photographic salon in 1902, this photo album, like the H. T. Payne albums, featured the two missions, local parks, and downtown locations. A distinct feature of the album was its emphasis on the blurred lines between Los Angeles as an urban setting and California's natural landscape through images of cactus gardens and Cawston's ostrich farm. The Historical Society's albums are significant in that they assumed the role of pictorial writing and preservation of history at a time when the motion picture was emerging as a form capable of the same task—with actuality films of the Spanish-American War or reenactments of historical events (such as Edison's *The Execution of Mary Stuart* in 1895) tapping into a desire to see the past and record history.[69] As we will see in chapter 3, both tourist attractions and photography in Progressive Era Southern California turned on a desire to experience history as well.

Not every Los Angeles photo album was created to provide view-ers with a proto-cinematic experience of Southern California life. Some albums at the turn of the century capitalized on the popularity of com-mercial photo albums in service of real estate and land development. The J. L. Le Berthon architecture company, for example, released its promo-tional photo album *Our Architecture* in 1904 to showcase the company's designed buildings around Los Angeles. The photographs by Claude S. Turner featured wide shots to show the buildings in full, accompanied by deep staging. Turner's photographs emphasize the wideness of the streets and use the corners of each building as a focal point—providing a three-dimensional sense of Los Angeles space familiar through ste-reoscopic albums. The following year, Le Berthon produced the album *Architecture of R. B. Young* (1905) depicting buildings shot in a similar manner, evoking the same sense of three-dimensional space, with images of the Stapleton Hotel, the Lankershim Hotel, and the Pacific Hospital attending to the beaux arts principles of allowing the sky to dominate the landscape within the frame.

Here I introduce Charles Fletcher Lummis (1859–1928), a fig-ure who will play a significant role in the following chapters. Lummis arrived in Los Angeles in 1884 after walking cross-country from Cincin-nati, a journey he would later document in his book *A Tramp across the Continent* (1892). Among all the regional boosters active in the Progres-sive Era, Lummis was perhaps the most vocal and well known, adopting a distinct California persona that was a performative embodiment of the California look and feel of the Payne stereoviews. His editorship of *Land of Sunshine* is a crucial component in the story of movie-made Los Angeles, as the publication brings together narration, mythology, and visual culture in a way that set the stage for the motion picture industry to assume the chief booster role and to transform the perception of the region. *Land of Sunshine*, the brainchild of Charles Dwight Willard of the Los Angeles Chamber of Commerce, promoted Southern California as a land of opportunity and the crystallization of American destiny by showcasing regional literary talent alongside sketches and generous use of photographic imagery. Articles on art, archeology, nature, wildlife, and regional history were endowed with greater impact through accom-panying photographs, often supplied by photographers affiliated with the Southern Pacific and Santa Fe Railroad Companies. Lummis also used his own photographs; responding to the vibrant culture of photography that was flourishing in the city, he became a photographer in his own right after arriving in Los Angeles, (though there is no documentation of his receiving any formal photographic training).[70] Taking advantage of breakthroughs during the 1880s in screen halftone processes—a technique for converting photographs into easily inked and printed dot patterns—Lummis embraced photography as a way to make the magazine's claims of California as a paradise real, working "primarily with 5 × 7 inch glass negatives and favoring the blue-toned cyanotype print process."[71] As the magazine increased in popularity and circulation from 1894 to 1902, the use of photographic halftones nationwide increased from 9 percent to 80 percent, while the older woodcut engraving process decreased dramatically. This "iconographic revolution," as Jennifer Watts observes, is comparable to the revolution in printing wrought by the Guttenberg press four hundred years earlier, invites comparison as well to contemporary web-based dissemination of multimedia.[72] Later, as readership expanded, the magazine held photography contests, soliciting readers to submit the best collection of out-of-doors views taken in Southern California, offering cash prizes of $5 to first-place winners and free subscriptions to runners-up. In response to the success of *Land of Sunshine* as an effective vehicle, in both literary and visual terms, for promoting semi-tropical California, Lummis remarked that the magazine "has more than a suspicion . . . that it will reveal some pictorial views about this extraordinary land, even to the majority of those who live here."[73]

"FOR THE ENCOURAGEMENT OF BETTER PHOTOGRAPHY"

Walter Benjamin reads the rise of the art photography during the early twentieth century as a redirected gaze back to "the pre-industrial prime" of photography. Photography, in this regard, is about extending the range of perception, or uncovering the "aspects of pictorial words which live in the smallest things, perceptible yet covert enough to find shelter in daydreams."[74] The panoramas of Carleton Watkins, for example, repurposed photographic language to expand perceptual telemetry, whether the recipient was experiencing a city in a novel fashion or witnessing the transformation of frontier land into manageable terrain. H. T. Payne's stereoscopic albums produced three-dimensional ground-level views of Los Angeles that emphasized the region's frontier status, engendering a distinct California feeling in the cultural imaginary. *Land of Sunshine* blended poetic written praise with both photographs and (as we will discuss in the next chapter) sketch images that celebrated this transformation *and* wildness. By contrast, the art photography community in Los Angeles during the early twentieth century demonstrated the power of a different way of seeing. A crucial subgenre of art photography that played a significant role in shaping the perception of Los Angeles as a place for image production and image consumption was pictorialism: an international movement that advocated for the photographer to "create" images rather than simply capture them. Southern California pictorialism called for the photographer's work to be individual and distinctive, invested with meaning. As part of the broader international movement, pictorialists in Los Angeles brought qualities to Southern California photography that bore striking similarities to cinematic practices: "dramatic references to art history," a willingness to incorporate professional studio practices, and a reliance on a "club and salon system . . . [with] its complicated relationships among many photographic communities."[75]

A critical moment in the history of art photography in Southern California was the 1914 founding of the Camera Pictorialists of Los Angeles by Louis Fleckenstein, Edward Weston, and Margrethe Mather. The primary aim of the club, and of the pictorialism movement at large, was to elevate the form to a painterly level: not replicating reality but using the photographic form to bend reality to the will of the artist. The club held annual exhibitions at the Los Angeles County Museum of History, Science, and Art (now the Natural History Museum of Los Angeles County in Exposition Park) until the 1930s. Though the work of each of the club's members plays a significant role in the story of Southern California art photography, Weston's work is of particular significance here because of how it intersects with other forms of Progressive Era photography and the other visual culture forms explored in this book, particularly in its visualization of the region's varied topography and climate and part of a transcendent experience. Weston arrived in Los Angeles in 1906, leaving briefly to receive what he felt was essential photographic training in Illinois before moving back in 1908. Inspired by the Photo-Secession movement of Alfred Stieglitz, Weston began experimenting with extreme close-ups, abstraction, and lighting effects, techniques that were becoming increasingly associated with motion pictures.[76] Writing about working in California for *Camera Craft* in 1939, Weston reflected on this early work in Southern California:

> I chose to work in the West, and here in California especially, because of the tremendous variety of subject matter to be found here. For instance: one day I was photographing along the old Butterfield Stage Route on the Colorado Desert, with the temperature around 120, heat waves shimmering over the dry washes. The next day I was up in the Laguna Mountains, among green meadows, brooks, and shady trees, looking down over a mile on the desert track I had crossed the day before. This is the kind of sudden contrast that makes California an exciting place to work. And because this kaleidoscopic quality of the state appeals to me so strongly, my secondary aim has been to record it.[77]

Weston's description of photographing the state recalls the appeal of its varied climate and topography that contributed to the development of outdoor shooting and the studio back lot in Southern California, as well as the influx of impressionist or plein air painters in Southern California during the late nineteenth and early twentieth century, upon which I will elaborate on in chapter 2. Weston was exposed to California plein air painting at the Panama-Pacific Exposition in San Francisco in 1915 as well as the stimuli of experiments by modernist artists. Pictorialists like Weston emphasized panoramic views, often using the "natural haze of the sun to emphasize the subjective perception" and imbuing the landscape with "symbolic value."[78] This approach would later have a profound influence on Ansel Adams, who also recognized the importance of locating the emotionally piercing aspects in the California landscape's "kaleidoscope quality." Adams, Weston, and documentary filmmaker Willard Van Dyke would later form the California photography group f/64, arguing that photography, ideally, should reveal "the inner folds of the awareness of the spirit."[79] This approach to photography asks us to reconsider our understanding of stasis in contrast to the moving image, or the framework that has traditionally been used to distinguish film from still photography. Rather than looking at still photography as an antecedent mechanism for photographic inscription, Louise Hornby makes a case for reading photography as part of a continuum of visual culture that has "entered into various stages of self-consciousness since its inception," and that modernism and the advent of cinema "coincided with one of those stages when photography sought a discrete identity."[80] Photographic stillness, she argues, is not an antithesis of modernism but rather an essential component of it, and it is therefore essential to read both still photography and the motion picture as part of a continuum of visual culture.

Pictorialism in California steered art photography toward an anti-booster role, positioning the form as a component of Mike Davis's debunking class of L.A. intellectuals (alongside writers like Upton Sinclair and modernist painters who challenged the conservative values of California plein air). The pictorialism of Weston, Fleckenstein, Mather, and others did the same in still form. A crucial aspect of this history, according to Mark Shiel, is that both the club and its tendencies coincided with the rise of the Hollywood studio network.[81] This is significant on two levels. First, the pictorialists, in their opposition to photography's industry and commercial functions, set the stage for the avant-garde cinema that emerged in Los Angeles during the 1920s: experimental art cinema constructed in opposition to the Hollywood studio system, which at that point had superseded other visual forms as the region's chief booster. As David E. James observes, filmmakers like Charles Bryant and Alla Nazimova during the 1920s, and later filmmakers like Maya Deren and Kenneth Anger, saw Los Angeles as an embodiment of contradictions and contested the "misrepresentations of class struggle by a popular culture of the establishment."[82] Art photography, like avant-garde cinema, responded to the contradictions of booster industry photography through de-emphasizing photography's reputation as a reality-based documentary form.

Yet at the same time, despite pictorialism's anti-booster leanings, the movement played a significant role, according to Ben Brewster and Lea Jacobs, in the development of cinematic narrative structure in general, owing largely to frame composition and the theatrical arrangement of mise-en-scène.[83] For example, the Southern California Camera Club, originating as the Los Angeles Camera Club in 1899 until its reforming and renaming in 1915, became part of a "growing Hollywood contingency by the 1920s," its members regularly lending their craftsmanship as cinematographers and camera operators on Hollywood motion pictures. Lorraine Arnold, Will Connell, and Fred R. Archer operated in Hollywood while simultaneously running the club they had founded under the motto "For the encouragement of better photography"; Connell would go on to publish *In Pictures: A Hollywood Satire* in 1937, a pictorial critique of Hollywood artifice with text provided by *The Grapes of Wrath* screenwriter Nunnally Johnson. This overlap between pictorialism, anti-boosterism, and film reveals art photography as part of a broader modernism project that, along with motion pictures and modern architecture (as I will explore further in chapter 6) has a complicated relationship with the booster industry of regional mythology and attempts to bring alternative realities into relief in the land of sunshine.

CITY SYMPHONIES

In 1897, the Edison Company shot one of the earliest known films set in Los Angeles: *South Spring Street, Los Angeles, California*. This actuality film, which runs for roughly half a minute, depicts a street scene with passing pedestrians and streetcars in what is now a portion of downtown adjacent to Little Tokyo. Here there are traces of two key functions of Progressive Era photography: inscribing a recognizable Los Angeles mise-en-scène and contributing to a photographic cartography of the city, both accomplished through the film's sense of spatial awareness.

Figure 1.4. Three frames from *South Spring Street, Los Angeles, California*, by Thomas Edison Manufacturing Co., 1897. (Library of Congress, Washington, DC.)

The Southern California look and feel, anticipated by the H. T. Payne stereoscopic albums (and other visual forms discussed in later chapters), can be experienced in *Spring Street* through displaying the characteristics for which the city would later become known, revealing "specific texture, volume, density, and appearance" in stark contrast to street scenes of other American cities.[84] Five years after this street scene was shot, actualities such as *The Cawston Ostrich Farm*, *The Firestone Parade*, *The Rose Parade at Pasadena*, and *The Santa Monica Road Races* replicated *Spring Street*'s presentation of Southern California life as the convergent point of the wild (or the frontier) and a newly envisioned conception of urban space.[85] *Spring Street*'s cartographic function is first announced through its accompanying description: "Advertised as a part of 'Southern Pacific Company Series.' . . . The following subjects were taken by our artist while traveling over the very extensive lines of the Southern Pacific Railroad Co. to whom we are indebted for many courtesies, and without whose co-operation we should not have been able to bring before the public these animated photographs of interesting and novel scenes."[86] For a spectator on the East Coast (or perhaps an American Mutoscope and Biograph filmmaker based in New Jersey), a scene from the end of the Southern Pacific line, advertised nationally as "avoiding the extreme cold of the winter months . . . making it a favorable route for tourists," is presented as populated with humans in motion in a way that patterns the imagination of the spectator familiar with the region through antecedent forms. Though not panoramic like later visions of L.A. or providing an aerial view like the Spence Airline for *Southern California through the Camera* or even the 1903 actuality from Roy Knabenshue's airship at on display in Chute's Park, *Spring Street* would set the stage for silent films that revealed Los Angeles from ground-level perspectives for those who had never set foot in the city.[87]

Mack Sennett's slapstick comedies are separated from the *Spring Street* by what Charlie Keil describes as the "transition period"—roughly 1907–13—when motion pictures were characterized by increased narrative complexity, greater individuation of characters, and more attention to "narratively relevant spatial relationships" achieved through mise-en-scène.[88] Sennett's comedies introduced the world to the Keystone Cops, Fatty Arbuckle, Mabel Normand and, of course, Charlie Chaplin, and as the camera followed these madcap comedians around Los Angeles in merriment and misadventure, there was an exploration, according to Mark Shiel, of "unfamiliar territory that was rapidly evolving before [the viewer's] eyes."[89] When Sennett showed his Keystone Cops chasing suspects around Echo Park, lions chasing humans around a two-story house, or an automobile dangling off a cliff above Santa Monica, the message to the viewer becomes just as much about "Look where we can go" as "Look what we can do." Coinciding with Los Angeles's transformation into the West Coast's largest city, the Keystone comedies "provided revealing descriptions of the shape of Los Angeles," an approach that Chaplin would carry into his own films after leaving Keystone—for Essanay, Mutual, First National, and eventual his iconic films for United Artists. In *City Lights* (1931), for example, Chaplin's Tramp character and a drunken millionaire drive home after a night on the town, the camera attached to the front of the car facing both passengers as the car whizzes through the city—passing by the J. W. Robinson Department Store (Grand and West Seventh), the B. F. Coulter Dry Goods Company (one block over), and the Ville de Paris Department Store on West Seventh and Olive (also featured in Harold Lloyd's 1923 film *Safety Last*).[90] In these films, L.A. locations are preserved in celluloid as palimpsest layers of the city, retrieved by the spectator through what is essentially a comedic repurposing of the phantom ride.

Phantom rides, according to Jan Olsson, were popular in Los Angeles well into the 1910s for their "dreamlike, almost hypnotic qualities."[91] Detailing a setting through a camera mounted onto a moving vehicle, this early cinematic forerunner to virtual reality, amusement park rides, and simulated travel resonates throughout L.A. cinema at all stages of film history. The opening shot of *Blade Runner* (Ridley Scott, 1982) serves as a notable example: a phantom ride through the sky as towers that dot the downtown skyline belch fire. In the nonfiction film *Los Angeles, ca. 1920*, however, the traditional single-shot aspect of the phantom ride is disrupted by editing that creates a similar day-in-the-life time lapse quality found in Muybridge's chrono-panoramas. In one instance, the viewer passes by a store selling silk shirts advertised for $6.85 (approximately $85 at the time of this writing), and a moment later, the camera passes by the First National motion picture studio offices, the employees stepping out of the building and onto the sidewalk to wave at the passing camera. The phantom ride then passes by the Victory Theater, which is playing Allan Dwan's *A Splendid Hazard* (Mayflower Photoplay Company, 1920), and then there is a cut to the Kinema Theatre on 642 South Grand, showing Mack Sennett's *Mabel and Fatty's Married Life* (1915).[92] Later the film cuts to a phantom ride traveling outside of the downtown area, past the Mack Sennett Studios near Glendale Boulevard and Alessandro Avenue in Edendale. The vastness that the city exuded in the *Spring Street* actuality and the H. T. Payne photographs is present in *Los Angeles, ca. 1920*, as the wideness of the streets in contrast to other cities is emphasized through the editing and staging of passing pedestrians and streetcars. The film also recorded history in the making as it passed the site of the Pacific Mutual Sentry Building at Sixth and Grand, capturing the moment that Los Angeles, according to David Fine, changed its sales pitch from trumpeting L.A. as a sunshine paradise to promoting the city as a cosmopolitan urban space; during the 1920s, Los Angeles came to be "promoted less like a Mediterranean Garden and more like a West Coast Metropolis."[93]

Los Angeles, ca. 1920 is one of the many "city symphonies" produced at the end of the Progressive Era (many of which are lost forever). City symphonies, a silent film genre that elevated the actuality film to the level of poetic city portrait, can also be read as rehearsals of photography's cartographic functions and a visual rendering of stadtbild. Films such as *Berlin: Symphony of a City* (Walter Ruttman, 1927) and *A propos de Nice* (Jean Vigo, 1930) offer a continuation of nineteenth-century photography's visual grammar for city transcription, while at the same time drawing on panoramic visions of cityscapes. In the case of Los Angeles, the city symphony genre has historically been used to serve both booster aims and debunker critiques, with both frameworks utilizing the same photography-rooted language for visualizing the city. On the booster side of the equation there is *Southern California Holiday*, produced by the Santa Fe Railway Company in 1953 and presenting an L.A. stadtbild rooted in a sense of vastness and perceived freedom of motion.[94] The twenty-five-minute documentary presents the city's typical street scenes as horizontal through a wide-angle lens and sweeping pans, offering very few shots that do not feature clear horizon lines and/or the full bodies of the city's residents in constant motion. What is also striking is that the connection between regional promotion and the railroad industry is also maintained: the film opens with a shot of a train crossing the Mojave

Desert as the voice-over proclaims that "there is probably no single area holding so much charm and beauty and the good things in life as Southern California." The "beautifully designed, Spanish type station" (Union Station in downtown) is the first Los Angeles location presented before the viewer is treated to a montage of views of Los Angeles sites that feel descended from the Edison actuality film. The variety of architecture in Beverly Hills, a product of the 1920s trend of Southern California eclectic (which I will return to in chapter 6), is also showcased in the film alongside activities of healthy living, industries based around oil and auto manufacturing, wildlife viewing, simulacra of the region's Spanish/ Mexican colonial past and, of course, the motion picture industry. What connects the *Southern California Holiday* to other L.A. city symphonies (and antecedent visual forms) is the sense that film is rendering visible what would otherwise be the city's invisible drama, a characteristic that ultimately brings the city symphony into dialogue with the panoramas of Muybridge and Watkins.

2

CALIFORNIA IN *PLEIN AIR*

In 1967, the California Institute for the Arts published a course information packet on its film program, known as the Cinemagraphic Division.
The program was advertised as "patterned after a professional motion
picture studio and staffed by professionally trained artists, designers, animators, and filmmakers." The motion picture, the school proclaimed,
was not taught "as a purely commercial art" but rather as a "significant
art form in itself, one due for an increasingly important role in the area
of fine arts," with the cinemagraphics student learning in an environment of "music, drama, painting, and sculpture."[1] Modeled after Walt
Disney Productions and staffed by Disney-trained artists such as William Hurtz (instructor 1963–68), the institute's cinemagraphics program
offers some interesting insight into the way that painted forms during
the Progressive Era played a crucial role in the development of the Los
Angeles visual arts world and how Los Angeles organized itself as a cultural economy.[2] Before 1961, the institute had been the Chouinard Art
Institute (founded in 1921) which, since the 1930s, had trained many
of Disney's animators as well as set designers and special effects artists
from other studios. Chouinard had, in effect, provided a model for Disney throughout the 1920s and 1930s of what a film training academy
could look like. While much has been written about the animators who
graduated from Chouinard—notably Disney animator Mary Blair and
Warner Bros. animator Maurice Noble—little scholarly attention has
been given to the faculty at Chouinard who trained film professionals.[3] Their history brings into relief a more complete picture of how the
turn-of-the-century arts scene in Los Angeles fostered the rise of the film

studio network. This chapter will explore painting in Southern California from roughly 1890 to 1920, a period in the region's history in which the techniques and style of Monet, Cézanne, and Matisse were applied to semi-tropical California's ecosystem.

First, I will explore California impressionism and how this movement supplied the region with visual narration. Often referred to as California plein air—drawing on the French *en plein air*, or "outdoors"—impressionism in California mythologized the Southland through light and color techniques that left behind formal strategies readily adaptable to motion picture production. Reaching back to earlier traditions of "American Eden" painting, California plein air used the region's natural beauty to fuel back-to-nature attitudes that contrasted sharply with the rapid urbanization of the Los Angeles area. Painters like William Wendt (1865–1946), Guy Rose (1867–1925), and Richard E. Miller (1875–1943) were steeped in the style of French impressionism and used California's terrain and climate to provide that style with a new lease on life, creating what Michael McManus described as a "beautiful anachronism."[4] For the most part, I will be using the term *plein air* rather than impressionism in large part to draw comparisons between the techniques of outdoor painting and filmic design practices, finding parallels between this art form and the use of California's natural landscape by the early studios.

Next, this chapter will look at the students of plein air and modern art that entered the motion picture industry and shaped evolving visual practices. Central to this story are members of the California Water Color Society.[5] Formed in 1921, the California Water Color Society infused plein air techniques with elements from cubism and realism to bring urban settings, rather than orange- and purple-toned sycamore canyons, to life. These artists emphasized everyday California life by bringing people and machines to California scenes that were familiar through photography, disrupting booster narratives while at the same time finding inspiration in the ways that plein air painters observed the natural world. As the Great Depression impacted Southern California, many of the Water Color Society members brought their talents to the film industry and adjacent fields: as Disney animators, designers of iconic film noir props, backdrop painters for films like *The Wizard of Oz* and *An American in Paris*, special effects artists who brought ancient worlds to life, and art teachers who trained the next generation of film creatives.

Last, this chapter will turn to art forms that challenged the popularity and relevancy of plein air during the 1920s. The decline of California impressionism coincided with the rise of art forms constructed in opposition to impressionism's aesthetics and booster affiliations. Modern forms like cubism, futurism, fauvism, and synchromism made inroads into the Los Angeles art scene due in large part to the European émigré filmmakers who championed these art forms, as well as art collectors who were willing to go against the tastes of L.A.'s conservative establishment. These oppositional forms connect with the history of Los Angeles cinema in two distinct ways. First, these modern art forms shaped Los Angeles into what David E. James describes as a "polynucleated site" for a variety of smaller cinemas working in tandem with and opposition to the Hollywood mainstream. In James's book *The Most Typical Avant-Garde: History and Geography of Minor Cinemas in Los Angeles*, he describes a "twilight zone" between industrial and nonindustrial film practices during the 1920s, in which modern art techniques were used to defamiliarize the narrative form that Hollywood had standardized by the end of the 1910s.[6] Second, modern art movements, either because or in spite of their position on the outskirts of the L.A. art scene from the 1920s through the 1940s, would shape approaches to production, animation, and special effects. Artists like Jules Engle, Knud Merrild, and Rico Lebrun, while not necessarily connected through style or technique in the way that plein air–trained film creatives were, recognized that Hollywood and its host city were preoccupied with light and movement and that film was the product of cross-pollinated art forms.

THE EUCALYPTUS SCHOOL

> Nature always challenges the capabilities of the imagination. . . .
> A pictorial representation is always a translation. Nature suggests ideas for interpretation, the artist supplies ideas of how interpretation is to be made.
> —Edgar Payne, *Composition of Outdoor Painting*

Albert Bierstadt's visits to California during the 1860s and 1870s provide a crucial starting point in sketching out the history of painting in

California. Steeped in the *luminist* style, Bierstadt imbued the state's landscape with symbolic and narrative meaning, layering these scenes with the visual language of American destiny.[7] Belonging to the Hudson River School tradition, paintings such as *Valley of Yosemite* (1864) and *Among the Sierra Nevada Mountains* (1868) anticipated Progressive Era booster literature through suffused light and sublime sensibilities, forecasting the future California mythmaking industry of Charles Fletcher Lummis through oil paint; Ansel Adams would photograph these same locations in 1935, infusing Bierstadt's luminist vision with the ideals of Edward Weston's f/64 circle. In response to Bierstadt, as well as painters like George Innes and James Abbott Whistler, a community of artists developed in Northern California that further advanced the Hudson River School ideas in visualizing in the Golden State. San Francisco, in sharp contrast to Los Angeles, had its "own academy of art with high professional standards and strong connections to European and American art centers," creating the ideal conditions to grow an art community.[8] Painters like William Keith (1838–1911), William Frederic Ritschel (1864–1949), and Mary DeNeale Morgan (1868–1948) would become known as Northern California tonalists, centered largely along the coastlines of Monterrey and Carmel.[9] Often referring to themselves as luminists to directly evoke the Hudson River School, Northern California tonalists preferred moody tones, muted colors, and soft contours. Their works were often shrouded in the fog and haze so common to the San Francisco Bay Area and the Monterrey Bay region, rendering the California landscape as sites of contemplation in low-key color harmony and diffused lighting.[10] For example, before traveling south to Los Angeles, Granville Redmond's (1871–1935) Northern California tonalist work was considered by some to be exceptionally evocative and moody despite a very limited color range (similar to the pictorialist's black-and-white art photography of the early twentieth century). While often referred to as part of the California impressionism tradition, Northern tonalism never really took hold in California and the rest of the nation, as Susan Landauer observes. The "tranquil and often melancholy landscapes" of the north were the "temperamental opposite of the sunny optimism sweeping through Southern California."[11]

A different story emerged in the Southern California sunlight. The population of Los Angeles jumped from nearly ten thousand in 1880 to nearly fifty thousand in 1890, and along with that came artists. As previously discussed, the arrival of transcontinental rail lines to Los Angeles stimulated the region economically, but at the same time it also directly fueled the growth of a local art community. As Jean Stern and Molly Siple have written, railroad companies like the Santa Fe and Southern Pacific initiated programs that offered artists free passage and board in exchange for paintings that could be used on railroad posters, handbills, advertisements, and calendars.[12] Thomas Moran and Edgar Payne, the latter a leading figure in the Southern California plein air movement, were notable California artists who took advantage of this program. Many of the painters who arrived in Los Angeles around this time had been born and educated in Europe, such as Austrian-born Franz Bischoff (1864–1929) and Prussian-born William Wendt. Other artists, such as Richard E. Miller and the California-born Guy Rose, studied in Europe before returning to the United States to apply their training under the California sun (both had done a residency at Monet's Giverny Colony in France). What is striking about the community of artists that formed in Southern California during the 1890s is that they saw themselves as outsiders, especially as their movement progressed into the early twentieth century and came into conflict with modern forms popular in Europe and on the U.S. East Coast. In contrast to Northern tonalists, these Southern Californians preferred lighter colors and celebrated the utopian promises of Southern California life promoted through booster publications like Lummis's *Land of Sunshine*.[13] In short, Southern California plein air was propelled and funded by turn-of-the-century boosterism, the movement directly influencing the visual marketing campaigns aimed at real estate and population growth.

Though Los Angeles at the turn of the century, according to Jean Stern, did not have substantial art establishments, the relationship between local artists and the California lifestyle industry embodied in Lummis's publications helped to turn Los Angeles into a convergence point for young artists.[14] It is no accident then that much of the initial Southern California plein air culture was centered around the Arroyo Seco, a dry riverbed running from the San Gabriel Mountains toward the L.A. River that was considered the region's center for bohemian life during the 1890s and 1900s. The natural environment of the arroyo was instrumental in the formation of the look and feel that Southern

California impressionism exuded. William Lee Judson (1842–1928), landscape painter and founder of a fine arts studio in Highland Park, "imported Manet's palette" to the Arroyo Seco, creating "his own brand of impressionism tempered by realism."[15] Elmer Wachtel (1864–1929), impressionist painter and violinist for the Los Angeles Philharmonic, was drawn to the "subtle but strong colors" of the area: the "brown-green of the grass . . . in mid-winter; the golden browns and yellows of October sunshine . . . ; violet and purple discerned in the distant hills; sycamores, yellow-pink to tender green at various seasons; and the pale amethyst sky over the La Cañada hills."[16] Forming what would be loosely known as the Arroyo group, this informal collection of painters who resided in the area emerged alongside prominent boosters who also called the Arroyo Seco home. Gutzon Borglum (1867–1941), the future sculptor of Mount Rushmore, worked with Lummis and studied art at the Art Institute in San Francisco with funding organized by Lummis and other Southern California land promoters. Upon returning to Los Angeles, Borglum would illustrate for *Land of Sunshine*, designing the cover and logo for the magazine, and later receiving art commissions from the Los Angeles elite through Lummis's connections.[17] Lafayette Maynard Dixon (1875–1946), a former illustrator for *Harper's Weekly*, worked alongside Borglum for *Land of Sunshine*, sketching mountain lions and other wildlife. Dixon was later described in an 1898 edition of the magazine as "the most promising illustrator on this Coast."[18] A connection between regional art and a popular image of Southern California emerges when one looks at the cover image of *Land of Sunshine*. A "half-page engraving of orange groves, palm trees, and snow-capped mountains stand in symmetrical perfection," portraying the land as one of "temperate days and cool evenings, verdant growth, and orderly landscapes."[19] The California look and feel in late nineteenth-century photography is presented here in ways that highlight the capacity of art forms to provide the land with narration and meaning.

Southern California plein air constructed what some scholars refer to as the state's social imaginary: a collective memory of a place that may never have existed but nevertheless is built in people's minds.[20] That these mental images of California spring to the mind's eye when prompted by booster rhetoric is the product of plein air's engagement with the natural landscape in three distinct ways. First, they emphasized the state's natural beauty in a manner that foreshadowed early Hollywood's signature

Figure 2.1. Cover page of *The Land of Sunshine* magazine, June 1894 (Huntington Library, San Marino, CA, call number 44214.)

practices of place substitution. Drawing on earlier traditions of American Eden painting and French impressionism techniques simultaneously, California plein air intensified the local population's connection to nature amid a period of rapid urbanization. In these paintings, the grassy hills and sycamore canyons of the Arroyo and beyond reinforced the state's emblematic colors, notably purple and orange, and provided an ideal environment to continue the legacy of the luminists, in which the primal aspects of nature are connected to a spiritual state of mind. Second, plein air painters brought a sense of nostalgia and escapism to California life. Utilizing the favorable advantages offered by the climate and terrain, these painters fueled back-to-nature attitudes through an emphasis on nature in stark contrast to urbanization, providing a sense of civic pride through visualizing the region's origins as a paradisiacal landscape. It also must be said that Southern California plein air constitutes a certain take on the concept of "the sublime," an overwhelming sense of awe in the face of physical greatness that was a feature of landscape paintings in Europe and North America from the early nineteenth century. Third, Los Angeles's location far from the world's art centers shielded the region from the grim realities found in other art forms, making plein air the dominant style until modern forms began to make inroads into Los Angeles during the late 1910s and early 1920s. While the movement faded in popularity during the 1920s, artists trained in plein air painting would utilize these techniques in film production design, animation, special effects, and educating future film creatives at L.A. art academies like Chouinard, Otis, and Scripps.

Edgar Payne, recounting his experiences as a plein air artist toward the end of his life, remarked that "nature must not be forgotten. The habit of continually painting outdoor motifs from imagination will eventually produce only 'studio pictures' without the feeling of real outdoor qualities."[21] Consider what the state's geography and natural environment afforded artists in contrast to elsewhere. In Europe, artists would have to travel great distances to find varied landscapes (deserts, mountains, snow, sea), often incurring risks, whereas from Los Angeles these landscapes were often within fifty miles or fewer. Painters like William Griffith (1866–1940) would travel in a wagon far from his home base in Laguna Beach before later shifting his focus to co-found the Laguna Beach Art colony and the Laguna Beach Art Association. Benjamin Brown (1865–1942), a quick and mobile artist known for his poppy field paintings, was often photographed with his portable, collapsible easel box in the hills above Pasadena.[22] Alson S. Clark (1876–1949), a French-educated World War I veteran, was known for driving far from Los Angeles to create large-scale paintings (often thirty-six by forty-six inches), producing these works at incredible speeds and without the aid of sketches. (It is worth noting that, even in the favorable conditions of the California sunshine, painting on this scale was not preferred by plein air painters, as too large a canvas made it difficult to respond to changing sunlight and weather conditions; roughly eighteen-by-twenty-four-inch pre-cut wood panels were preferred.) The advantage provided by these natural settings, as well as the inherent abstraction of these paintings, freed these images from what André Bazin would call "the complex of resemblance."[23] Impressionism finds its emotional charge in atmosphere and by showcasing its differences from the objective reality associated with the photographic image. This was a quality of plein air revered by boosterism, as the promise of realism is discarded in favor of dissolving objects into smaller elements to be coded with narrative meaning.

Maurice Braun's (1877–1941) *Land of Sunshine* (date unknown) embodies
the optimism of the Lummis magazine of the same name, brought to life
through orange-toned rolling hills and sun-bathed sycamore trees. Guy
Rose's *The Oak* (1916) uses the titular tree, nearly gold-toned, to upstage
the setting painted in the "high key of nature" and "alert to every impression of beauty," as friend and fellow plein air painter Antony Anderson
(1863–1939) remarked.[24] Paul Grimm's (1891–1974) eucalyptus paintings
celebrated this import to Southern California's Edenic garden, whereas
Franz Bischoff would do the same with roses—both artists using regional
flora to advance a growing cultural perception of Southern California
life. Layering the landscape with metaphors of American destiny, much
as Bierstadt's California paintings had done previously, the Arroyo group
and other Southern California plein air painters visualized the rhetoric
of boosters like Lummis, Nordhoff, and McGroarty, participating in a
broader proto-cinematic mythology industry.

William Wendt is a crucial figure in both the story of plein air's connection to the booster industry, as not only does his work strongly exemplify the form's capacity for narrativizing landscapes but also his career
was instrumental in the formation of the Los Angeles's art community
on the eve of movie industry ascendancy in the region. Referred to as the
"Dean of Southern California Landscape Painters," Wendt first came to
California as a tourist during the 1890s, eventually settling in the region
and founding, along with other prominent Los Angeles–based artists,
the California Art Club in Pasadena. Singled out by critics for the "bril-
liancy of light and strength of color" in his work, Wendt made a name
for himself within and outside of California by lending his paintings to
travel writers as illustrations and to postcard companies, placing his
paintings in heavy circulation throughout the 1900s and 1910s.[25]
His painting *Land of Heart's Desire* (fig. 2.2) was converted to a sketch
illustration for use in booster John S. McGroarty's mythologizing ode to
California life, *California: Its History and Romance* (1911), a work cited
by early filmmakers Al Christie and the Horsley Brothers (founders of
the Nestor Film Company in 1911) as inspiring their move to the Golden
State.[26] *Land of Heart's Desire* would also become a popular painting featured in plein air exhibition circuits both within California and outside
the state—notably at the 1910 Art Institute of Chicago exhibit and at the
1915 Panama-Pacific International Exposition in San Francisco.

Figure 2.2. *Land of Heart's Desire*: illustration of William Wendt's 1910 painting of the same name featured in John S. McGroarty's *California: Its History and Romance* (1911).

Wendt's use of complementary colors and popular optical theories of the period proved to be lucrative for him and other plein air painters. In *Head of Amarillo Canyon* (fig. 2.3), gold, orange, and purple are "keyed to a fever pitch," embodying the state's color palette made popular through other forms of visual booster promotion.[27] California becomes a staging ground in this painting for exploring the idea that true colorists are the "descendants of Impressionists," liberating secondary tones to bring "motion and kinesis" to nature scenes.[28] Furthermore, one of the by-products of impressionism, as Sarah Street and Joshua Yumibe note, was an embracement of new color paints and chromatic experiments, and the work produced by Wendt and his plein air contemporaries exemplifies the connection between artistic experimentation and California nature culture.[29] Responding to these ideas about color and motion, cinematographer John Alton would later write in *Painting with Light* that a crucial element of shooting outdoors in California was that there were different types of daylight, each providing a slightly different mood and sense of movement, just as plein air painting offers examples of what

Figure 2.3. *Head of Amarillo Canyon*, by William Wendt, 1897. (Private collection.)

Figure 2.4. *Poppy Fields Near Pasadena*, by Benjamin Brown, date unknown. (Private collection.)

different forms of daylight could do emotionally. "When we are out-side," remarked Alton, "we see pictures within pictures. We feel their vibrations; some of them bring memories, [while] others appeal to us because they bear messages."[30] These vibrating and kinetic secondary colors of California connect to the booster industry in striking ways that still have resonance in contemporary California life. For example, the prominence of these colors in the California citrus industry's box labels and advertisements, explored further in the next chapter, are an example of the California palette that was advanced by plein air and still experienced in California grocery stores today.[31] There appears to be little coincidence, then, that the movement's birth coincided with the first New Year's Tournament of Roses in Pasadena and its "display of botanical pyrotechnics."[32]

Benjamin Brown (1865–1942), who co-founded the California Art Club with Wendt, used a strikingly similar palette of orange, gold, and purple in his work, notably in his paintings of California poppies. Poppies and other prominent California wildflowers were popular subjects for Brown, an interest he shared with other plein air painters like John Marshall Gamble (1863–1957), Mary DeNeale Morgan, and Franz Bischoff. Southern California flora would loom large in these paintings, just as much as the California color palette, through poppies, wildflowers, sycamores, oak trees, yucca and, crucial to the story of plein air, eucalyptus. Originating in Australia, this naturalized immigrant was initially planted in 1877 by the Southern Pacific Railroad Company for the purpose of advertising to prospective buyers "the productive quality of its land," testing the value of wood for industrial purposes, and to "remove the sterile and forbidding appearance" of the company's stations.[33] Writing about the tree in his book *Eucalyptus* (1895), Abbot Kinney "celebrated the genius" of Californians in transforming "unlovely gums—scrawny, ashy, monotonous and depressing in their native Australian brush—into handy adornments."[34] A second wave of eucalyptus growth in California took place between 1907 and 1913, the heyday of California plein air and a time when civic planners were largely rejecting East Coast and European models for nucleated growth of city spaces, opting instead for regional design to be neither urban nor rural. The center of plein air culture, Pasadena, was an exemplar of this approach, taking beautification seriously and, as Jared Farmer notes, creating gardens *with* eucalyptus rather than forests *of* eucalyptus.[35] It appears to be no accident that by the end of the Progressive Era, California plein air was derisively referred to as the "Eucalyptus School" by East Coast art critics.

The role of nostalgia in California plein air is also significant to the story of Los Angeles. In some cases, this was accomplished through paintings featuring allusions to California's Spanish colonial past, with some images being in black and white for books that presented this mythologized history in poetic terms (as seen with Wendt's *Land of Heart's Desire*). In other cases, the paintings evoke a sense of belonging and a call to engage with the landscape as a form of civic pride. Yet nostalgia in these paintings also draws attention to the historical and cultural layers that they preserve. The palimpsest, according to Vincent Brook, is the master metaphor for representing the cover-up and the "bleeding through of L.A.'s historical layers," and reading plein air painting as a precursor to filmmaking in Los Angeles provides a site for staging a recovery of historical layers displaced by urbanization and cultural erasure.[36] Early filmmakers, arriving in California at the height of the plein air movement, were enticed by a social imaginary of the state that excluded the rapid urbanization taking place at the same time. These images of the state can be read as palimpsest layers preserved in oil paint. As Mark Sandberg argues, the varied geography and "rich array of settings" available in California appealed to filmmakers looking to relocate, and plein air painters, by keeping the rise of urbanity and city expansion outside the frame, strengthened this perception of the state.[37] In contrast to the photographic documentation of the rise of downtown Los Angeles during the nineteenth century, as well as the Edison actuality at the end of the century, plein air preserves the wild landscape of the region as a palimpsest layer, an environment that early filmmakers in Los Angeles witnessed before its eventual erosion. Performing a scholarly retrieval of this palimpsest layer reveals plein air as intensifying Angelenos' connection to nature amid the transformation of the city, fueling back-to-nature attitudes and connecting the California social imaginary to booster rhetoric of nostalgia and escapism. Even toward the end of the movement, these paintings, such as Joseph Kleitsch's (1882–1931) *The Old Post Office* (1922) and *Old Laguna* (1924), offer bittersweet views of a Southern California still clinging to its frontier status. As the 1920s were a key moment in L.A.'s formation, the decade in which the city began to

topographically resemble the city presently known to us, Kleitsch's paintings (and those of other plein air artists producing work in the 1920s)
can be seen as preserving a Southern California "third space"—a physical
location where real (first space) and imagined (second space) narratives
overlap and "disrupt binary and linear historical understandings of a
place and its people."[38] In California plein air, nostalgia is something
that comes not from the past but rather sideways, as Svetlana Boym
observes—a feeling of being out of time and place with a rapidly evolving world, such as the people of Los Angeles would have felt from 1900
to 1920 as the city grew into the West Coast's largest cultural economy.[39]

   Two crucial events in California history during the Progressive Era
propelled the California impressionist movement onto the national
stage and linked the form to a rapidly expanding form of Southern California identity. The first was an effort to build a permanent art museum
in Los Angeles that coincided with the rise of the Arroyo group and California impressionism. The initial attempt to build an L.A. art museum
was by the Ruskin Art Club—the first women's club in Los Angeles,
named after the famous English art critic John Ruskin—in 1892.[40] While
that attempt was unsuccessful, the first permanent display of paintings
opened later in 1894 at the Los Angeles Chamber of Commerce, coordi-
nated with the head of the Los Angeles School of Art and Design, Louise
Garden MacLeod, a Ruskin Art Club member. The chamber "was at first
reticent," as Nancy Moure notes, but when they realized "what potent
propaganda California landscapes effected . . . they became quite enthu-
siastic about it."[41] The efforts of the Ruskin Art Club were also a catalyst
for the 1895 formation of the Society for Fine Arts in California—whose
mission was "to advance the knowledge and love of art through exhibitions, by lectures, and instruction"—and the Painter's Club, formed in
1906 in the Arroyo Seco.[42] Writing about the Painter's Club in a 1911
article for *Out West* magazine, C. P. Austin describes the group as "always
earnest, though sometimes beneficial, [and] sometimes farcical."[43] The
efforts of the Ruskin Club and affiliated organizations eventually found
success with the creation of the Los Angeles Museum, which opened
in Exposition Park in 1913 under the leadership of curator Everett C.
Maxwell. Though the museum initially lacked art exhibitions, the first
important one was held in 1916, when Maxwell assembled the paintings that had been on display at the Panama Pacific Exposition in San

Francisco the year before, many of which were from notable California impressionists. The Los Angeles Museum still exists today in the same location as the Natural History Museum of Los Angeles County.

The second crucial event for California impressionism came in 1915 with the Panama-Pacific International Exposition in San Francisco, which popularized the movement on both a state and national level. The exposition opened on February 20, 1915—ostensibly to celebrate the opening of the Panama Canal, but it was also a commemoration among San Franciscans of the city's recovery from the 1906 earthquake.[44] By-products of the exposition were a celebration of California art and technology and a boost to the rising film industry. Early film pioneer William Selig, for example, was honored at a banquet (alongside William Randolph Hearst) for his contributions to California arts and culture. Yet, crucial to the story of plein air, the display of works at the exposition from painters like Benjamin Brown (the bronze medal winner) and William Wendt (the silver medal winner), whose *Land of Heart's Desire* painting was featured, amplified an interest in serious art forms and created new art lovers out of the attendees. The exposition also provided opportunities to study other artists and styles and for styles to mingle; photographers like Edward Weston experienced plein air and modern art form, and each of these forms (and others present at the exposition) comingled with each other and, ultimately, motion pictures, an emerging art form. Most important, the exposure given to California impressionism connected the movement to a growing wave of cultural populism, embodied by the increasing legitimization of the motion picture as an art form through the exposition and new established practices in photography. The exposition, as Jasper Schad notes, made a "progressive vision for art" a reality in Los Angeles, diminishing the "hierarchical distinctions between high art and popular art."[45]

During the movement's initial phase, wealthy boosters of the Arroyo Seco were the primary buyers of Southern California plein air paintings, yet by the mid-1890s the Los Angeles Chamber of Commerce's support of this art movement signaled that California impressionism was destined to have a life outside of the state and be wedded to a popular imagination of the region. Following the Panama-Pacific Exposition, the circulation of Southern California plein air imagery beyond the traditional exhibition circuit or gallery showings played a critical role in advancing popular cultural images of the state. By the 1910s, there had been a clear shift in the way these images circulated and who viewed/possessed them. In a 1916 article for the *American Magazine of Art*, critic Mabey Urmy Seares discussed Wendt's success at the exhibition, noting that the artist was well known outside of California, "perhaps best known in Chicago, where many of his paintings hang in public or private galleries."[46] Seares also noted that much of Wendt's expanding popularity could be attributed to the use of his paintings as book illustrations (as seen in McGroarty's *California: Its History and Romance*) and as postcards or miniature prints, which were in heavy circulation around the 1910s. Fueled by the tourism industry, travelers were invited to take a little bit of California home with them in the form of small plein air prints of Wendt's California color palette, Bischoff's roses, or Grimm's eucalypti. Popular resorts and hotel chains were instrumental in the spread of these images, notably the Biltmore Hotel group, owner of iconic hotels in downtown Los Angeles and what is now La Cañada Flintridge near Pasadena; while the Flintridge Biltmore no longer exists (currently the building is the Flintridge Sacred Heart Academy), the downtown Biltmore (or Millennium Biltmore) still displays plein air paintings alongside photographs from the early Academy Award ceremonies held in the hotel ballroom.

During the 1910s, circulating plein air images and creating a familiarity with their style and subject matter was limited to media outside of motion pictures. Cinema would not be a vehicle for spreading the style through the public consciousness until the 1920s at the earliest. Additionally, there is little documentation of California plein air painters working in the production design of early Hollywood during the Progressive Era, despite attention the movement received at the Panama-Pacific Exposition. There were, however, some painters who worked simultaneously in art and in the motion picture industry. The work of Granville Redmond, a deaf painter who started his art career in Northern Californian tonalism before moving to Los Angeles, provides an interesting case study of plein air's overlap with the burgeoning Hollywood film industry. Like Benjamin Brown, Redmond was known for his paintings of poppies and other wildflowers on the wild outskirts of Los Angeles. His paintings were routinely converted to postcards and miniature-sized paintings for tourists to take home. Yet painting was not Redmond's only trade. He was also an actor who worked primarily for Charlie Chaplin, appearing in at least six of Chaplin's films. Redmond would paint on the Chaplin studio lot between takes, often with Chaplin himself pausing to admire Redmond's work. Chaplin eventually gave Redmond his own art studio at Chaplin Studios, and in return the artist notably taught Chaplin sign language and how to use one's face to tell stories visually. In an interview for the *Silent Worker*, Chaplin credited Redmond with inspiring the famous bread roll dance sequence from his 1925 film *Gold Rush*, noting that Redmond was "tailor-made for this work" and that he did not need to speak, for his face and hands could tell a story.[47]

Another Hollywood plein air painter was Hobart Bosworth (1867–1943), who had started his career working as a stage actor in Los Angeles during the 1900s and eventually was hired by Selig Polyscope to star in his debut film, which would be the first narrative film shot in Southern California: *The Count of Monte Cristo* (Francis Boggs, 1908). Bosworth would continue working for Selig, appearing as several iconic characters—such as the titular wizard in *The Wonderful Wizard of Oz* (1910), *Davy Crockett* (1910), and *The Sea Wolf* (1913)—until joining the Thomas H. Ince Studios in the early 1920s. At Ince, Bosworth would spend his mornings painting before he was needed on set, producing work steeped in the plein air style. In a Thomas H. Ince studio tour film from 1920, Bosworth is shown painting outdoors, with the title card reading: "The paint and brush occupy Hobart Bosworth before his march to the studio."[48] In an interview with the *Los Angeles Examiner* in 1918, Bosworth stated, "I want to paint pictures of the desert whose beauty has me a fast captive in its charm . . . that is the work that I love."[49]

Despite (and in some ways because of) California impressionism's connection to boosterism, the movement faced criticism in the early 1910s from Los Angeles's progressive and conservative circles alike. On the one hand, the movement was championed by *Los Angeles Times* art columnist Antony Anderson, whose articles during this period focused heavily on the promotion of local artists.[50] Plein air, as Anderson wrote, "is not a plaything for idle hands, but the expression of a strong soul's aspiration toward the ideal in life."[51] On the other hand, progressive Los Angeles groups were uncomfortable with an "emphasis on surface beauty . . . and its habit of dematerializing objects."[52] Additionally, the conservative Los Angeles press viewed California impressionism through a lens of xenophobia in the wake of World War I, describing the

Figure 2.5. Granville Redmond and Charlie Chaplin on the set of *A Dog's Life* (1918). Chaplin is forming the letter *d* in American Sign Language. (University of California–Berkeley Library.)

movement as a "fetish of European superiority."[53] There was also criticism within the movement itself; William Wendt, for example, argued against meddling with nature: "Nature has more to say than can be caught in a minute [and] we landscape painters should mix our brains with our paint."[54] Much of these criticisms (and to some extent, some of the success) of California plein air can be attributed to Los Angeles's location far from the world's art centers, shielding the region not just from other art movements but also from the grim realities found in other art forms, and yet this insulated bubble provided unsustainable. Toward the end of the 1920s, California impressionism declined in popularity. The movement, after all, was "the style's final instalment," according to Donald D. Keyes.[55]

The movement's decline can be attributed to several factors, but there are two that, paradoxically, foreshadow the movement's eventual impact on the cinematic arts. First, plein air artists found it increasingly difficult to compete with other art forms, notably cubism, futurism, and modernism. Added to this, the appearance of these other forms in motion picture décor, set design, and visual marketing campaigns raised their visibility in the public sphere. Impressionism was ill equipped as a movement to counter the popularity of these other forms when they were appearing with regularity in the signature production design styles of films from MGM and RKO. Modernism, gaining a foothold in Southern California through architecture and visual art during the 1920s, also became more associated with California progressivism, placing the style and its affiliated ideologies in stark contrast with plein air. These modern forms presented a challenge to the regional boosterism evoked by plein air, and thus the movement itself fell out of favor, largely because of its historical association with the Arroyo group. Davis's Debunker intellectual classes throughout the 1920s and the 1930s—whether through literature, cinema, or other visual art forms—created an environment that was increasingly hostile to nostalgia and mythmaking.

The second reason, the Great Depression, made it more difficult to sell artwork for conspicuous consumption, forcing artists to look to other industries to make ends meet. The works of this movement, no longer championed by art establishments, fell out of the public view, a challenge to preserving the legacy of California plein air. As art tastes had shifted over the midcentury, many of the impressionist works in private collections were sold or given away by heirs with little interest in the style. In 1977, the Los Angeles County Museum of Art auctioned off much of its plein air collection, as the museum's "interests lay elsewhere."[56] Even today, much of the work of impressionists resides in private collections or with Southern California resorts and hotel chains, so they are often difficult to track down and study. Yet there were also many important efforts during the 1970s to preserve the history of California impressionism through education, retrospectives, and museum collections. In 1972, Nancy Moure curated the first post–World War II exhibition of California plein air art at Pomona College, titled *Los Angeles Painters of the Nineteen Twenties*. In 1975, Moure privately published a three-volume set on California art, the third of which highlighted the seemingly forgotten contributions of early twentieth-century plein air art: *Dictionary of Art and Artists in Southern California Before 1930*. In response, important collections arose around the state that also played a crucial role in preserving the memory of California impressionism, notably in the Museum of California/Oakland Museum, the Bowers Museum of Cultural Art in Santa Ana, and the Laguna Art Museum in Laguna Beach, Orange County. Finally, much of the renewed interest in California plein air toward the close of the twentieth century is owed in part to the work of Jean Stern and the Irvine Art Museum. Operated jointly by the University of California at Irvine and the Museum for California Art, the Irvine Art Museum houses one the largest collections of California plein air in the state and engages in "interdisciplinary projects, research, publications, seminars . . . and educational outreach" aimed at "expanding [an] understanding of California Art."[57]

CHASING THE LIGHT

> It must be remembered, too, that shadows change rapidly and if the work is not completed in time, changing shadows may alter the entire arrangements. When the sun is on [the] extreme right or left of the painter, especially if it is low, light and dark areas are more likely to be equally divided and, therefore, more difficult to arrange. Although the latter situation may, in some instances, give a proper inequality of values, in the average landscape looking more nearly towards the sun or partly away from it generally presents a better arrangement of masses.
>
> —Edgar Payne, *Composition of Outdoor Painting*

At a panel hosted by the *Plein Air* podcast in May 2019, three film industry professionals—Mike Hernandez (Dreamworks production designer), Sharon Calahan (lighting cinematographer for Pixar), and Bill Cone (set designer for Pixar)—highlighted the ways that early twentieth-century California plein air painting established techniques that were highly adaptable to filmmaking. First, plein air artists learned firsthand how color changes and moves. Light, according to the panelists, is what plein air painters should focus on first, otherwise they are just chasing light. Second, plein air painting trains artists to work quickly to produce visuals within restrictive time frames, with Hernandez especially noting that working in crunch time is a significant factor in film art techniques.

Third, plein air painting trained artists how high-key lighting in atmosphere color can be used to create a higher range of storytelling. In fact, high-key lighting, as Bill Cone notes, is exactly what the plein air artist is working with when painting outdoors, recalling art critic Antony Anderson's characterization of Guy Rose's work as attuned to the "high key of nature." The plein air artists tended not to paint in the middle of the day—when the sun is overhead and there are no shadows—instead opting to paint early or late in the day. Fourth, plein air painting also impacted the way that the rule of thirds is utilized in outdoor shooting. Finally, like method acting, plein air painting encourages artists to draw upon an experience and feel of life when creating levels of light and temperature. "Cinema is about storytelling . . . with temperature and light," according to Calahan, and if you're not used to channeling emotions and life experience into this process, "it can show through your painting."[58]

Returning to the Chouinard Art Institute, I would now like to sketch the evolution of plein air techniques from the Progressive Era to present-day film design. The school was founded in 1921 by Nelbert Murphy Chouinard, an artist who moved to Pasadena in 1909 and became steeped in California impressionism and the Arroyo Seco art and culture community.[59] Chouinard first taught art at Hollywood High School and the Otis Art Institute before she purchased a two-story house on West Eighth Street, near Alvarado Street, which would become her namesake art school's first location. In 1929, she moved to 743 South Grand View Street, near the Otis Art Institute and Westlake Park (now known as MacArthur Park). The Westlake District during the 1920s and 1930s was, according to Jean Stern, the "vibrant heart of the Los Angeles art community," and during this time, the Chouinard Art Institute would play an important role in the development of cinema art of various expressions.[60] In 1929, Walt Disney approached Chouinard and arranged to have his animators take classes on temporary scholarships, and by 1961, Disney took over financial ownership of the Chouinard Art Institute. This merger resulted in the school being renamed the California Institute of the Arts, and in 1972 the school was relocated to Valencia, a suburb of Santa Clarita. Yet because Chouinard operated as a cinematic arts school since 1929, the institute can be read as providing Disney with a template for what a film training academy could look like.

In 1936, the Chouinard School of Motion Picture Arts was founded, a crystallization of programs that had previously, throughout the early 1930s, trained motion picture creatives. Its mission statement: "Dealing with art as a factor in the production of motion pictures." In the previous year, there had been a class on motion picture set design offered by Harold W. Miles (an art director associated with RKO, MGM, and Paramount) that covered "script analysis . . . choice of architectural styles and their appropriateness to the story . . . the problems of dressing sets . . . [and] the problems of photography as related to design" and included sections on "design, perspective, figure drawing, quick sketches, interior period designs, costume history, architectural drawing, still life, history of interior, furniture design, and landscape composition."[61] By 1939, the Motion Picture Arts school, under the directorship of Miles, stated in program literature:

> The Chouinard Art Institute trains students for the motion picture industry in subjects that are within the scope of an art school. Courses in the fundamentals of art, such as drawing and composition, have in the past equipped students for interesting and remunerative work in the animation studios. The same background, plus the interior and architectural training, have placed students in the art departments of many major studios as set designers, sketch artists, or set decorators. . . . Several years ago this natural function was organized into a definitive training as the Chouinard School of Motion Picture Technical Arts, and it is taught by men who are outstanding in their respective fields.[62]

One of the instructors at Chouinard during this period was Millard Sheets (1907–89), who had made a name for himself in the region as an art teacher, administrator, architectural designer, muralist, and water colorist. When not teaching at Chouinard, Otis, or Scripps, Sheets used his watercolor painting to depict the grim realities of the Great Depression, his paintings of Bunker Hill residents living in poverty preserving an entirely different palimpsest layer of L.A. history than those of his plein air forerunners. What makes Sheets a significant figure in this story is that he, as well as many of his Chouinard students, were members of the California Water Color Society, an organization whose history provides a bridge between the heyday of California plein air during the Progressive Era and film design tenets practiced today.

The California Water Color Society was formed in Los Angeles 1921, holding its first exhibition that year at the Los Angeles Museum.[63] The group was influenced by California impressionism, with some of the original members trained in the plein air form, but also borrowed heavily from cubism, realism, and California scene painting, the last a term coined by art critic Arthur Millier to refer to landscape paintings of everyday life in California. Though overlapping stylistically with California impressionism, a distinguishing feature of California scene painting was its inclusion of urban settings populated with machines and people, as well as traditional landscapes. Scene painting, according to Gordon T. McClelland and Jay T. Last, was a regionalist art form that "documented scenes and activities of everyday life on the Pacific Coast . . . California cities, and industrial sites," defined by a "large format, free broad, brush strokes, and strong rich colors."[64] The rise of the society and scene painting during the 1920s came at a time when painting and photography began to merge in their visions of California. When looking at the work of Millard Sheets and other society members, along with pictorialism and later the documentation of the Great Depression through photography and painting, there occurs a peeling back of L.A. palimpsest layers to reveal more vivid insights into California life outside the glittering Hollywood image; for this one need look no further than Sheet's Bunker Hill paintings (such as *Angel's Flight* from 1931), in which the realities of downtown life are sharply contrasted with the booster promise of Los Angeles as the pinnacle of American destiny.

As the Water Color Society membership grew throughout the 1920s, the regional art scene became increasingly shaped by California scene painting, and by the end of the 1920s, many of these artists were regularly sending their work to art shows throughout California and nationwide—generating further attention to the region and its art culture.[65] As California began to feel the impact of the Great Depression during the early 1930s, the members of the society and other scene painters discovered that they simply could not make a sustainable living selling paintings during the national economic crisis. To make ends meet, these artists entered the motion picture industry—some as animators for Disney and Warner Bros., some in special effects departments as matte painters, and others in ancillary fields like education (teaching at the Chouinard Art Institute) and marketing (poster design and painting portraits of movie stars). The Water Color Society had several hundred members by the 1930s, but the core circle that maintained the strongest affiliations, according to Gordon McClelland and Jay Last, were the ones who took day jobs in the motion picture industry.[66]

In evaluating the impact of the Water Color Society members on film practices, first consider the production of two films separated by over five decades. First, *The Wonderful Wizard of Oz* (Francis Boggs, 1910), shot at the Selig Polyscope studios in Edendale, Los Angeles—with Hobart Bosworth in the title role. As mentioned in the introduction, 1907 to 1913 was a transition period for Hollywood in which motion pictures were characterized by an increased narrative complexity, a greater individuation of characters, and more attention to "narratively relevant spatial relationships" achieved through mise-en-scène, and *The Wonderful Wizard of Oz*'s production conditions bridge the transition period to California visual culture in striking ways.[67] Although the film is shot entirely on sets, away from the California sunshine that allegedly had drawn early film pioneers to Los Angeles, the use of painted backdrops foreshadows the relationship that would develop two decades later between the production design and motion picture artists who were educated in the California plein air style. The film's cyclone scene was achieved through moving an impressionistic painted background (a matte painting) around the set with the camera stationary: an effect like the moving circular panoramas of the nineteenth century. Like the phantom rides in city symphonies such as First National's *Los Angeles, ca. 1920* (discussed in the previous chapter), the cyclone scene from *The Wonderful Wizard of Oz* utilizes the effects of impressionism to generate in the spectator the thrill of embodied perception, while at the same time advancing the film form even further into narrative complexity, in stark contrast to the cinema of attractions that marked the Edison actuality period.

The second film highlighting the relationship between scene painting and optical illusions is *Planet of the Apes* (Franklin J. Schaffner, 1968). The iconic ending set piece—the Statue of Liberty submerged in the sands of Malibu—was realized through the work of special effects artist Emil Kosa Jr. Kosa, a Czech immigrant who started his career designing theatrical backdrops during the 1920s, was a member of the California Water Color Society alongside animators, backdrop painters, and the art teachers who trained industry professionals.[68] As was true of so many California artists of his generation, the Great Depression made it difficult for Kosa to make a living from selling art, and in 1933, he joined the newly formed special effects department at 20th Century-Fox. The true magnitude of Kosa's thirty-five-year career with Fox is difficult to determine, as much of the credit for his early work was taken by department head Fred Sersen. Some of Kosa's notable achievements, however, include the iconic 20th Century-Fox logo (which he designed shortly after joining the studio) and his Academy Award for Best Special Effects for *Cleopatra* (Joseph L. Mankiewicz, 1963); he brought the ancient world to life through combining his technical expertise as a scene painter with the principles of optical illusion. As Gordon T. McClelland notes, 20th Century-Fox's special effects department during Kosa tenure "was an acknowledged leader in the field of motion pictures and particularly in the area of matte shot art."[69]

While some the Water Color Society members lent their talents to special effects, there were others who entered the art departments as concept artists and production designers. A by-product of plein air's influence on the society painters was a strong understanding of the way that the rule of thirds, a crucial component of cinematographic composition, is utilized in outdoor painting. This made plein air techniques highly adaptable to producing indoor backdrops and matte paintings used to replicate outdoor settings within a studio environment. Scottish-born George Gibson, trained at Chouinard by Frank Tolles Chamberlain and Millard Sheets, started his film career in 1933, working at 20th Century-Fox alongside Emil Kosa Jr. before joining MGM in 1934. At MGM, Gibson worked for famed art director Cedric Gibbons, who eventually put him under a full-time contract with MGM in 1939 after his work on the sets for *The Wizard of Oz* (1939). As with Kosa, it is difficult to determine the full impact of Gibson's career before his retirement in 1969, but the number of films that he worked on is believed to be over one hundred, with backdrop sets often as large as 60 by 150 feet. Other notable films include *An American in Paris* (1951), *Brigadoon* (1954), and *The Shoes of a Fisherman* (1968), "for which he recreated the frescos of the Sistine Chapel."[70]

The influence of plein air can also be felt in the work of animators who were members of the California Water Color Society. Mary Blair, a Chouinard graduate, started working in the animation industry in 1940, first at Ub Iwerks Studio and then at Walt Disney Studio later that year. Her notable works at Disney include *Dumbo* (1941), *Saludos Amigos* (1942), *The Three Caballeros* (1944), *Alice in Wonderland* (1951), *Lady and the Tramp* (1955), and the It's a Small World ride, which premiered at the Disneyland theme park in 1966. Ralph Hulett, also a Chouinard graduate, joined the Disney Studio in 1937 and worked notably on *Pinocchio* (1940), *Fantasia* (1940), *Peter Pan* (1953), and *The Jungle Book* (1967). The work of Hulett, Blair, Phil Dike, and others are linked through three crucial techniques derived from plein air: concept art, color scripts, and sequence lighting. Concept art in animation would become known as art produced quickly to develop work and to demonstrate a project's progress for other craftspeople who would work on the same project at later stages. This process can be traced to the plein air artists and their ascendant skill at producing visuals quickly under time restrictions. A color script was a method for mapping out the color, lighting, and emotional beats within an animated film. This is largely rooted in the mood and connotations certain colors evoke and can be traced to plein air's emphasis on life experience in painting. Finally, sequence lighting is the design plan for maintaining a continuity of light sources within a particular sequence of an animated film, considering the fact that light changes and has movement (another feature of plein air).

The last Water Color Society contribution that I would like to highlight (though there are scores of others deserving of a book-length study in their own right) is the art of portrait painting as both a form of star promotion and as set décor, embodied strongly by the career of Swedish-born painter Christian Von Schneidau. Arriving in California in 1917, Von Schneidau studied plein air techniques under Richard E. Miller, one of the original California impressionists and a former member of Monet's Giverny Colony Turning his craft largely toward portrait painting, Von Schneidau developed a reputation as a painter of the stars, with his portraits of Mary Pickford being among his most famous. With this reputation carrying his film industry career into the 1930s and 1940s, Von Schneidau was routinely hired by prop departments in Hollywood to create paintings as either set decorations or as crucial plot points,

such as the portrait from the noir classic *Laura* (1944). At the time of
this writing, much of Von Schneidau's work in motion picture in unac-
counted for—believed to be lost, improperly archived, or fallen into private collections.

The impact of plein air techniques on film design philosophy
contributes to the idea that cinema was a product of world building
and environments, and that the original Los Angeles movie-making
networks can be read as multimedia organizations from the outset.[71]
Though plein air is not the only art style that fueled Hollywood's formation in this manner, the movement's links to Progressive Era booster
campaigns, especially in cementing a particular expression of Southern California social imaginary, speaks to a conflict between two cur-
rents of film innovation. James Tweedie writes that the dominant strands
of film theory tend to affirm either (1) the idea that film is a "modern
medium . . . because it uses technological innovation to present a more
accurate vision of the world than other arts," or (2) that film is "modern
precisely because it takes liberties with reality and shapes the world."[72]
At first, plein air's influence on the cinematic arts appears to endorse
the latter perspective. It could be argued that an impressionistic style
for rendering the world, fused with film's formal techniques, challenges
the "tired old idea" that films "advance the cinema only to the degree
that that they subvert the illusionist codes of popular movies."[73] A more
complicated story emerges, however, when one considers that plein air
painters sought to reproduce a certain kind of reality effect, and that
their works' distribution alongside regional photography was more
about patterning, rather than liberating, the mind of the spectator. Furthermore, as the cinema became increasingly recognized as a legitimate
art form (through events like the Panama-Pacific Exposition and other
historical factors), the modern forms that rose in Southern California in
opposition to plein air's reputation also intersected with the Los Angeles film network. These styles also merit scholarly attention to further
illustrate California art's engagement with Tweedie's dual tendencies
of filmic innovation.

VISUAL MUSIC

Moving beyond the Progressive Era into the 1930s and 1940s, we see cinema constantly enhanced by art movements, notably surrealism and expressionism. Yet there remains a continued noticeable convergence between the film industry and the distinct features of California. As Paul Karlstrom has observed, the role of the film industry in the local economy allowed popular culture to take on a greater significance than it did elsewhere, and through the cross-pollination between popular art and film, Los Angeles "had come to embody (physically and psychologically) change, freedom, and mobility."[74] Some important themes that emerged from the L.A. modern art scene of the period, according to Karlstrom, were a Hollywood-influenced preoccupation with light and movement, an openness to nontraditional forms and sources, a distance from the influence of the New York art scene (a defining feature of early twentieth-century California impressionism as well), and new ideas about color harmony.[75] There were some artists who recognized the expressiveness of "cinematic devices" through their art, such as Lorser Feitelson and Man Ray.[76] Other artists working in the film industry were Jules Engel and Rico Lebrun, who worked for Disney and taught animators how to draw animals for *Bambi*; June Wayne, who operated a lithography business and later founded the Los Angeles Women's Building in 1977; and Stanton MacDonald-Wright, who collaborated with ceramist and film special effects pioneer Albert King.[77] Although there is not a convenient set of styles and influences that binds the modern artists of 1940s Los Angeles, their overlap with Hollywood is significant, as the film industry was instrumental in distributing Southern California imagery to receptive international audiences.

Charting the influence of modern forms on cinematic design in Los Angeles reveals intersecting histories between modern art and plein air even before the arrival of motion pictures to Southern California. In 1901, William Wendt traveled to New York and Boston, primarily due to his inclusion in the Society of American Artists exhibition with his *Cornish Coast*. Back east, Wendt saw hundreds of paintings and society shows, declaring, "While in New York I saw pictures until my brain reeled and my feet were worn and sore from 5th Ave. pavement. God, but I was tired of pictures such as I saw. Away from the unwholesome, unhealthy productions of so many painters, with nature undefiled, I hope to take courage again and trust that my mind may be normal enough to interpret her sanely."[78]

Wendt's words summarize the plein air/booster position on the modern forms that had yet to take hold of Los Angeles. The city's position at the frontier would continue to insulate the city for some time, and yet several events would ensure that synchromism, modernism, cubism, futurism, and other related forms would overtake plein air as a dominant force in the Los Angeles art scene. For one, the 1913 Armory Exhibit in New York, though taking place on the opposite end of the country, demonstrated the power and influence of these advancing forms within the American art world. Marcel Duchamp, Edward Hopper, Pablo Picasso, and Robert Henri were shown alongside Van Gogh, Cezanne, and Gauguin; Robert Henri's landmark Macbeth Gallery art group the Eight would later inspire the formation of modern artists operating in Los Angeles during the 1920s dubbed the Group of Eight. Yet a crucial factor in Southern California life that ultimately intersected with a growing interest in modern art forms was the shift in regional booster culture. Modern forms embraced ideals at odds with boosterism's utopian promises, and as such anti-mythmaking art forms found powerful allies in the literary world and alternative art scene. If Southern California boosterism supplied California plein air with a set of subjects and focus of technical expertise that informed Hollywood studio practices in a variety of ways, then the Southern California debunker class responded with modern art, which also supplied Los Angeles cinema and the city's film industries with a variety of narrative techniques through art and production design. An early indication that a wave of debunker art forms was about to crash upon plein air's booster ideologies was the 1923 exhibition from the Group of Independent Artists of Los Angeles, which Mike Davis describes as a "united front for the 'New Form', including Cubism, Dynamism, and Expressionism" whose adherents "attacked the landscape romantics—the Eucalyptus painters, Laguna seascape painters, Mission painters, and so on."[79]

Though the popularity of impressionism among the Los Angeles cultural elite provided a difficult environment for modern art to gain a foothold during the early 1920s, modern art in Los Angeles during this time found support from individuals inside and outside of the motion picture business, ultimately transforming the city from the last bastion of impressionism to a center for modern art. "If cosmopolitanism existed anywhere in Southern California," remarks William Hackman, "it was Hollywood, an intellectual and cultural oasis occupied by transplanted New Yorkers and European immigrants."[80] Director Josef von Sternberg, for example, owned one of the city's "most formidable collections of modern art," as modern aesthetics and film had enjoyed a close symbiotic relationship in the European cinema environment where von Sternberg began his career.[81] Here we can see an overlap between motion picture practices, California art, and a different Los Angeles intellectual class alongside Mike Davis's Boosters and Debunkers: the Exiles, German, Austrian, and other European immigrants—intellectuals, architects, composers, and filmmakers—who found Los Angeles an ideal environment where, during the spread of fascism throughout Europe during the 1930s, the vibrant culture of Weimar Germany could be given a new lease on life at the edge of the Pacific.[82] Outside of the filmmaking community, the family most synonymous with modern art in Los Angeles during the 1920s were the Arnsbergs. Located on Hillside Avenue in Hollywood, the Mediterranean Revival home of Louise and Walter Arnsberg has housed, since 1927, modern works collected since the 1913 Armory Show; in 1933 architect Richard Neutra built a sunroom for the home for the display of works by Duchamps.[83] Writing of his encounter with the Arnsberg house in 1949, L.A. modern art museum curator Walter Hopps credits this shrine to emerging modern forms as "an exciting assault on the eyes" and as the origin story of the L.A. modern scene that would dominate well into the 1960s through architecture and the pop artists of the famed Ferus Gallery.[84]

Though modern art is ostensibly unified in its opposition to plein air's nostalgic romanticism, its stylistic variations make its influence on cinema in Los Angeles somewhat more difficult to map than plein air's. One modern form that warrants further investigation is synchromism, primarily because its guiding principles are highly comparable with film design thought. Additionally, synchromism's history in California overlaps with the story of film art education in the region, in particular the history of Chouinard sketched out earlier. In short, synchromism held that light and color were analogous to music: pitch in sound relates directly to luminosity of color, tone in sound equals hue in color, and intensity of sound corresponds to saturation of color. As the artist Percyval Tudor-Hart observed, "The twelve harmonic intervals of the musical octave . . . have corresponding sensational and emotional qualities of those of twelve chromatic colors."[85]

One student and admirer of Tudor-Hart was Stanton MacDonald-Wright who, prior to his exposure to Tudor-Hart's color theories, had trained under Warrant T. Hedges at the Art Students League in Los Angeles. Encouraged by Hedges to pursue avant-garde styles (and to steer away from the regional plein air zeitgeist moment), MacDonald-Wright pursued his art studies and career in Europe before returning to Los Angeles to assume directorship of the Art Students League. In 1923, he wrote *A Treatise in Color* for his students, in which he furthered the analogy between color and sound. His perspectives on color and emotion were based on nature and observation: "As nature recedes from the eye, it becomes blue-violet or violet, while as it advances it becomes more yellow or orange."[86] MacDonald-Wright also established the Group of Independent artists of Los Angeles the same year, further entrenching modern forms in opposition to the "eucalyptus painters . . . who perpetuated the [mythology of Southern California's past]."[87] He would later go on to teach at Chouinard alongside Millard Sheets, color theorist Hans Hoffman, and Mexican muralist David Alfaro Siqueiros, placing synchromism at an intersection with plein air's legacy. A program for a February 1927 exhibit on synchromism at the Los Angeles Museum summarizes MacDonald-Wright's contributions to the L.A. art scene and further suggests connections between the style and narrative film language: "The Synchromists desired to express by means of colour, form which would be as complete and simple as a Michelangelo drawing, and which would give subjectively the same emotion of form that the Renaissance master gives objectively. They wished to give images of such logical structure that the imagination would experience their unrecognizable reality in the same way our eyes experience the recognizable reality of life."[88]

Writing in 1949, cinematographer John Alton argued that the way we receive light sensations of different colors is a lot like a concert of light played by a hundred different musical instruments. In other words: "a symphony of visual music."[89] Music, Alton notes, is an "audible picture" of what the composer may have had in mind. This echo of synchromist principles in Alton's approach to cinematography is not to suggest that there are concrete connections. Rather, it is to invite further exploration between the art styles that overlapped with film art education in Los Angeles during the 1920s and 1930s, a time period during which Alton honed his craft in Los Angeles as a photographic lab technician.

Finally, the Group of Eight is also worthy of consideration when exploring the intersection between late Progressive Era L.A. art and the rise of the film industry in Southern California. The Group of Eight also exhibited at the Los Angeles Museum in 1927, with the objective of "creative experimentation and individual expression, rather than emulations of the formal experiments of European or American moderns elsewhere."[90] It is possible that the group took its name from a 1908 Macbeth Gallery exhibition in New York titled *Robert Henri and the Eight*, and when Henri visited Los Angeles in 1925, he was hosted at Otis and Chouinard by Group of Eight members who also taught at these institutions. Painters like Mabel Alvarez, Clarence Hinkle, Donna Schuster, and Édouard Vysekel used these teaching positions, accompanied by exhibitions at the Los Angeles Museum, to broaden the concept of modern art through a "Cezanne-esque attention to surface design." Additionally, several of the group members (and affiliated painter and sculptor Gjura Stojana) were mentioned frequently in the diaries of Edward Weston and other L.A. pictorialists. As Susan M. Anderson observes, the definition of modernist art was often reduced to "a narrow set of practices emphasizing the formalist elements of abstractions" from the 1930s through the 1960s, whereas contemporary scholarship seeks to "restore the concept of modern art to the broadness of the 1920s."[91] Here, I position modern art's influence on cinematic language, overlapping with and in opposition to booster-affiliated art forms, as part of this larger scholarly broadening project that Anderson describes.

3

SELIG BUILDS A ZOO

The West was no longer "wild" by the dawn of the twentieth century. In the movies, however, the Wild West continued through Los Angeles, a city that cinema depicted as the "last manifestation of the Western movement" and the "end of the frontier."[1] This is a largely because in Los Angeles the concepts of "wild" and "urban" are viewed as "variable qualities and processes," and the city's end-of-the-frontier status is quite literal. L.A.'s metropolitan area is "now bordered primarily by mountains and desert rather than farmland," and has the longest "wild edge" of any major non-tropical city, roughly 675 miles. In cities like Portland, Seattle, and Vancouver, the growth of the "urban" has traditionally been seen to decrease the "wild," whereas the growth of L.A. as an urban space has paradoxically increased the wildness of the region.[2] The mountain lion, for example, a symbol of Southern California's wildness that graced the logo of booster Charles Fletcher Lummis's *Land of Sunshine* magazine, now lives in the Santa Monica Mountains, hemmed in by major freeways and foothill neighborhoods (Calabasas, Malibu, Topanga, and others). Los Angeles's reputation as a wild and untamed space figures strongly in movies set there, as Andersen's *Los Angeles Plays Itself* explores effectively through noir cinema and disaster movies. Los Angeles–set cinema appears to have anticipated the symbiotic relationship between urban and wild in Los Angeles, entrenching the city's end-of-the-frontier status in the public consciousness. This chapter explores how this conception of Los Angeles as a perpetual frontier space is the by-product of visual culture practices at the turn of the century that cemented the region's reputation as a land for place substitution.

For Ben Stanley, both the "frontier" and Los Angeles are places "saturated by the hyperreal" that exist "as both . . . material reality and celluloid fantasy."[3] Photography, as we saw in chapter 1, captured the material reality of the Southern California frontier (and the frontier city of Los Angeles in rapid transformation) on collodion plates and dry plates, later to be transformed into proto-celluloid fantasy through panoramic exhibitions, stereoscopic technology, and mass-distributed photo albums. Plein air painters, by contrast, harnessed the region's Mediterranean sunlight, a different form of material reality, to create near-celluloid fantasies of the Southland, leaving behind a set of techniques that later informed the creation of fantasies through actual celluloid. The "saturation by the hyperreal," however, suggests that the frontier was ultimately tamed into a simulacrum of its former self, a make-believe vision of the West that was ultimately absorbed by Los Angeles and culturally repurposed. By the dawn of the twentieth century, the rapidly changing landscape of Southern California, according to Charles Wolfe, "occasioned innovative thinking about the relationship between physical environments and the production of images," approaches to visual storytelling that were inevitably absorbed by Hollywood as the film industry superseded the influence of other forms by the mid-1910s.[4] This chapter looks at how Los Angeles's development into a motion picture capital was fueled by a preexisting visual attractions industry centered on the region's natural landscape and innovations in mass media inspired by this physical environment.

First, this chapter considers how ideas about health and wellness informed the development of California as a site of proto-cinematic transformative experience. The land's promise of health cures was an integral component of boosterism's sales pitch, contributing to a narrative of California that would underscore the state mythology encoded in photography, painting, and eventually cinema. At the dawn of the Progressive Era, California agribusiness played a significant role in promoting a Southern California pastoralism and cementing the state's reputation as a health sanctuary through a variety of mass-distributed visual marketing: citrus crate labels, brochures, and promotional railway boxcars that shipped these products around the country.[5] Fueled by travel writings and publications on new healthy living philosophies, the citrus belt became emblematic of what the state had to offer the weary traveler looking to escape the realities of the American East Coast and Midwest (places that California visual culture positioned as embodiments of an obsolete style of living). From this health and wellness industry emerged a literal weary traveler who came to embody Southern California boosterism: Charles Fletcher Lummis, whose *Land of Sunshine* and *Out West* magazines employed the California visual languages that emerged through and alongside the photography and paintings discussed in previous chapters to transform boosterism into a mythmaking industry, in collaboration with artist, poets, and playwrights.

Next, this chapter looks at how the tourist industry envisioned California as both a physical and psychological playground, defining the terrain as a place where one could redefine and transform oneself. Los Angeles towards the end of the nineteenth century, according to Kia Afra, was an "open shop town" whose "innovations in tourism and a robust visual culture played a direct role in its rapid growth."[6] This chapter also considers California tourist attractions as a form of protocinematic experience, anticipating Tom Gunning's characterization of early cinema as related "more to the attractions of the fairground than to the traditions of legitimate theater."[7] As this chapter highlights, there is a paradoxical relationship between Gunning's "cinema of attractions" and turn-of-the-century tourist attractions. For Gunning, the cinema of attractions privileges "theatrical display" over "narrative absorption," whereas "narrative absorption" was a goal of many Southern California tourist attractions. Attractions such as the Mount Lowe Resort in the hills above Altadena, for example, were concerned with creating enclosed and immersive narrative worlds, supported by their attendant visual cultural forms, as much as with providing leisure and respite. Visual promotion of these attractions, often in collaboration with the same railroad companies that collaborated with photographers and painters, emphasized the immersive experience of these sites and sights with brochures, guidebooks, newspaper advertising, souvenir posters and maps, postcards, and other ephemera. It seems hardly a coincidence that the 1929 *Southern California through the Camera* magazine, introduced in chapter 1, contained a section on California tourism featuring images of sunbathing and camel tours through Death Valley (escorted by tour guides dressed in Arab Bedouin costumes), declaring that "there is much to see in this vacation land and there is a wide choice of modes of travel."[8]

Finally, this chapter explores the ways that Los Angeles's development into a motion picture capital was motivated by a relationship between the region's natural landscape and innovations in mass media inspired by this physical environment. Centering on William N. Selig's Polyscope Studios as a case study, I show how the performative aspects of California nature and wildlife viewing culture were extrapolated into motion picture industry practices. It was not random happenstance then that early Hollywood found its marketing strength and appeal in its "erasure of site specificity from the fictional world of film," as Mark B. Sandberg argues.[9] The Southern California attractions industry had, by the time Selig started to explore the potential of moving his operations to the West Coast, demonstrated to the rest of the country how the region's varied geography and "rich array of settings" provided ideal conditions for immersive and participatory experiences.[10] California tourism, when viewed alongside other attendant visual forms like painting and photography, aided film pioneers in envisioning what a cinematic spectator could potentially be and how spectatorial psychology could be harnessed through the visual language of the motion picture. Taking advantage of the state's idealized terrain, the ascendant film studios established practices of place substitution for which Hollywood would become known domestically and internationally. This chapter frames this transformation of Los Angeles as introducing the city as a film setting that is somewhere, nowhere, and anywhere simultaneously—a space where possibilities appear limitless.

CALIFORNIA FOR HEALTH, PLEASURE, AND RESIDENCE

Visualizing California began in the late eighteenth century with drawings of the region's flora and fauna from direct observation. These were visual records created by explorers traveling along the California coastline or by naturalists stationed in Alta California's pueblos, missions, and presidios. Among the earliest known California nature images were ornithological drawings created during a French expedition by Jean-Louis-Robert Prevost of a California thrasher and a pair of California quail in Monterey in 1786. These images, according to Anthony Kirk, were "often fundamental to the success of the endeavors" of explorers and "played an essential role in these grand enterprises."[11] Illustrations of California flowers, often hand colored, soon followed, with golden poppies becoming a popular subject that would be emblematic of California, reinforced by the late nineteenth- and early twentieth-century California impressionists, as discussed in chapter 2. These artistic renditions of California would soon turn to ethnographic studies of the region's native people, with notable examples from Russian artists who visited California's shores during the early nineteenth century: Mikhail T. Tikhanov's *Balthazar* (1818) and Louis (Ludwig) Choris's *Indian of California* (1816), for example.[12] As discussed in chapter 1, the daguerreotype faced several challenges posed by painted forms, notably the theatricality and emotive power of the California nature artists' brush and imagination. Toward the end of the century, painting was the primary mode of visualizing the potential of California's flora and agricultural industry, highlighting the promise of healthy living and economic prosperity associated with this aspect of California life.

This social imaginary of California—largely a product of photography, painting, and other visual forms—played a significant role in the creation of the interactive California exhibition at Chicago's White City World Fair exhibition in 1893 (often referred to as the World's Columbian Exposition). Literature promoting the exhibition cited its visual features, which had already been made familiar to the nation through visual marketing: "A mock Spanish Mission with Moorish flourishes . . . the 100,000-square-foot hall furnished with redwood paneling and redwood wainscoting . . . garden produce on redwood counters . . . wine bottles in redwood display cases . . . [announcing] the plentitude of California."[13] In the grand hall, the land of sunshine was renarrativized in a large, interactive, and tactile form, reenacting the California literature and promotional material of health and agribusiness that had peppered the national landscape over the previous decade. The orange, a symbol of California distributed to exhibition attendees, provides a useful starting point in exploring the growth of Southern California from a literal end of the frontier to a revered center for health and well-being—agribusiness serving as a metaphor for personal transformation promoted through the state's readily recognizable visual signifiers.

The Spanish Franciscans were the first to bring orange trees to California, and each of the coastal missions, starting with San Diego (constructed in 1769), featured a garden that included several citruses. The mission at San Gabriel (present-day Pasadena area), for example, contained an orchard of roughly four hundred oranges on six acres, planted around 1804 but falling into disrepair after secularization in 1834.[14] It seems no accident then that by the early twentieth century, Los Angeles–area Craftsman bungalows were advertised with illustrations of these homes "flanking an abundant orchard, presumably a dwelling for a typical California grower."[15] By 1880, the California citrus industry had rebounded and focused its attention on a potential East Coast migratory audience. A wave of agribusiness literature emerged that aimed to link California citrus culture with the state's promise of healthy living and sound mental health. Notable works include *Orange Culture in California* (Thomas A. Gary, 1882), *The Great Interior Fruit Belt and Sanitarium of Southern California* (L. M. Holt, 1885), *The Orange: Its Culture in California* (William Andrew Spalding, 1885), and *A Treatise on Citrus Culture in California* (Byron Martin Lelong, 1888). Spalding wrote, "Orange culture gives healthy occupation to the mind as well as the body," suggesting an explicit link between California agriculture and the health movement that would propel westward migration to the state. Holt described "the citrus groves of San Bernardino County as one vast sanitarium, where an entire generation of middle-class Americans [could recover] from the fatigues of city life."[16] It is also important to note that by "city life," Holt highlights the effects of life in East Coast cities, foreshadowing the stark contrast that Los Angeles booster literature would draw between Southern California life and traditional American city life, further elaborated on by plein air painting. Additionally, while H. T. Payne's and other photographic albums telegraphed the state's promises of transformational experiences, these images also documented the growth of the citrus belt, and the citrus industry in Southern California was placed at the center of a pictorial narrative of semi-tropical California.

Capitalizing on the success of these publications, the Southern Pacific Railroad partnered with the California State Board of Trade in the winters of 1888–89 and 1890–91 to send promotional railcars called California on Wheels to states east of the Rockies. More than a million people visited these decorated trains and left with fruit samples and promotional literature whose authors "always made sure to include [images] of floral novelties such as yard palms and palm-lined allées."[17] Following the California on Wheels tours, state and world's fairs held in Chicago, Iowa, and other midwestern locations featured exhibitions about "exotic and fertile" land in Los Angeles, promoted with brochures from the same companies operating with Southern Pacific and personally financed by leading businessmen in Los Angeles. That the campaign was orchestrated by the Los Angeles Chamber of Commerce is significant on two levels. For one, the California on Wheels tours were organized on the eve of the chamber's involvement with the local Los Angeles art community, which ultimately resulted in the embracement of the emerging Southern California plein air movement as a powerful visual booster of California life. As discussed in the previous chapter, the California color palette, exemplified by the paintings of William Wendt and Benjamin Brown, was present in brochures, box labels, and the sides of the traveling boxcars—enshrining the state's colors of gold, orange, and purple in the public imagination before the "Eucalyptus School" would later elevate this palette to new heights. Second, the chamber of commerce would succeed the Southern Pacific as the chief regional booster by the end of the century.[18] Campaigns like California on Wheels, the co-opting of nostalgic and utopian plein air art, and partnering with publications like *Land of Sunshine* positioned the Los Angeles Chamber of Commerce to establish the ideal conditions for the motion picture's arrival to the Southland and, ultimately, the city's formation into a global city of visual entertainment.

As the initial success of agribusiness was underscored by health literature, it is important to consider the broader industry of health and travel literature that emerged during the 1870s, setting the stage for Lummis's *Land of Sunshine* and other effective forms of visual boosterism by the end of the century. As mentioned in chapter 1, Charles Nordhoff's book *California for Health, Pleasure, and Residence* (1873), according to Kevin Starr, "single handedly stimulated significant migration from the East and from Europe."[19] Los Angeles is not mentioned nearly as much as San Francisco, as the book was written years before the completion of the Tehachapi Loop and the opening of the Southland by rail travel from the East. Yet what is mentioned about Los Angeles is worth noting, as the city and surrounding area are framed as a site where nature and civilization are engaged in a mutually beneficial relationship: the oranges of the San Gabriel mission are cited by Nordhoff as "surely one of the most beautiful objects in nature"; the people of Los Angeles "do not think it needful to build fireplaces, and scarcely chimneys, in their houses"; Los Angeles provides "remarkable relief" for consumptives; and olive trees, almond trees, and English walnut trees, on Nordhoff's recommendation, are certain to flourish in Los Angeles.

> Certainly in no part of the continent is pleasure traveling so exquisite and unalloyed a pleasure as in California. Not only are the sights grand, wonderful, and surprising in the highest degree, but the climate is exhilarating and favorable to an active life; the weather is so certain that you need not lose a day, and may lay out your whole tour in the State without reference to rainy days, unless it is in the rainy season; the roads are surprisingly good, the country inns are clean, the beds good, the food abundant and almost always well cooked, and the charges moderate; and the journey by rail from New York to San Francisco, which costs no more than the steamer fare to London, and is shorter than a voyage across the Atlantic, is in itself delightful as well as instructive.[20]

Another notable work was Archduke of Austria Ludwig Salvator's 1878 book *Eine Blume aus dem Goldenen Lande oder Los Angeles* (A Flower from the Golden Land, or Los Angeles), which stimulated a wave of European migration to Southern California with promises of land conducive to a healthy lifestyle.[21] Describing the region as populated by "extraordinarily healthy" people and the "best state in the Union for health, wealth, and happiness," Salvator finds Los Angeles, when viewed from a distance, "entrancing at every angle" and conducive to uplifting the spirit.[22] Additionally, Salvator's book features lengthy descriptions of the geographical layout of Los Angeles, the Arroyo Seco, the estates at the city's edge, and the streets of downtown which, when accompanied by the Los Angeles photography of the late nineteenth century, can be read as laying the groundwork for the cartographic role that early L.A. cinema would later play. Salvator's and Nordhof's writings vividly sketch the California look and feel that would be captured by H. T. Payne's photographs and projected to the rest of the country through photo albums and later rendered vibrantly through plein air oil paint in works shown in galleries and dispersed around the nation in miniature postcard form. Thus, the

California health and travel literature of the 1870s and the agribusiness literature of the 1880s can be read as the blueprints for the Southern California social imaginary that would be advanced by Lummis and his Arroyo group.

OUT WEST

Responding to the writings of Salvator and Nordhoff, Charles Fletcher Lummis traveled to Southern California in search of good health, arriving in the state in 1885 after a 143-day footsore walking journey from Ohio.

> It was the last day of January. The ground was carpeted with myriad wildflowers, birds filled the air with song, and clouds of butterflies fluttered past me. I waded clear, icy trout brooks, startled innumerable flocks of quail, and ate fruit from the gold-laden trees of the first orange orchards I had ever seen. Pretty Pomona gave me pleasant lodgings that night and the next day, February 1, 1885, a thirty-mile walk through beautiful towns, past the picturesque old Mission of San Gabriel, and down a matchless valley, brought me at midnight to my unknown home in the City of the Angels.[23]

After his arrival in Los Angeles, Lummis became the editor of the *Los Angeles Times*, and later, drawing on his own life-as-performance-art persona and skills as a deeply charismatic booster and regional promoter, editor of *Land of Sunshine* (founded in 1894; renamed *Out West* in 1902). These publications promoted Southern California to the rest of the country as a paradisiacal land of healthy living—with illustrations from local artists (some of whom also traveled to Southern California for health) and photographs from photographers that were affiliated with the railroad companies. During the Progressive Era railroads routinely worked in tandem with boosters like Lummis, *Los Angeles Times* founder Harrison Gray Otis, and Otis's successor Harry Chandler, a real estate speculator who would later help found organizations like the Automobile Club of California as well as iconic locations such as the Hollywood Bowl. After establishing a reputation for himself nationwide, Lummis settled in the Arroyo Seco, constructing a rustic stone Craftsman house he named El Alisal (Spanish for The Alder Grove). Today, El Alisal, known as the Lummis House, is a registered Los Angeles historical landmark, a short drive from Southwest Museum of the American Indian, founded by Lummis.

The first thing to note about both *Land of Sunshine/Out West* is its use of the region's flora and fauna as iconography. The reader is treated to an image of a mountain lion on the cover page of both magazines, as well as an illustrated floral arrangement around the publication's title. The phrase "lavishly illustrated" also graces each cover page, signaling the evocative use of sketch art and photography that Lummis so strongly championed. Inside, articles on California art, archeology, and regional history are presented in what Kevin Starr describes as "the right sort of New England tone"; born in Massachusetts, Lummis had envisioned *Land of Sunshine/Out West* as the West's answer to the *Atlantic Monthly.*[24] Accompanying photographs of vast western landscapes, of date palms in the canyons and dry riverbeds in the Mojave Desert or Coachella Valley, and of Joshua trees and yucca plants recall the panoramas of Watkins or the stereoscopic images of O'Sullivan and his Los Angeles–based successors throughout the 1870s. Slices of regional cultural life, such as photographs of drying red chilis hanging from the entryway to a Spanish-style hacienda, visually market a California style of natural living in which the lines between outdoor and indoor living are indistinct, a defining characteristic that would later be used to sell modern homes after the Progressive Era. Photos of Los Angeles, Pasadena, and Santa Barbara hotels, some of which look like they could be at home in an H. T. Payne or Historical Society of California photo album, are used in advertisement sections proclaiming them "the newest and finest of the great pleasure resorts of California."[25] And images of the state's fauna, including the enormous sun fish (which itself would become a tourist attraction in Southern California during the early 1900s), provided a portrait of an untamed land, an image of the Los Angeles area that informed filmic depictions of the city well into the twentieth century. As Edwin R. Bingham noted, *Out West* had attained a vast international circulation by 1907 (across much of Europe, New Zealand, and China), and by the time Lummis left the magazine in 1909, *Out West* was used as a promotional handout by the Los Angeles Chamber of Commerce.[26] This collaboration with the chamber, combined with the promotional power of *Land of Sunshine/Out West*'s visual narration of Southern California, is but one illustration of the fact that, as Norman Klein observes, by the early 1900s, boosterism in Los Angeles had developed "into virtually a public service corporation" centered around three industries: real estate, transportation, and tourism.[27]

If we examine issues of *Land of Sunshine* and *Out West*, we can see how Lummis figured into a category of turn-of-the-century writers (including Jack London, Stephen Crane, and Richard Harding) that David Fine terms the "cult of the physical." These were literary personas who associated American landscapes, ecosystems, and natural living with their narratives on the human condition.[28] There is something highly performative about the way Lummis self-presented after immersing himself in Southern California life: he wore cowboy or ranchero hats, serapes, and Native American hand-crafted belts; later in life, he dressed completely in white. Lummis would even adopt the name Don Carlos, styling himself in the manner of a landowner from the Spanish/Mexican colonial era, which I explore further in the next chapter. In this sense, *Land of Sunshine*, *Out West*, and Lummis's other publications are about more than the land and its people—they document a personal transformation through California's mythical qualities. Each edition of *Land of Sunshine* and *Out West* featured an advertisement from the Los Angeles Chamber of Commerce beckoning readers: "For health and happiness and a home, come to California." And why wouldn't they? After all, this is exactly what Lummis did in 1885. Advertisements for Navajo blankets, *Ramona* toilet soap, and regional food and wine were just as much invitations to participate in this transformational California lifestyle as they were intended to promote commerce. If we look at pre-cinema visual culture in Southern California as providing a template for the burgeoning film industry on how to construct ideal spectators, ready and willing to immerse themselves in a virtual environment, then the story of Lummis reveals a person who was a pre-cinematic version of such spectators—living life as a movie before there were movies.

In the pages of *Land of Sunshine* and *Out West*, nature and wildlife are presented as contributing heavily to California's status as a place of renewal and identity reconstruction. "Walks in any direction in Los Angeles," according to an article by contributor Harold Stanley

Channing, offers one "unusual attractions" and "ample recompense," with views of the San Gabriel Valley from the top of Eagle Rock as a notable example.[29] In a later issue, Juliette Estelle Mathis declared that "blood rushed to [her] head" as she "cried in frantic delight" at the sight of golden seas of sunflowers, buttercups, and poppies.[30] The California condor, now extinct, is celebrated in the same issue by nature author Theodore S. Van Dyke, who writes that the bird, larger than the more commonly known Andean variety, possesses movements that "becloud the secret of sailing or soaring that has so long puzzled all philosophy."[31] Years later, in a 1908 edition of *Out West*, poetry in praise of eucalyptus and sidewinder snakes and articles on caves and Southern California bungalow gardens continue *Land of Sunshine*'s tradition of using nature to foreground a distinct California identity. Yet curiously, both publications reveal that an overlap between nature and visual attractions had fully developed in Southern California by end of the nineteenth century. Trips to Santa Catalina Island are advertised before the table of contents as early as 1895 in editions of *Land of Sunshine*. Editions of *Out West* recommended weekend getaways to Escondido, San Jose, Brookdale near Sequoia Park, San Mateo (advertised as the "floral city"), Paolo Alto ("the greatest educational center of the west"), and the Pacific Grove resort in Monterrey. Rail lines were advertised as well: special routes "through the orange groves" to Riverside and Redlands, as well as Santa Fe or Los Angeles Limited routes to and from Chicago. The partnership between tourism, real estate, the chamber of commerce, and *Land of Sunshine/ Out West* reveals a network of interlocked enterprises and industries that constructed the "ideal Californian" through landscapes of sights and experiences. "From the late nineteenth century," according to Susan Davis, "tourism in Southern California has been a place-building business," and along with the "California-ness" promoted through the pages of Lummis's work, this appears to foreshadow the use of Los Angeles, and indeed the state of California as a whole, as a land of place substitution in early cinema and during much of Hollywood's "golden era."[32]

TAMING THE FRONTIER

In 1888, the real estate market in Los Angeles collapsed. While the city's population had multiplied by 400 percent over the previous five years, reaching about fifty thousand, business infrastructure had not kept pace sufficiently to provide jobs for that many people. "The economy of L.A.," according to Norman Klein, "was too primitive for a city of 50,000," and in a "race against time, the new chamber of commerce turned towards the only industry that promised immediate returns—tourism mixed with real estate speculation." By 1900, tourism accounted for over a quarter of all business revenues in the city, "more than all manufacturing combined and second only to agriculture."[33] The Southern California tourism industry that had firmly entrenched itself at the heart of the regional culture at the turn of the century overlaps with the photography and paintings discussed in the previous chapters on two levels. First, the images of Southern California visual culture and the attractions of Southern California tourism are wedded to affirmations of American national identity. Like plein air and photography, visual marketing of Southern California tourism was connected to "expressions of patriotism and affirmations of one's American citizenship," as Stacey Camp observes, and the region's status as the end of the frontier can be viewed as a defining feature of the near-cinematic fantasy that tourists could participate in through Southern California's industry of attractions.[34]

This industry of immersive tourist experiences was anticipated in large part by antecedent forms of visual culture, and in the case of Southern California, many of the forms discussed in previous chapters positioned westward expansion and American destiny as something one could participated in by engaging with visual culture. For example, John Banvard's *Mississippi* panorama of 1846 (discussed in chapter 1) enlisted the spectator as a participant in westward expansion and the discovery of an America going through a radical transformation. In panorama paintings, optical mastery of the scene is denied, and the viewer is required to navigate ways through the spectacle, a quality that Banvard's *Mississippi* would share with cityscape panoramas and Civil War battle panoramas during the latter half of the nineteenth century. In another example, the California nature paintings of Bierstadt not only imbued the landscape with narrative meaning, they also sparked tourism to the region and influenced the designation of Yosemite and other locations as national parks.[35] Years later, the paintings of William Wendt, Maurice Braun, and other plein air painters would update this narrative through new ideas of color and motion, as well as allowing their paintings to participate in the tourist industry through reproduced postcards and miniature take-home prints sold by hotels and resorts. In photography nature and the "wild" aspects of the Los Angeles area would play a major role in bringing California's look and feel into the public consciousness. H. T. Payne's photo albums, for example, featured many images of Washington Park, site of a panorama exhibition established in 1887, which incorporated the park's vegetation and natural landscape as theatrical set dressing. Yet the Payne albums also featured stereoviews of Eaton Canyon, Santa Monica beach camps, orange groves, and rows of poplars, as well as a heavy emphasis on yucca plants and palm trees. The palm tree would have such an exaggerated presence in nineteenth-century photography, postcards, and paintings that the tree would become a symbol of "the Arcadian good life of Southern California."[36] Hotels built in the wake of these photo and stereoscopic albums would use palm trees in their logos and promotional material to evoke these feelings, and by the 1920s, most of the major Hollywood studios had stockpiles of palm trees for sets, movie premieres, and glamour photos of stars like Rudolph Valentino and Joan Crawford.[37] Each of these forms entrenched a popular perception of semi-tropical California as a place that was unlike America yet at the same time an embodiment of the American dream.

When hiking down to the heavily photographed Eaton Canyon from one of the San Gabriel Mountain resorts, there is a sense that one is participating in a near-cinematic experience where the boundaries between civil and wild are intentionally porous. Along this route, Los Angeles could also be experienced as the national imaginary envisioned by literature and visual culture, as a place that could be simultaneously anywhere and nowhere. One such attraction was the Mount Lowe Resort, where the wild and the civilized comingle, and where literary boosterism's romanticized California destiny is promised through the visual marketing of this resort as an immersive experience.

The San Gabriel Mountains provide an interesting starting point to look at turn-of-the-century California tourism, largely because this range, according to Mike Davis, "constitutes the biological core of an

Figure 3.1. A Pacific Electric brochure of Mount Lowe Resort tourism, 1913. (Courtesy of the Michael Patris Collection, Mount Lowe Preservation Society, Inc. San Marino, CA.)

urban wilderness, sustaining the largest population of coyotes, black bears, and mountain lions."[38] By the 1890s and 1900s, wildlife viewing in the San Gabriel Mountains became an immersive experience, with some tourist sites encouraging "visitors to reenact animal removal campaigns, as well as reenact the 'taming' of the frontier"; just as early cinema responded to a desire to see the past through depicting historical events on film, Southern California tourism produced an attraction genre that allowed visitors to participate in a romantic interpretation of the region's history.[39] The Los Angeles Mount Lowe Resort and Railway, for example, the final stop of a railway line that started at the departure dock for Santa Catalina Island tourism, attracted over 3 million tourists from 1895 to 1936. The route would later become a part of Pacific Electric Railway Company, with its iconic "Red Cars" operating throughout Los Angeles County. Ye Alpine Tavern, a resort hotel, opened in 1895 atop Mount Lowe; this themed hotel foreshadowed the California eclectic house designs of the 1920s and the city's propensity for Hollywood-inspired simulacra.[40] The Pacific Electric route and Ye Alpine Tavern overlap in the sense that they contributed to a remapping of the region from two different perspectives. On the one hand, the Red Car routes helped to map the Los Angeles basin in a literal sense, as new transportation routes fueled the decentralized growth of the L.A. area into a region-based megalopolis of loosely connected communities and attractions. On the other hand, the Mount Lowe Resort, along with similar attractions scattered throughout the region (such as *Ramona* tourism sites, discussed in the next chapter), highlights semi-tropical California as an anywhere space where one can cast oneself in a theatrical reliving of the past. Today, the San Gabriel Mountains, one of the steepest ranges in North America, is visited annually by nearly 30 million tourists who come for the popular outlooks, streams, and picnic grounds, despite the fact that much of the thousand-square mile range consists of inaccessible canyons and ravines that act as wildlife redoubts.

Another important tourist attraction during the Progressive Era was Santa Catalina Island, which, like the Mount Lowe Resort, combined nature viewing as a near-cinematic experience based on looking with a coordinating visual marketing campaign that emphasized the "wildness" of the California tourist experience. The island has operated as a tourist community since the 1890s, with the proximity to wildlife a major selling point. As Camp notes, the region's large sunfish played a significant role in the island's early years of tourism; visitors could pose for photographs riding taxidermized sunfish in the surf off the island's popular beaches.[41] The 1910s and 1920s saw a rapid increase in tourism centered on the port of Avalon, in partnership with Pacific Electric, whose visual marketing advertised the island's natural attractions and framed Catalina tourism as an experience where one could become immersed in the wild without venturing a great distance from civilization. Travelers began their journey in glass-bottomed boats that allowed tourists to see "strange under-sea life in all the charm of its natural state."[42] Once on the island, the tourist would encounter the bison, an anticipated experience because of the heavy emphasis of this creature in Pacific Electric advertisements. Local newspapers promised "dozens of beautiful canyons abounding with wild goats, doves, and quail," and advertised "sport fishing" and "wild goat shooting."[43] By 1921, the All-Year-Round Club enthusiastically supported the construction of the port city of Avalon on Santa Catalina, and later stimulated tourism to the city by running wintertime "sunshine ads" in cold states: full-color illustrations of Avalon harbor and the St. Catherine Hotel that heralded Catalina holidays as "no trip like this in all the world . . . where every minute has pleasure in it."[44] By the end of the 1920s, with the Catalina Casino completely built and featured in All-Year-Round Club and Pacific Electric advertisements, Santa Catalina tourism was "generating tourism dollars from nearly 1 million annual travelers."[45]

What both attractions reveal is a continuation of the formal strategies of California photography and an anticipation of what Nanna Verheoff identifies as the "museal function" of earlier cinema, in which "touristic impulses are apparent in a popular mix of curiosity" and nationalistic links to education and mastery over environment.[46] Southern California photography and regional tourist attractions employed Aby Warburg's notion of pathos formula in their address to the spectator/participant.[47] Pathos formula, a formal aesthetic strategy for organizing art in such a way that the viewer can experience the subject matter emotionally from a safe vantage point, is used in tourism and photography to augment a sense of Southern California vastness and the freedom afforded by these surroundings. The Mount Lowe Resort and Santa Catalina Island transport the pathos formula from still images to the actual world existing outside of the frame, placing navigational control of the fantasy in the hands of the person experiencing the immersive attraction. By contrast, the bridging of education with mastery of environment in these attractions can be read as a pre-cinematic form of defamiliarization, or the making of something familiar from literature or visual culture feel wholly new and unique to the participant. Actuality films, rooted in experience and theatricality, capitalized on this process of defamiliarization as they turned their lenses on many other local tourist attractions soon after the arrival of this early cinematic genre to Southern California. Cawston's ostrich farm, pigeon farms, alligator farms, and panoramic views of the Santa Monica and San Gabriel Mountains offer examples of the cinematic form tapping into this defamiliarization process and pathos formula of Southern California tourism, all while reinforcing the L.A. stadtbild featured in tourist promotion and other visual culture forms.

When we look at the ways that the Mount Lowe Resort and Santa Catalina Island were marketed as experiences (more than simply as attractions), we see how the porous boundaries between the wild and the civilized shaped an ideal California traveler. The romanticized California life put forward in the writings of Nordhoff, Salvator, and Lummis, becomes a lived experience that the tourist can try on for short periods of time, furthering the immersive qualities found in other popular turn-of-the-century attractions such as panorama exhibitions (both painting and photography) and the exhibition halls of world's fairs. The tourist participates in the taming of nature and the frontier, a narrative of American expansion made familiar to the nation through literature, photography, and theatrical experiences like Wild West shows. The San Gabriels, according to Camp, served as a "local frontier" where this narrative could be "acted out," along with other locations that were less than a day's journey from Los Angeles; just as the plein air painters discovered varied landscapes fifty miles or fewer from Los Angeles, so too could the tourist looking to "enact mythical heroism," whether coming from L.A. or from afar.[48] Tourists to Catalina Island similarly found a landscape that was "choreographed to tell a story of national progress and ascendency," a real natural setting visually marketed and promoted in a way that provided the location with hyperreal qualities.[49] Beyond the Progressive Era, there was a continuation of this overlap between the tame and the wild and between the indoor and the outdoor in tourist attractions, notably with the "centrally planned, media-infused environment" of the modern theme parks of Southern California.[50] The Adventureland attractions at Disneyland, since the park's opening in 1955, exemplify the practice of immersive, role-play experience through place substitution; the frontier taming that one could participate in at the Mount Lowe Resort can be seen as anticipating the frontier taming that passengers on Disneyland's Jungle Cruise ride were invited to experience. Looking at the history of Southern California tourism from a broader perspective, from roughly 1880 up to the present, we can see a continuing cycle of tourist attractions as a template for immersive narrative experience and, in turn, film narratives providing inspiration for tourist attractions as immersive experiences.

"OUR LITTLE STUDIO"

Though there have been differing accounts of what exactly was the first narrative film shot in the Los Angeles area, it is generally agreed by scholars to be the fourteen-minute *The Count of Monte Cristo*, shot in late 1907 by Francis Boggs. At the time, Selig Polyscope was on the verge of extinction, buckling under the weight of copyright suits from Edison. Selig authorized Boggs and cameraman Thomas Persons to travel to Southern California to shoot a scene where Edmond Dantes (played by Hobart Bosworth in his film debut) emerges from the ocean to proclaim that "the world is mine." This scene from *Monte Cristo*, according to Andrew Erish, may have been a "scouting expedition to test the viability of a production unit based in Los Angeles," as Selig had visited the city in the fall of 1906 to assess its potential for business.[51] A year after *Monte Cristo*, Selig felt confident enough to "send a full company of players and technicians to establish a West Coast base," declaring that "nowhere, but in the real West could the proper atmosphere and wide vistas be found."[52]

On August 16th, 1909, Francis Boggs sent a message to "Colonel" William Nicholas Selig from the Perkins Hotel in Portland, Oregon. Boggs had just returned to Portland the previous day from Astoria, where he had shot "educational features of the Columbia River salmon fishing" and a narrative short titled *The Fisherman's Bride*. In the letter, Boggs mentions that he will be "taking the company back to Los Angeles."

> Our little studio is in pretty good shape to work in now, and we are going after some good acting pictures. There are many great locations near Los Angeles that we have not touched yet, and we are going to get them. I appreciate more than I can tell your consideration regarding the matter of overworking. I realize that perhaps during the heated term, I may have become a little too

strenuous,—still I am ambitious to get results, and I feel as much
pride in this race for supremacy that the firm is making, as you do
yourself. I know we have got the American firms beaten for productions, and if we can catch the Biograph on the acting, we will
have them,—to use a slang phrase "tied to the post" in every way.
From now on, I am going after the acting strong, and will also keep
up the scene end too.[53]

Selig first experienced California during the late 1880s when he
moved to Northern California for health reasons, first finding work at
a fruit farm and then performing magic in San Francisco as "Selig the
Conjurer."[54] After touring up and down the California coast, his attention soon turned toward motion pictures after encountering Edison's
Kinetoscope at a tour stop in Dallas in 1895. Seeing the potential for
film as a form of narrative entertainment, Selig circumvented the Edison
patent by borrowing from the blueprints to the Lumière model, and in
doing so developed his own Selig standard camera and the Selig Polyscope projector.[55] Selig made a reputation for himself as a filmmaker who
made actualities in the West's rugged frontier, the genre soon becoming one of his signatures. With many of his early westerns drawing on
antecedents in traveling Wild West shows, such as Buffalo Bill's Wild
West, Selig first used Colorado as a shooting location during the early
half of the 1900s before eventually settling in Los Angeles following the
success of The Count of Monte Cristo. Francis Boggs and Selig Polyscope
film workers arrived in Los Angeles on March 21, 1909 and created an
outdoor studio using the drying yards behind the Sing Lee Chinese laundry at 751 South Olive Street between Seventh and Eighth Streets. Their
first production (and complete studio film in Los Angeles) was The Heart
of a Race Tout.[56] On August 24, 1909, the Selig Pacific Coast Studio in
Edendale was officially completed, its name appropriately evoking the
regional mythos that Selig and other filmmakers had been drawn to. By
the end of November 1909, Selig's Los Angeles branch had produced
approximately fifty one-reel films.[57]

In the run-up to Selig Polyscope's arrival in Los Angeles, the 1906
San Francisco earthquake damaged the theatrical community, but Los
Angeles supported two full-time theater companies and was part of
the Orpheum vaudeville circuit, from which additional players, sets,

costumes, and props could potentially be recruited.[58] Drawing on talent from local theater groups like Roscoe "Fatty" Arbuckle and Hobart Bosworth, Selig's films would feature more bombastic performances, in stark contrast to D. W. Griffith's more subtle and subdued performances. As the Edendale Studio was under construction, Selig Polyscope would film its first westerns in Los Angeles: *Ben's Kid* (1909), featuring Arbuckle, and *Across the Divide* (1909), with interiors shot in Selig's temporary downtown L.A. studio and exteriors shot at Camp Follow's in the San Gabriel Canyon above Azuza. Beginning in 1910, "the film trade press recognized the studio's aesthetic and symbolic value and made images and descriptions of them key components of its emerging attention to the region."[59] "Virtually every American motion picture company," by the early 1910s, "came to embrace Selig's aesthetic of making Westerns in the West" and by 1912 Biograph, Kalem, Bison, and eventually Pathé followed his lead by establishing studios in Los Angeles.[60] According to the *Los Angeles Times*, "Despite the tremendous output of cowboy and Indian pictures, the local directors say that the demand for them, especially in Europe, is still greater than any other class."[61] Perhaps the most revealing statement came in 1911 from *Moving Picture World*, which credited Selig as the "first to discover the photographic advantages of Southern California," a recognition of the region's ability to provide place substitution that had been effectively anticipated by the tourism industry and its visual promoters.[62]

The next phase in Selig's transformation of the Los Angeles environment into a movie factory came in 1912 when Edgar Rice Burroughs wrote *Tarzan of the Apes*, further stoking a national interest in exotic tales at a time when motion pictures were attending to this fascination through visualization. Before *Monte Cristo*, Los Angeles's local animal parks had also provided a site for popular actualities that sold Los Angeles and Southern California as an ideal location for wildlife viewing, including a 1903 short from a Los Angeles pigeon farm and another 1903 film of Cawston's ostrich farm, the latter of which makes an appearance in the *Los Angeles and Southern California Photo Album* produced by the Historical Society of Southern California that same year. Selig, who had already made a name for himself in the previous decade as a filmmaker of animal safaris, visited the Hagenbeck Zoo in Hamburg in 1913, "where he drew inspiration for the creation of his own private zoo and for productions featuring wild animals."[63] Also inspired by the menageries in the Los Angeles area and the region's culture of wildlife viewing, the Selig Zoo opened in 1913 in Lincoln Heights, northeast of downtown Los Angeles. With initial visual advertisements depicting journeys to the attraction by automobile and train, the zoo would serve two critical functions in L.A.-based film productions from the mid-1910s until the mid-1930s, drawing on some of the guiding principles behind California tourism's attraction genres.

In the summer of 1915, the Selig Polyscope Company ran *The Movie Special*: a train journey from Chicago to California and back again. Passengers on board the train were extras in the Polyscope-produced western *The Seven Suffering Sisters* (William R. Coleman, 1915), which was shot over the duration of the journey on the train and outside during stops (no print is known to exist today). Tickets cost $128 (roughly $2,750 today), and the train made several stops in California that were of great significance. The first was in San Francisco for the Panama-Pacific International Exposition: a world's fair celebrating the opening of the Panama Canal, during which William Selig himself was honored at a banquet (alongside William Randolph Hearst) for his contributions to California arts and culture. Since the movies were still struggling to be viewed as a respectable art form, this was seen as a PR move more than anything else.[64] The next stop was a tour of the Selig Polyscope Studios in Los Angeles—located in Edendale—and then on to the Selig Zoo in East Los Angeles, a thirty-two-acre wildlife menagerie that, in addition to catering to L.A.'s white middle-class population as a public spectacle, also served as a movie-animal rental house and faux wilderness movie set for major studios and independent producers right up into the early 1930s.

Some of the zoo's notable "animals stars" were felines who worked with silent era animal trainer Olga Celeste (known in the industry as the "leopard lady") and Jiggs, the first chimpanzee to play the character of Cheetah, born in 1928 and debuting in *Tarzan the Ape Man* (W. S. Van Dyke, 1932). The zoo's second function was to provide shooting spaces for film productions set in exotic locations. The simulated environments of animal enclosures, designed to collapse the distance between the real world of the visitors and the imagined world of the zoo's designers, were repurposed into simulated environments designed to collapse the distance between the real world of film spectators and the imagined world of the filmmakers. The zoo would eventually close in the mid-1930s after reduced attendance, disrepair, and damage from a flood, and many of its statues and installations were dispersed to other parts of the city (life-size elephant and lion statues are at the Los Angeles Zoo today).

What connects Selig Polyscope and the Selig Zoo to the other studios that emerged in Los Angeles during the 1910s, like Universal Studios and the Thomas H. Ince Studios (or Inceville) was that they provided a template for future Hollywood studios as mini-environments, mini-cities, and mini-ecosystems. Los Angeles provided such an idea space for this studio model to flourish that a 1916 issue of *Photoplay* reported that Inceville was recognized as a town by the U.S. government, with fully functioning restaurants and a fire department.[65] One can also look to the creation of Disneyland decades later as an indication of how much these motion picture practices of building environment and experience were embedded in the subconscious of Los Angeles–based filmmakers. The way that studios during the 1910s and 1920s used visuals to forge a relationship between themselves and their audiences further illustrates the connections between the rise of Hollywood and the established practices of the Southern California tourism industry, as movie fandom can be read as another form of commodified lived experience.

A LAND OF PLACE SUBSTITUTION

By the 1930s, the practice of place substitution and fictionalizing locations—a by-product of Southern California tourism adopted by early American cinema—was firmly in place as Hollywood's signature qualities, for which it was known internationally. Promotional material for Paramount Studios would openly advertise these practices by including a location map of California that signaled, with a great level of self-confidence, places in California that have stood in for somewhere else (fig. 3.2). This was accomplished, in part, through what Jennifer Bean describes as "an unprecedented fascination with the 'place' of motion pictures": environments stripped of geographically specificity and reengineered for an optimal engagement with the senses.[66] For example, Mount Lowe is a specific location in the southern portion of the San Gabriel

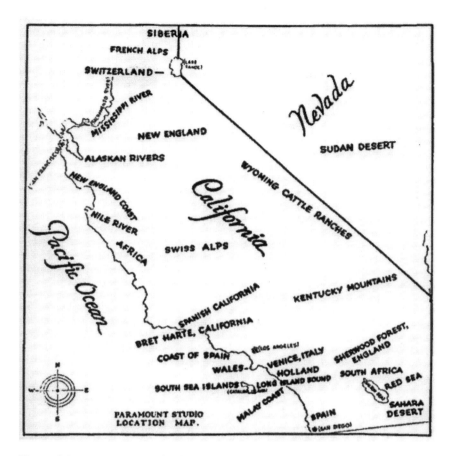

Figure 3.2. Paramount Studios' promotional location map, 1937. (Marc Wanamaker, Bison Archives, Beverly Hills, CA.)

Mountain range with identifiable features (for example, California sage brush and oak trees, Mount Wilson at an elevation 5,710 feet, Eaton Canyon, Occidental Peak, etc.), and yet at the same time, the Alpine resort cast the location as any portion of a mythologized western frontier of the nineteenth century. On film, the San Gabriel Mountains have played themselves (*E.T.: The Extra-Terrestrial*, 1982), an unspecified nation at war (*Fear and Desire*, 1953), Africa (*Tarzan* films of the 1930s), and a range of western locations, past (*Out West*, 1918) and contemporary (*Deadwood*, television series, 2004–6). An hour's drive from Mount Lowe, in the city of Chatsworth on the northeastern end of the San Fernando

Valley, lies Iverson Movie Ranch, which originally started as a homestead (with flora and topography similar to the San Gabriels) and eventually became the location of over two thousand film shoots. D. W. Griffith's *Man's Genesis* (1912) and Cecil B. DeMille's *The Squaw Man* (1914) were early films shot here; Iverson's Ranch would go on to be Africa, Asia, the South Seas, the Wild West, and alien planets in films such as *The Gold Rush* (1925), *The Good Earth* (1937), *The Treasure of the Sierra Madre* (1948), *The African Queen* (1951), and *In Cold Blood* (1967). Hollywood, according to Allen J. Scott, is two things: a place in Southern California, "a particular locale-bound nexus of production relationships," and it is everywhere, a "disembodied assortment of narratives."[67] As Hollywood's host city, Los Angeles can be read as possessing both of these qualities, at first occasioned through pre-cinema visual culture and then advanced through a Los Angeles that was made by movies, resulting in a symbiotic relationship between a film industry and a city that fostered it. Southern California tourism—as a crystallization of photography and painting's formal strategies and ties to boosterism—provided an immersive model for early Hollywood filmmakers on how a spectator's mind could be both patterned and liberated.

4

DON CARLOS

The All-Year-Round Club's *Southern California through the Camera* features a section titled "Old Spanish Missions" containing a photo taken in the courtyard of an unspecified adobe mission (fig. 4.1), accompanied by a statement proclaiming: "Nowhere in the United States is there architecture so flavorful of ancient lands." What is interesting is that the picture was not taken by a tourism company, nor is it drawn from one of the H. T Payne albums or any of its contemporaries. Rather, the image is

Figure 4.1. "Nowhere in the United States is there architecture so flavorful of ancient life in foreign lands." All-Year-Round Club, *Southern California through the Camera* (1929). (Huntington Library, San Marino, CA, call number 128028.)

from an unidentified film credited to First National Pictures, featuring an actress in a Spanish colonial era costume in the garden courtyard of the mission.[1] Later in the magazine, a section called "Moving Pictures" features an image from the same film (fig. 4.2), with a caption reading: "Below is a scene from a motion picture where one of California's old Spanish Missions supplies the background."[2] It is also revealing that First National's studios were modeled on the Spanish missions that graced the California coastal regions from San Diego to San Francisco. The studio was "designed entirely in the old Spanish style," as reported in 1926 by the *Los Angeles Times*, "and within [its] walls may be filmed, from time to time, photoplays symbolic of the olden Spanish regime of California."[3] In *Southern California through the Camera*, images from Hollywood's interpretation of Southern California's past are seen as more appropriate for promoting tourism than documentary photography of the actual sites. As we saw in the previous chapter, the movies recognized, in part through an established regional tourism industry, that California locations could be any *place*. Yet these scenes from *Southern California through the Camera* point to a recognition of California as playing both any place and any *time*. While early filmmaking

Figure 4.2. "Moving Pictures." All-Year-Round Club, *Southern California through the Camera* (1929). (Huntington Library, San Marino, CA, call number 128028.)

in Los Angeles has used a broad range of historical periods as settings, California's eighteenth- and nineteenth-century Spanish/Mexican past is of great significance to the story of Hollywood's ascendancy in the region, due in large part to how a mythologized version of this past was used to market the region in strikingly proto-cinematic ways.

Each aspect of Southern California visual culture explored in the previous chapters was, in varying degrees, informed by what would eventually become known as the "Mission Legend": an evocation of Southern California's pre-statehood Spanish colonial/Mexican ranchero past viewed through rose-tinted nostalgia and understood in mythical terms. The Mission Legend has received a large amount of scholarly attention since the 1946 publication of Carey McWilliam's *Southern California: An Island on Land*, with the focus primarily on how the construction of the state's creation myth knowingly or unknowingly sidestepped the atrocities visited upon California's indigenous population. Returning to Vincent Brook's concept of the palimpsest as a master metaphor for the cover-up and the "bleeding through" of Los Angeles history, critical engagement with the Mission Legend's legacy has served as a retrieval of these layers to recontextualize the history of Los Angeles's formation as a cultural economy. In recent years, cinema and media scholars have exhumed palimpsest layers to renarrate the story of Hollywood's rise by returning the marginalized voices of L.A.'s Mexican American community, which played a significant role in the city's visual culture scene in the 1920s. In *Cinema between Latin America and Los Angeles: Origins to 1960*, scholars like Colin Gunckel, Jan-Christopher Horak, Jacqueline Avila, Desirée J. Garcia, and Lisa Jarvinen explore the "considerable, ongoing role that Los Angeles has played in the history of Spanish-language cinema" from the Progressive Era to the early 1960s.[4] In *Mexico on Main Street: Transnational Film Culture in Los Angeles Before World War II*, Gunckel focuses on the immigrant film culture of Mexican Americans, which centered largely in the downtown area of Los Angeles. His work is a palimpsest layer retrieval of the city's cultural history that offers a "competing vision" of the transformation of the city during the early twentieth century. These works, alongside other scholarship on Mexican American Los Angeles during the early twentieth century, play a significant role in shaping the ways that this chapter participates in a debunking process still taking place.

In this chapter, I am interested in exploring the Mission Legend's role in California's turn-of-the-century industry of attractions, in which immersion and participation were geared toward inviting the visitor to take part in a mythologized past to which most had no cultural connection. Just as photography fueled a visual mapping of the region, later advanced through motion pictures, the Mission Legend remapped California under the sign of territorial appropriation. As part of the larger industry of tourism in California, the Mission Legend recast real locations as spaces for transformative experiences, just as Mount Lowe and Santa Catalina did. At the same time, it was more than just space being remapped; it was time as well. The filmmakers who arrived in California during the early twentieth century—enticed through visual culture informed by this redrawn California past—brought the Mission Legend to life cinematically, using the developing practices of place substitution to locate the otherness of this mythologized past and ensuring that Hollywood, as the region's chief booster by the 1920s, controlled the terms under which the territory would be mapped. Yet, just as we have seen with any other form of boosterism, there is a form of debunking that countered it—whether using the same literary or visual forms or radically oppositional ones. A crucial difference, however, is that this debunking of California boosterism, and its attendant visual forms, is still occurring, driven by an excavation of the region's historical palimpsest layers through scholarship and activism. Studies that explore the links between Chicanx history and urban planning, such as David R. Diaz's *Barrio Urbanism*, complement the literature on Mexican American film culture in Los Angeles, just as scholarship in urban studies has bolstered the writing of the previous chapters. Examining the Mission Legend's role in the formation of Los Angeles as a cultural economy brings into relief the social and cultural mechanisms that pasted each palimpsest layer over the real Latinx story of the city.

This chapter starts with the phenomenon of "*Ramona* tourism," a proto-cinematic industry of pilgrimage by dedicated fans of Helen Hunt Jackson's novel to sites in Ventura County and San Diego County where crucial moments of the novel were believed to have taken place. What is striking about *Ramona* tourism is how this blending of fact with fiction lent itself so effectively to visual marketing practices that contributed not only to the growth of the Los Angeles area but also to the popularity

of mission era–themed culture. *Ramona* tourism, in this sense, also provides an example of Southern California tourism in the late nineteenth
century as offering the same promise of near-cinematic experiences
and practicing the same forms of place substitution as the nature and
health tourism explored in chapter 3. This was a period of contraction,
according to Carey McWilliams. On the one hand, the 1880s were an
intense transition period where "the typically Spanish appearance of
Southern California towns" was demolished in order to refashion the
region in the likeness of traditional Anglo America.[5] On the other hand,
the Arroyo group of boosters embraced the *Ramona* mythology and the
Mission Legend at large, appropriating Spanish/Mexican/indigenous
history to distinguish California from the rest of the nation (contrasting
with the Anglo heritage manifest in "Old America," for example) and as
part of a larger culture of attractions as proto-cinematic experiences.
Charles Fletcher Lummis, the booster known for *Land of Sunshine, Out
West, A Tramp across the Continent*, and other works exalting California's romantic qualities, is less known for how he incorporated *Ramona*
mythology and fandom into his nationwide promotion of California.
Lummis's visual marketing of the novel's prime tourist destinations,
largely through the popular *Home of Ramona* (1888) picture book, provided a foundation for several film adaptations in the early twentieth
century. Other boosters and "Arroyians" capitalized on the legacy of the
Mission Legend through other visual cultural forms, notably theatrical
works. Journalist, poet, and playwright John S. McGroarty, discussed in
previous chapters, celebrated the Spanish colonial past through poetry
and other works of literature, some of which were avidly read by early
filmmakers who arrived in California during the early 1910s. In this
chapter, I consider McGroarty's *The Mission Play*, first staged in 1912, as
a work that orchestrates visual culture around the prevailing mythology
of the Mission Legend. *The Mission Play* notably combined the popularity of the *Ramona* novel with the pervasiveness of the Spanish Colonial
style in L.A., and its reception can be read as a testimony of the endurance of this myth industry into the twentieth century.

Finally, I look at the Mexican American visual culture that was developing in Los Angeles along a parallel track, often constructed in direct
opposition to the Anglo-dominated Hollywood culture that the Mission
Legend helped to construct. A crucial aspect Mexican American visual

culture during the 1910s and 1920s is that it played a significant role in the construction of downtown Los Angeles, another parallel storyline that complements the story of downtown's rise through photography and other forms of visualization (another retrieval of a palimpsest layer performed through important recent scholarship). The *revista* theater, a popular form of social-political comedy originating in Mexico, is an important component of this story, as this form of popular entertainment synthesized other visual culture forms and fueled the growth of a theater network in the downtown area whose legacy continues to the present.

RAMONA

[Los Angeles] is only a hundred years old, and that is not time enough for such a song to simmer. It will come later, with the perfume of century-long summers added to its flavor.
                    —Helen Hunt Jackson, "Echoes in the City of the Angels"

"The most important woman in the history of Southern California never lived," according to Dydia DeLyser.[6] Helen Hunt Jackson's novel *Ramona*, published in 1884, is the story of an adopted half-Scottish/half–Native American woman named Ramona who falls in love with a Tongva man named Alessandro. Outraged, Ramona's family, the Mexican Moreno family, exiles the couple from what is believed to be present-day Rancho Camulos in Ventura County to Temecula, northeast of San Diego. Ramona and Alessandro are soon married and start a family on a homestead, but eventually American settlers threaten their livelihoods in the wake of U.S. statehood. Their child eventually dies of illness and Alessandro is shot by the Anglo settlers. The popularity of the novel played a crucial role in the growth of regional migration and the California tourist industry—an industry that ultimately contributed to a cycle of erasure and rebuilding that permeates Los Angeles history. This cycle is best described by David Fine, who observes that first Anglo Americans obtained land built by Spanish/Mexican subjugation of the indigenous population, and then Anglo Americans dismantled, destroyed, or allowed to fall into decay this Spanish American colonial legacy, and finally, Anglo Americans recovered this past culture and repurposed it to attract more Anglo Americans to California.[7]

The strength of *Ramona* tourism lies in how it weaves fiction into the fabric of fact.[8] The town of Camulos in Ventura County, approximately fifty miles to the north of Los Angeles, was the end point of two railroads in 1881: the Southern Pacific and the Santa Fe. The development of this hub expanded the number of travelers to the Southern Pacific line between Los Angeles and San Francisco, largely thanks to *Ramona* enthusiasts as new riders.[9] When the Southern Pacific built a station near Camulos, the company advertised the destination as the "Home of Ramona" in brochures and station maps, capitalizing on *Ramona* fandom as a way to increase revenue and distinguish itself from competing rail lines in Southern California.[10] As Carey McWilliams remarked in *Southern California: An Island on Land*: "Trains regularly stopped at . . . [the Home of Ramona] so that wide-eyed Bostonians, guidebooks in hand, might detrain, visit the rancho, and bounce up and down on the bed in which Ramona slept."[11] Rancho Camulos, owned by the Del Valle family during the 1880s, was believed to have been the "Home of Ramona," and as early as 1886, tourists would come to the family ranch and ask where Ramona and Señor Moreno were.[12] The family capitalized on this, publishing visual material of their own and featuring "Home of Ramona" on wine labels and letterheads. By 1906, postcards from Rancho Camulos asked: "Have You Read Ramona?"[13] Throughout the twentieth century, wildflowers from Rancho Camulos and from the alleged Ramona and Alessandro marriage site near San Diego were pressed into copies of the book.[14] The present-day Camulos, according to Vincent Brook, still maintains its "Spanish Fantasy Past" through its promotional material, which advertises the location as a place "where the history, myth, and romance of old California still linger."[15]

As with plein air painting during the Progressive Era, postcard circulation played an important role in spreading the *Ramona* myth and developing a popular social imaginary of Southern California during this period. Each *Ramona* tourist location—Ramona's home, her school, her marriage place, and Alessandro's grave—was the subject of tens of thousands of postcards circulated around the country during the late 1880s and into the 1890s. Some postcards even featured staged scenes from the novel using performers in costume, such as a Native American woman named Ramona Luba, whom postcards identified as "the Real Ramona."[16] The *Ramona* postcard and souvenir market continued into the early twentieth century, with "Ramona's Marriage Place," a rundown adobe house near San Diego, overtaking Rancho Camulos as the most popular tourist attraction It was purchased and restored in 1910 by real estate developer John D. Spreckels, whose restoration included a souvenir shop, which offered "dried flowers from the courtyard, souvenir teaspoons, postcards, and other *Ramona* curios . . . sold by the dozens."[17] While these practices greatly contributed to the region's reputation as a land of innovative visual culture, it is here that we return once again to Charles Fletcher Lummis, whose direct engagement with the legacy of Jackson's novel would add an extra layer of sensuous involvement to this legend.

By the late 1880s, California's Spanish/Mexican colonial past was familiar to the coutry through the photographic industry. Images of Mission San Gabriel and Mission San Fernando appeared in popular photo albums of the late 1870s and 1880s, presented as sites of the region's hallowed ground. At the same time, a key ingredient of the success of *Ramona* tourism was the novel's "place descriptions . . . accurate even to the details of roof tiling," which caused tourists to identify these places as real.[18] Both photography and the novel's descriptions converge in Charles Fletcher Lummis's *The Home of Ramona*, one of his underdiscussed contributions to California visual culture, produced in Camulos by Charles Fletcher Lummis and Company in 1888. Lummis, as mentioned above, became so enamored with the California Mission Legend that he nicknamed himself "Don Carlos."[19] The Mission Legend plays a strong role in both of the magazines Lummis edited, *Land of Sunshine* and *Out West*: rail travel to Rancho Camulos was advertised, articles explored the history of missions and historical figures, and romantic portrayals of Mexican ranchero life, on which "Don Carlos" Lummis modeled much of his persona, were presented as a life to aspire to in the face of urbanization. *The Home of Ramona*, produced years before the first issue of *Land of Sunshine*, provides some of the crucial groundwork for the pictorially lavish promotions of California that Lummis would become internationally renowned for at the turn of the century.

Lummis's book—five and a half by nine inches, featuring ribbon-tie binding and ten photographs—capitalizes on the reputation of Ramona's home at Camulos as a real place. What is striking about *The Home of*

Figure 4.3. *The Home of Ramona*, from Charles Fletcher Lummis and Company, 1888. This first image serves as an establishing shot of Camulos. (Huntington Library, San Marino, CA, call number 252770.)

Figure 4.4. *The Home of Ramona*, from Charles Fletcher Lummis and Company, 1888. Ramona's tree, shot inside the "straight walk shaded by a trellis." (Huntington Library, San Marino, CA, call number 252770.)

Ramona is how it seems to anticipate film storyboards and silent cinema. In the opening pages, Lummis states that "no novel of strong purpose can be pure fiction" and that Jackson's novel is the "*Uncle Tom's Cabin* of the Indian." One of the first images acts as an establishing shot: a panoramic wide shot of Camulos in blue tint (a process known as cyanotype). Next, the reader is treated to a series of shots around Ramona's home: the *placita* (the courtyard of Ramona's home, taken from the roof on the opposite side), *Ramona's* tree and the "straight walk by the trellis," the veranda, and the chapel—with each location accompanied by a descriptive passage from the book. What is also fascinating is that the images feature two human figures—a man and a woman—dressed in historical period clothing. The staging of these images, their mise-en-scène, and their progression would be echoed twenty-two years later in D. W. Griffith's 1910 seventeen-minute adaptation of Jackson's novel, the first of four film adaptations.

Griffith, having himself played Alessandro in a touring stage version years earlier, shot the film in Camulos—the film's opening title card proclaiming: "The actual scenes where Mrs. Jackson placed her characters in the story." The film features no close-ups, just a tableaux of (mostly) wide shots that harken back to the panoramic vision that was deeply embedded in the established California visual culture at the turn of the century, as well as evoking the imagery of Lummis's *The Home of Ramona*. These landscape vistas in Griffith's film demonstrate, as Eileen Bowser suggests, that Southern California "tended to produce freer positioning of cameras," and in publicity material for his *Ramona* film, Griffith highlighted his use of such long shots.[20] This film would be one of the twenty-one films that Griffith shot in early 1910 with an explicitly Californian setting; Griffith had also worked on another Mission Legend film earlier in the year (also starring Mary Pickford) called *The Thread of Destiny*.[21] *Motion Picture World* writer Louis Reeves Harrison described *Ramona* as a "special feature" and its audience as "unusually large, quiet, rather above than below the average in quality," composed largely of "earnest looking . . . businessmen who ordinarily stay away from motion pictures."[22]

At the same time, Griffith's *Ramona* arrived at a time when California's Native Americans had been significantly weakened by droughts and Anglo immigration.[23] Added to this, the film engages in what Vincent

Figure 4.5. Mary Pickford as Ramona and Henry B. Walthall as Alessandro in D. W. Griffith's *Ramona* (Biograph Company, 1910).

Brook refers to as "redface casting," which can also be seen in the 1936 Henry King film version.[24] In Griffith's film, Alessandro and Ramona are played by Henry B. Walthall and Mary Pickford, who at the time were Biograph Company stock actors. Alessandro is portrayed as a "naïf," and the film's view of white superiority is revealed "primarily through the performance codes": Walthall's Alessandro acts, toward the end, "in the unchecked histrionic, rather than verisimilar, manner, and it is this shift in [behaviors]—and not his race—that justifies his removal from the face of the earth in the cold-blooded way that nature eliminates the unfit."[25] "If, indeed, Griffith's *Ramona* [catered to] refined upper-class bejeweled audiences," as Vincent Brook observes, spectators who began "arriving at the theater in automobiles" in the 1910s, then the film's role in "lifting the movies from the gutter," coupled with the racial politics of its creation, can be read as an extra layer of whitewash to a Los Angeles palimpsest layer.[26] Put simply by David Fine, *Ramona* film adaptations do for California what *Gone with the Wind* does for the American South, an interesting rejoinder to Lummis's comparison between Jackson's novel and Harriet Beecher Stowe's.[27]

Other adaptations of *Ramona* are a feature-length version released in 1916, directed by Donald Crisp for William Horsley's studio at Melrose and Bronson, and starring Adda Gleason and Monroe Salisbury.[28] This was followed by a 1928 version directed by Native American director Edwin Carewe and starring Mexican American actress Dolores del Río in the title role. The final version was Henry King's 1936 Technicolor adaptation, with Loretta Young and Don Ameche in the starring roles. It is the Edwin Carewe version, however, that further illustrates the connection between Los Angeles visual culture and the ascendancy of Hollywood cinema in striking ways. Though shot in black-and-white photography, the film's first title describes the story as set in the "colorful days" of the early California Spanish dons, setting up the historical chronology of the story through juxtaposing the California ranchos with panning for gold. The Moreno house is adorned with creeping vines, potted plants, and Mexican blankets draped over the walls—the home exemplifying the Mediterranean villa or Spanish Colonial Revival designs that were popular home designs in Los Angeles during the 1920s. Not only does this architecture upstage the action throughout the film, there is also an emphasis on nature and the wild California landscape that would have already been familiar to audiences through photography and tourism culture; Ramona is shown with a parrot early in the film, and in the scenes that follow, trees and other distinct forms of California flora are foregrounded within the frame.

Also noteworthy is the film's marketing, which capitalized on the enduring popularity of the *Ramona* myth and the Mission Legend embedded in established Southern California visual marketing practices. A *Moving Picture World* article on April 28, 1928 detailed the premier of the film at the United Artists Theater on Broadway in downtown, describing the location as the "city's business commercial thoroughfare in Downtown Los Angeles," affirming Tina Olson Lent's view that downtown Los Angeles was constructed during the 1920s in the form of a classic American city to symbolize the end of Los Angeles's frontier status.[29] The article further describes the theater's lobby at the premiere as decorated with mission era décor and featuring indigenous Californians making "blankets, pottery, slippers, and straw hats" as patrons filed in.[30] The film

Figure 4.6. Dolores del Río as Ramona in Edwin Carewe's *Ramona* (United Artists, 1928).

was also promoted on the airwaves through a song written specifically for the film. "Ramona," with music by Mabel Wayne, lyrics by L. Wolfe Gilbert, and sung by Dolores del Río became a popular hit and was rerecorded with different singers at various points throughout the twentieth century.[31] The theatricality behind the film's promotion had a precursor in another crucial chapter in the story of the Mission Legend and Southern California visual culture, one that combined this mythology with local theater and pageantry: John S. McGroarty's *The Mission Play* (1912).

While the *Ramona* myth stoked the imagination of boosters like Lummis and filmmakers like Griffith, the poetry of John Steven McGroarty also played an important role in the state's national reputation as a land of mythmaking. Known as "the Poet of Verdugo Hills," McGroarty arrived in Los Angeles in 1901. In addition to a distinguished career as a journalist for the *Los Angeles Times*, he wrote several works that championed the region as, in his words, the "Land of Heart's Desire," notable among them *California: Its History and Romance* (1911) and *The*

Mission Play—a three-hour stage production that showcased a romantic portrait of California's mission past in stunning pageantry. A 1908
article for Lummis's *Out West* magazine by William Albert Curtis, titled
"The First Theater in California," observes that, at the time of publication, the theater industry in California had a reported investment
of $7 million and "two hundred showhouses of various types and sizes
from San Diego to Mendocino."[32] Many of the actors from the California
stage during this period would later be recruited by early Hollywood film
studios, notably Hobart Bosworth, who would work for Selig Polyscope
and later Thomas H. Ince Studios. Additionally, over a decade earlier, in
1894, La Fiesta de Los Angeles debuted, a parade promoted by boosters
that showcased Mexican-American culture, itself largely indebted to the
popularity of *Ramona*; the festival was discontinued in 1916 although
there have been numerous attempts since to revive it.

By 1911, the appropriate conditions were in place for a theatrical
pageant celebrating California's Spanish/Mexican heritage, and for such
event to be readily received by a Los Angeles Anglo population already
steeped in *Ramona* mythology and Mission Legend iconography. A special playhouse was built in the San Gabriel Valley in the Mission Revival
style specifically to show the play, seen by an estimated 2.5 million people between 1912 and 1929.[33] Funded by an umbrella organization of
L.A. businessmen and *Ramona* enthusiasts called the Mission Legend
Association (largely underwritten by Henry E. Huntington), *The Mission Play* featured a cast of nearly three hundred, a pipe organ, choral
singing, mime, and dancing in "celebration of the Franciscans in Alta
California."[34] It was said by one journalist that a tourist "who went to
California and failed to see Catalina Island, Mt. Wilson, and *The Mission Play* is considered to have something wrong in his head."[35] As one
of the Progressive Era's most popular visual attractions, *The Mission Play*
demonstrated broadly the effectiveness of establishing a mythological
whitewashed view of the state's colonial legacy as a usable past. The play's
venue, reconstructed in 1927, can still be visited today; near the cities
of San Gabriel and Alhambra, it is situated on Mission Drive near South
Ramona Street.

Ramona tourism and *The Mission Play*, viewed together, offer an
origin story of early film's capitalizing on the popularity of the Mission
Legend in terms of story choices, the use of California as a land of place

substitution, and the growth of other visual culture forms that were adjacent to the motion picture industry. Set in Old California, Johnston McCulley's *The Curse of Capistrano* serial in 1919, for example, grew out of the popularity of the Mission Legend and became the basis for the iconic Zorro character in film and television throughout the twentieth century. Though Paramount Studios advertised the Santa Barbara/ San Luis Obispo region of California as "Spanish California," the San Fernando Valley and Sunland/Tijunga area of Los Angeles adequately supplied the setting for Fred Niblo's *The Mark of Zorro* (1920), staring Douglas Fairbanks in the title role; the Disney television series, starring Guy Williams in the title role, made use of Iverson Ranch (discussed in the previous chapter), whereas, by contrast, the Anthony Hopkins and Antonio Banderas vehicle *The Mask of Zorro* (Martin Campbell, 1998) was filmed in Mexico, as California was no longer the land of place substitution by the end of the century. Spanish Colonial Revival architecture, though dating back in California to the late nineteenth century, was celebrated at the 1915 Panama-Pacific Exposition and revised into a miniature residential style that could be reproduced as livable movie sets. As Merry Ovnick notes, *The Mark of Zorro* was coded in visual design practices that ran parallel to a "taste for historical revival and fantasy styles" in residential architecture that "was reinforced by exposure to Hollywood" production design, an issue that I return to in chapter 6.[36] This interweaving of early Los Angeles, the Mission Legend, an emphasis on the otherness of an imagined past, and near-cinematic modes of experience further contributed to the palimpsest layering of a forgotten history. Yet from the perspective of contemporary scholarship on L.A. and cinema, exploring these connections brings the mechanisms of this palimpsest layering into relief for critical interrogation and the writing of competing histories.

TEATRO CALIFORNIA

In contrast to the Mission Legend myth industry, consider an overview sketch of competing histories, beginning first with the literary debunkers who operated in similar circles to McGroarty and Lummis, and then bridging over to a vibrant culture of Mexican American theater that constructed downtown on a parallel track to the visual culture explored in previous chapters. Novelist and activist Mary Austin was, at the turn of the century, briefly affiliated with Charles Fletcher Lummis's *Land of Sunshine* group as well as the loosely connected but influential bohemian Arroyo group that operated largely around the Pasadena area. Her first book, *The Land of Little Rain* (1905), was a collection of essays on southwestern pastoral life. Having witnessed firsthand the Owens Valley water scandal of 1913—depicted (and transported to the late 1930s) by screenwriter Robert Town in *Chinatown* (1974)—Austin wrote *The Ford* (1917), dramatizing these events through what some have called a "panoramic novel." The 1920s, which David Fine notes as the decade when Los Angeles literary history began, provided the debunker class with the "familiar and assessable literary image" of the "Deceptive Dream Maker"—the Hollywood director/producer as an extension of the Lummis/McGroarty/Chandler booster set; such figures would play an important role in Evelyn Waugh's *The Loved One* (1948; adapted into the 1965 Tony Richardson film of the same name), Budd Schulberg's *What Makes Sammy Run* (1941), and F. Scott Fitzgerald's unfinished *The Last Tycoon* (published posthumously in 1941).[37] This form of antiboosterism would also energize Davis's category of noir intellectuals, who saw the failure of the American promise in Los Angeles as more pronounced when contrasted with the booster images of the city projected through Hollywood culture; it should not surprise that between the 1940s and 1950s, "approximately 20% of the films in the noir cycle were set in and filmed on location in Los Angeles and identified as such in the narratives."[38]

Shifting the focus to downtown, consider first the history of one of the earliest motion picture theaters that displayed the legacy of stereoscopic photography in a unique way. One of the earliest film exhibitors in Los Angeles was Theodore L. Tally, who opened a parlor on South Spring Street in downtown Los Angeles in 1896 and screened actuality films with the newly released Edison Vitascope. Tally later opened the Lyric Theater at Third and Main in downtown in 1902 (originally opened as the Electric Theater but later renamed the Lyric upon the addition of vocal numbers to accompany films). In 1906, he opened Tally's Broadway on Broadway and Spring, relocating to a larger venue on Broadway in 1910. The Broadway introduced an elevating orchestra and, in 1912, he installed a large pipe organ built by the Murray Harris Company—probably "the first organ ever used in a movie show."[39] The significance of Tally's contributions to both film history and Los Angeles visual culture, however, can be seen in the coverage of his screening of *Madame Butterfly* in a 1915 edition of *Moving Picture World*. "Hear Tally's great pipe organ and orchestra" proclaims the article, which featured an image of Tally himself standing in front of an advertisement whose optical effects recall stereoscopic photography techniques: the advertisement, behind a glass frame, featured Mary Pickford as Cio-Cio-San in costume in a Japanese garden (cut out and pasted on cardboard), a backdrop with painted-on trees and an image of Mount Fuji painted onto a transparent sheet placed over the background.[40] Decades later, in 1962, Murray Schumach wrote about the demise of Tally's Broadway and the neighborhood in the *New York Times*, lamenting that "neither the building nor the block is glamorous today" and both had been "obliterated by squalor and indifference."[41] Though the story of Tally is considered central to the story of the first motion picture theater network in Los Angeles, it is useful to provide a contrast to the lesser-discussed history of Mexican American theaters that operated in the same area and impacted the Los Angeles cultural landscape in equally important ways.

The Mexican Revolution ended in 1917, but violence continued sporadically into the 1920s.[42] In the first quarter of the twentieth century, an estimated 10 percent of the population fled Mexico to the United States to escape political violence and economic hardship. This migration also coincided with a massive population growth and development, spearheaded by city planners, that was aimed at putting a greater physical and discursive distance between immigrants and native-born Euro-American populations arriving in droves from other parts of the United States, as well promoting Los Angeles as the opposite of the "congested and heterogenicity of the East Coast cities" (despite the fact that the city had the largest non-white population outside of Baltimore).[43] During the 1910s, the Hollywood industry rose in Los Angeles alongside a process of Americanization that "relied on depictions of non-whites as vulgar, inferior, or in some cases blood thirsty," an image that would adopt further consequences as Mexican labor and political activism stoked a fear of socialist radicalism, a fear that shaped Los Angeles politics heavily during this period.[44] As early as 1917, the Mexican government formally complained to President Woodrow Wilson about offensive stereotypes of Mexicans and Mexico in Hollywood films, and boycotts were organized in Mexico of films by Paramount, Metro, and Famous Players–Lasky over concerns of these depictions.[45]

At the same time, the development of downtown Los Angeles during the first few decades of the twentieth century—demographic growth, industrialization, and the expansion and transformation of urban space—"coincided with the widespread explosion of commercial leisure nationwide. These changes were largely shaped by the popularity of vaudeville and the feature film, the rise of Hollywood fan culture, a concurrent expansion of ethnic entertainment and press cultures."[46] Some notable venues and institutions provide illuminating cases in point. In 1909, Tally's Electric Theater began operating as Teatro Electrico to attract a Mexican audience. Other venues that followed were the Teatro Plaza (established 1911) and the Teatro Metropolitan (established 1912), which, during the week of Mexican Independence Day in 1918, held a series of events for the benefit of the Mexican Protective League.[47] The Teatro California, at 808 South Main Street, opened in 1918 and operated until its closing in 1988, serving as a grind-house theater in its later years. Finally, the Grand Opera House on 110 South Main Street was rechristened Teatro Mexico by the 1920s, and by this time Main Street, now home to several Mexican institutions, was the location of the offices of the newspaper *El Heraldo de Mexico* (346 North Main Street).

If vaudeville was a precursor to film that eventually turned into a tributary of film talent, Mexican American Los Angeles had its own popular theater practices throughout the early twentieth century. The *revistas*, short for *teatro de revistas* (theater of reviews), were a popular theater practice at the turn of the century that was geared toward social/political commentary, and as Jacqueline Avila observes, Los Angeles was the perfect spot for revistas as it already boasted a large Mexican population and a "lively theater culture."[48] Revista companies traveled to Los Angeles from Mexico throughout the 1910s and 1920s, giving performances that were largely a fusion of different forms of theater entertainment, notably vaudeville, burlesque, and the French revue, and often relying heavily on familiar stock characters (such as the *pelado*, or vagabond character) and satirizing Mexican politics from an expatriate perspective. Some of the notable by-products of the revistas, ones that intersected with both

Hollywood and Mexican film culture, were the establishment of venues, largely in the downtown area, and the success of many of the talent involved. One venue, the Teatro Capitol, was located at 340 South Spring Street, starting in 1903 as the Casino Theater before eventually changing its name to the Capitol Theater by 1929 (the theater was demolished in 1952). As revistas declined in the early 1930s in the wake of sync-sound cinema, many popular performers found work in both American and Mexican cinema, including Lupita Tovar, who starred in *Santa* (1931; the first Spanish-language sync-sound film) and the Spanish-language version of Universal Pictures' *Dracula* (George Melford, 1931). Additionally, behind-the-scenes talent also found work in the motion picture industry, such as Guz Aguila, a revista librettist who was exiled to Los Angeles in 1924 and "gave voice lessons to Hollywood stars and to performers from the local Mexican stage."[49]

By 1930s, the population of Los Angeles exceeded 2 million and the Hollywood movie industry was generating nearly $130 million a year in ticket sales. 1 would like to conclude this chapter with two moments in this decade that can be read as part of what Norman Klein describes as an "anti-tour": exploring locations where there had once been something as a method for revealing the process of cultural erasure and to stage a historical memory retrieval. *Plaza de Los Ángeles*, a historic landmark across the street from Los Angeles's Union Station, is the site of the original 1781 settlement El Pueblo de Nuestra Señora la Reina de los Ángeles sobre el Río Porciúncula, or the Pueblo of Our Lady the Queen of the Angels on the Porciúncula River. In the same year as the American Revolution was winding down, Immanuel Kant was publishing his *Critique of Pure Reason*, and a twenty-five-year-old Wolfgang Amadeus Mozart completed his thirteenth opera, a multiracial party of forty-four settlers founded this pueblo alongside a roaring river flowing into the Pacific Ocean. Within the site of this settlement stands Olvera Street, a location that had been repackaged by the Los Angeles Chamber of Commerce (under the directorship of *Los Angeles Times* editor Harry Chandler) into an attraction that harnessed the power of the mythology that had played such a strong role in selling the city as the land of personal transformation over the previous decades. Two works of narrative art during the 1930s foreground divergent tracks of the Mission Legend's legacy and its broader connections to cinema and visual culture in the post–Progressive Era years. The first is William M. Pizor's 1937 short documentary about Olvera Street— *A Street of Memory*, directed by William L. Prager. The historical district was shot on vericolor film by Alvin Wyckoff, a cinematographer whose career began in 1914 with the Mission Legend–themed film *The Rose of the Rancho* (Cecil B. DeMille, 1914), remade in 1936 in a film directed by Marion Gering and starring John Boles. Olvera Street, a few blocks away from the site of the 1897 Edison Spring Street actuality, is described in Pizor's film as a place that "throbs with the spirit of the past" and a "never-ending procession of different designs." This tour of California's past, narrated by actor Wallace MacDonald, can be read as a revised Los Angeles actuality that celebrates the mythology that drew filmmakers, some of whom were involved in the short's production, westward during the 1910s.

The second (competing) example is the mural *La América Tropical* (1932) by Mexican painter David Alfaro Siqueiros, a visiting instructor at the Chouinard Art Institute alongside Millard Sheets and other members of the California Water Color Society. Unveiled near Olvera Street on October 8, 1932, *La América Tropical* depicts, through stark Marxist and anticolonial imagery, the impact of imperialism, capitalism, and military violence on Mexico's indigenous population. The painting was partially covered in 1934 and then fully whitewashed over in 1938 after city authorities deemed Siqueiros's painting indecent and anti-American. The mural has since been recovered through a 2012 restoration project funded by the Getty Foundation. These two examples construct what Edward Soja describes as a city's third space: a physical location where real (first space) and imagined (second space) narratives overlap and "disrupt binary and linear historical understandings of a place and its people."[50]

A Street of Memory can be viewed as both a reinforcement of a social imaginary and as another addition to the palimpsest layer foisted on Los Angeles's image by McGroarty and Don Carlos. As an *imago*, the film functions as a historical document, revealing how embedded the process of cultural memory erasure (and its audio/visual codes rooted in pre-cinema Mission Legend visual culture) was at the time of its release; the real Olvera Street, a palimpsest layer waiting for retrieval, is absent from the film, and instead the viewer is treated to a cinematic continuation of the tradition of place substitution that is wedded to Southern California visual culture and dominant film industry. *La América Tropical*, by contrast, was turned into a whitewashed palimpsest layer because it countered the very process of erasure that ultimately leads to obscurity. Both examples highlight the importance of the Chicano cinema movement that arose in the late 1960 and continues to the present day as both a form of cinematic anti-tour and restoration of cultural memory to the city. Films like *My Family* (1995), directed by Gregory Nava, for example, offer a new set of imagos that renegotiate the terms of Los Angeles's cultural memory of the Progressive Era with what Bruce Williams characterizes as a dual address to Spanish- and English-speaking audiences, as well as a cinematic recovery of a history obscured by the *Ramona* myth and Mission Legend.[51] Including Chicano cinema as a key component of the broader Los Angeles cinema revisualizes Los Angeles history with a new set of images, constructed in sharp contrast to the placitas and verandas of Don Carlos's world.

5

OFF THE RECORD

In the previous chapters, I explored the key role that visual culture played in cementing a social imaginary of Los Angeles and its surrounding environment as a space for transformation and self-actualization. Experiencing Southern California photography and painting by the turn of the century, one discovered a place that was simultaneously the American destiny crystallized and completely unlike anywhere else in America. The visitors encountering California tourist attractions experienced this space in a way that allowed them to act out fantasies, often linked to a historical past that never really existed but rendered believable by visual marketing networks and media circulation. The motion picture industry, recognizing California's potential to be an "anywhere space," reorchestrated these visual forms and pre-cinematic narrative practices and firmly assumed control of writing the booster narrative of Los Angeles and the state at large. Here, I would like to turn toward the ways in which early Hollywood controlled the reception of Southern California as the home of the American film industry and the industry's reputation as a place-substitution enterprise. Controlling this narrative of Los Angeles as an anywhere space required the early studios to engage with public consciousness in a twofold approach: journalistically and through the creation and circulation of its own visual cultural forms that were designed to control the reception of the business and its products. In a sense, one could argue that the early studio moguls adopted the Charles Fletcher Lummis model of boosterism in that they were selling a place and idea through poetry and lavish visuals, spearheading a form of neo-boosterism that would shape the perception of Los Angeles throughout the twentieth century.

This chapter considers the ways that the early Los Angeles film-making network consolidated into what Benedict Anderson termed an "imagined community." By dominating the developing Los Angeles cultural economy and visual culture industry, the growing studio network defined the contours of its self-made image and controlled how this image (and that of its location) was received internationally. For Anderson, an imagined community is one where a socially constructed group is joined through shared culture and iconography, "conceived as deep horizontal comradeship."[1] This analogy suggests that Hollywood is a state of mind as much as a real place populated with real people, ascribing a greater significance to the "imagined" part of Anderson's term. Added to this, the fact that the majority of what we consider Hollywood is not actually situated in the city of Hollywood (as has been the case since at least the late 1920s) further compounds the notion of this film community as "imagined"; most of so-called Hollywood is like Los Angeles itself, scattered throughout a decentralized territory that Charles Jencks calls a "heteropolis": where the "internal space of the city decomposes into a multiplicity of finely grained micro-territories."[2] Maintaining control of how this imagined community was received and maintained required a myth-making machine on par with the boosterism industry that attracted the movies to Southern California in the first place.

In exploring how Hollywood controlled its reception toward the end the Progressive Era, I turn to the concept of "paratext": things that are exterior to a text that influence how the text is received (marketing material, fan culture, collectables and ephemera, and so on). In previous chapters, we have seen examples of how pre-cinema visual culture in Southern California can be viewed as paratexts of the region's development during the Progressive Era; the photography of Watkins, Muybridge, and Payne, for example, shaped the ways that settlers from the East Coast and Midwest could look at and think about California life. The next section of this chapter looks at how film journalism, trade magazines, fan culture, and early film historiography were used to control the public perception of the industry's newly founded home in Southern California, as well as the corporate image of Hollywood studios and the reception of the films they produced. Some of these forms were rooted in established visual culture practices in Los Angeles and elsewhere, while others evolved in response to Hollywood's needs in the immediate moment.

I start by looking at how the early studios controlled publicity and reception through their engagement with established journalism and via their own publications and public relations organizations. As Jan Olsson argues, journalism, "apart from being a source that reflects film culture's strides and transgressions from the perspective of news," plays an integral role in repositioning "cinema's cultural purchase."[3] This chapter explores how film journalism in Los Angeles contributed to how motion pictures were perceived as an emerging cultural expression regionally and nationwide. I then explore the fan culture that emerged alongside the ascendant Hollywood community, a strong feature of a broader early twentieth-century Los Angeles visual culture. As theatrical impresarios had learned before the birth of cinema and during the early years of motion pictures, expanding and building on the relationship between performers and their fans was a "reliable method for increasing the respectability of the entertainment they offered," a practice that lent itself effectively to promoting motion pictures both before and after they moved to Los Angeles.[4] I conclude with a look at the behind-the-scenes and studio tour films that constructed spectator-entertainer relationships and brand recognition.

"AN ISLAND WITHIN AN ISLAND"

The work of journalist and labor advocate Carey McWilliams is important to understanding the formation of Los Angeles into the nation's most robust cultural economy by the end of the Progressive Era, largely because of McWilliams's recognition of how "Los Angeles lends itself uniquely to image-based analysis."[5] Los Angeles, McWilliams wrote, was constructed on a "giant improvisation . . . that created its past, unviewable save through the fictive scrim of its mythologizers."[6] In 1946, McWilliams published *Southern California: An Island on Land*, an exploration of the region's history through the lens of anti-boosterism and counter-histories—"neither a romantic nor a debunker" portrait, as one reviewer noted.[7] The book features a chapter on the Los Angeles film industry: "The Island of Hollywood." Here, he argues that Hollywood is not just a city within a larger-city but also a state of mind, "an island within an island."[8] "The community of Hollywood," McWilliams writes, "is made up of people engaged in the production of motion pictures, few of whom live in the [city of Hollywood]. Where motion pictures are made, there is Hollywood." On one level, this view suggests that Hollywood as a state of mind has informed the way that other facets of daily Los Angeles life are conducted. Supporting this view, McWilliams cites the inevitable manner in which Hollywood industry practices informed other aspects of American culture: the use of klieg lights for produce markets or the way that attendants at drive-in restaurants were modeled on movie theater ushers, for example.[9] On another level, this characterization of Hollywood suggests that the film industry exhibits the features of an imagined community, affiliated horizontally through a sense of belonging, and spanning across what McWilliams would call "the Los Angeles archipelago" of neighborhoods and enclaves. He concludes the chapter with observations on the growing tensions within Hollywood that would provide the basis for the House Un-American Activities Committee hearings and the subsequent Hollywood Blacklist that occurred a few years after the book's original publication. Ultimately, McWilliams provides a counter-history to the systematic erasure of cultural memory that marked Hollywood's evolution throughout the twentieth century, a quality that this imagined community would share with its host city.[10]

History is written by the victors, as the saying goes. If we choose to view, as Vincent Brook does, Hollywood history as a palimpsest layer obscuring other L.A. histories, then it becomes necessary to view the creation of this layer as the result of Hollywood writing its own history.[11] Two crucial features of the early writing of Hollywood history were (1) how this historiography was interwoven with the film journalism that emerged during the early twentieth century, and (2) the role that Los Angeles itself played in how the history was written. History books and studio-led publications on motion picture history that emerged toward the end of the Progressive Era and shortly thereafter tapped into a cultural familiarity of Los Angeles by directly mentioning specific locations and characteristics of Southern California. The social imaginary of Los Angeles that had been made available through photography, painting, and the tourism industry since the 1880s provided journalists and film historians with useful references, metaphors, and imagos: idealized images of Los Angeles that, through their association with Hollywood in the industry's promotional material, advanced boosterism's aspirations beyond its Progressive Era heyday.

One of the earliest examples of film journalism in Los Angeles was when the Vitascope premiered at the Orpheum in Los Angeles in 1896, an event attended by both Edwin S. Porter and Theodore L. Tally, the latter of whom would purchase the projector and use it to grow the earliest motion picture exhibition network in the city. The Los Angeles press was quite taken by the invention, whereas newspapers elsewhere, as Jan Olsson suggests, ignored the novelty of moving pictures. The *New York Tribune*, for example, took little notice of the invention, disputing its newness and "belittling the novelty value of Edison's projector."[12] By 1910, "film matters were seldom addressed in the daily press," although many trade papers that were dedicated exclusively to moving pictures "often elected to reprint the few articles that had managed to find their way into major newspapers."[13] Some notable film trade publications included *Views and Films Index* (established in 1906) and *Moving Picture World* (established in 1907). *Variety* started reviewing films in 1907, and that same year *Billboard* also launched a film column. By 1930, entertainment industry reporting and celebrity culture had catapulted Los Angeles to a position rivaling Washington, DC, and Yew York in press corps size.

To chart the growth of film journalism in Los Angeles from the 1900 to 1930, it is useful to start with the ways that motion pictures in Los Angeles grew alongside the thriving theatrical stage community during the century's first decade, as an overlap existed in operations, public relations, and entertainer-spectator relationship building. During the early 1900s, theater attendance in Los Angeles was largely facilitated by the Theatrical Guide Company Offices at the Burbank Theater Building in downtown Los Angeles (Main Street, between Fifth and Sixth Street). At the time, the Burbank Theater, which had opened in 1891 with 1,580 seats, was under the management of Oliver Morosco, who by the mid-1910s managed a network of theater companies in Los Angeles and San Francisco. Morosco produced plays in New York City and had founded the Oliver Morosco Photoplay Company with movie producer Frank A. Garbutt; the company was responsible for supplying the motion picture industry with talent from the L.A. stage. (The company would merge with Famous Players–Lasky in 1916.)[14] Every Saturday, the Burbank Theater published the *Los Angeles Theatrical and Amusement Guide*, which was distributed to "all theaters, hotels, and other public resorts" and "mailed to any address in the United States for $1.00 a year."[15] The guide advertised plays in and around the L.A. area, local tourist attractions (such as Angels Flight, the "most unique pleasure resort in the world," and Pavilion Park, which offered "fares 5¢ with liberal ticket reductions"), and Southern Pacific trips to to locations like Lake Tahoe. Starting in 1903, the guide began advertising shows of "new moving pictures" at venues such as the Cineograph Theatre (Court Street, one block north of First Street between Spring and Main) and the Lyric Theater which, on a weekly basis, featured a "new program of Biograph Views." By the middle of the decade, traditional theater venues began to incorporate motion pictures into their daily programming and there was soon an overlap in attendees. By the close of the decade, a new Los Angeles–based theater weekly trade paper, the *Rounder*, started promoting motion picture venues and printed film reviews.[16]

As film was decreasingly viewed as an activity beneath the sophistication of middle-class intelligentsia, theater venues adopted a set of practices aimed at keeping both theatergoers and moviegoers informed of future programming and maintaining their exhibition equipment constantly on the cutting edge. First, theaters took their cue from an established practice of East Coast motion picture companies, issuing "their own house organs" with exhaustive accounts of films, often illustrated with production stills: Edison's *Kineograms*, *Universal Weekly*, and *Essanay News*, being notable examples. An early adapter of this practice was T. L. Tally, whose theater chains produced a weekly publication called the *Tallygram*, printed from the offices of Tally's Film Exchange at the corner of Sixth and Broadway. Second, film exchanges were established in Los Angeles, mostly in the downtown area in close proximity to the bustling theater community around Broadway and Main Street. Both the Clune Film Exchange (727–29 South Main Street) and the Los Angeles Stereopticon and Film Exchange (112–14 Court Street) started operations in 1906, offering "moving picture machine accessories and repairs," "Edison Kinetescope spot lights," "Selig Polyscope stereopticons," "films for sale or for rent," "illustrated song slides," and "electric pianos."[17] The Kleine Optical Company of California operated the Kosmik Film Service out of the Pacific Electric Building, specializing in lenses, lamps, and "motion picture machines of all kinds."[18]

The worlds of theater and cinema began to separate during the early 1910s around the time of the rise of motion picture studios, and with that shift came a new industry of journalism and literature aimed specifically at motion picture venue owners and film exhibitors. In 1910, *Moving Picture World* published F. H. Richardson's *Motion Picture Handbook: A Guide for Managers and Operators of Motion Picture Theaters.* Richardson's guide instructed theater managers in operating projectors, wiring, appropriate light levels, advertising practices, proper management of employees, and how to select an ideal theater location. Later, the *Motion Picture Mail* grew as an industry newspaper for film exhibitors and theater owners during the 1910s, costing about 10 cents per issue. The December 16, 1916 issue featured a two-page ad for Paul Trinchera's *A Song of Strife*, a World War I film starring Alice Hollister and Pauline Curley that "Deals with the Tragic Problems of All Wars by Conquest"— setting the tone for how the film should be marketed by theaters. The issue also contained an article on Famous Players–Lasky's acquisition of Paramount Studios, informing theater owners that "the Capitol stock of the Famous Players Lasky Corporation is $12,500,000 and that of Paramount is $10,000,000. . . . There will be no change in administration in either the parent or new subsidiary company." The issue concluded with a reminder to exhibitors not to "fail to get the Special Christmas Number of the *Motion Picture Mail*."[19]

The establishment of film studios in the Edendale area at the start of the 1910s propelled this culture of entertainment reporting around theater and motion picture exhibition to an international level as correspondents from East Coast motion picture trades established a permanent presence in Los Angeles. *Motion Picture World* covered the rise of early Hollywood from at least 1910, and *Photoplay*, which had been established in Chicago in 1912, soon followed with a mode of address that was "tipped in favor of working-class women."[20] "The idea that Los Angeles was too controlled by uptight, conservative Anglo Midwesterners to nurture anything but artless conformity," argues Hillary Hallett, "eased the erasure of the movie industry's dynamism from most histories of the city's development."[21] Consider the role of individual personalities within the world of the Los Angeles film press; this phenomenon bolstered the fan culture that provided studios with paratextual control over reception. By 1910, *Motion Picture World* started running a new column in direct response to the rise of film stars in the Los Angeles film industry, some drawn from the local stage and others relocated from the East Coast: "Picture Personalities" answered letters from fans about the personal lives of performers like Florence Lawrence and Mary Pickford, resituating cinephilia as a participatory experience that involved a relationship to film stars with relatable interior lives.[22] Adela Rogers St. Johns, who started her career in 1913 with Hearst's *Los Angeles Herald*, was hired by *Photoplay* to write a weekly gossip column, eventually earning St. Johns the nickname "Hollywood's Mother Confessor," as she "socialized with many of her subjects," especially her friend Frances Marion.[23] Later in life, St. Johns wrote a memoir of her experience as a Hollywood reporter titled *The Honeycomb* (1969). As Hallett points out, "The reorientation of fan culture towards women during the 1910s, as exemplified by the popularity of columnists like St. John, was sped by the creeping conviction among many industry insiders that their good fortune depended on catering to the female trade," drawing upon strategies that theatrical impresarios had learned decades earlier: "attracting ladies with new kinds of plots and heroines enlarged their audiences and increased the respectability of the entertainment they offered."[24]

Alongside the deliberate reportage of *Motion Picture World* and *Photoplay* arose gossip columns and early examples of a growing motion picture tabloid industry. It is generally believed that the gossip column originated in Hollywood during the 1930s and 1940s, with a notable figure in the rise of this industry being Hedda Hopper (born Elda Fury), who began her Hollywood career during the 1910s and was affiliated with Charles Fletcher Lummis and the Arroyo group during this period. Yet gossip columns and rumor mills were features of early Hollywood throughout the end of the Progressive Era, with reporters and private investigators often frequenting industry hotspots and establishments close to the studios. One gossip newspaper, operating out of the San Fernando Valley, was the *Universal City Club Snooper*—originating in 1915 around the same time as the founding of Universal Studios at its present-day location. Nightclubs, cafés, and restaurants popular with celebrities—such as the Café International, Musso and Frank Grill, and later the Brown Derby—were frequented as often by celebrity journalists as by the celebrities themselves.

A defining feature of late 1910s/early 1920s Los Angeles film culture, one facilitated by industry journalists and fan culture, was a consolidation of the motion picture industry under the umbrella term *Hollywood*, solidifying the reputation of the film industry as Los Angeles's alter ego. In the summer of 1921, *Photoplay* used "Hollywood" to stand in for "the whole industry and personality writ large," contributing to this view of early Hollywood as an imagined community.[25] At the same time, a growing industry of independent filmmakers, operating outside of the majors, imagined a different form of filmmaking and moviegoing audience. This world of independent film was served by a film press that catered to different modes of cinephilia and industry needs. Wid Gunning, a former theatrical play critic, serviced a growing independent cinephile culture through *Wid's*. A December 8, 1923 issue on the production of Erich Von Stroheim's *Greed* (1924) opened with an editorial titled "Make Way! The Author Comes!" arguing for the importance of good writing as a corrective to wasteful overhead costs. This was followed by "It's Going to Be an Independent Year," an article by Gunning discussing the advantages of independent filmmaking over big studios: "The big producing executives made a rather fatal blunder in my opinion. . . . For many years, theatre owners have rather belittled independents, feeling that no creative unit could really succeed unless in some manner there was an association with the magic forces of the big corporations like Paramount, Metro Goldwyn, Universal, Fox, First National, etc." Gunning observed, "I have always believed and will always believe in unit production. . . . The making of what might be termed commercial product in a commercial manner naturally becomes somewhat more efficient when organized for quantity production, but most everyone today knows that there is a much greater profit from fine films than there is from the so-called commercial type, with really less possibility of loss from the better film if it is intelligently made." Gunning concluded that the "one thing which has blocked independent production for the last two years or more has been the lack of an efficient distribution and sales method which would bring a proper and fair return."[26]

Beyond the English-speaking world of Los Angeles cinema theaters, Los Angeles expanded into the movie capital during the 1910s at a time when the demographics of the city diversified and refashioned L.A. along ethnic lines. Along with these shifts emerged film publications that were specifically designed to service these communities. As discussed in chapter 4 a Mexican entertainment culture, centered on revistas and motion pictures (both from the United States and Mexico), grew in the downtown area alongside the rise of the Anglo-oriented Hollywood film industry and its L.A. exhibition venues. Los Angeles English-language newspapers operated on both sides of the border during the early twentieth century, with many of its moguls holding vast land investments in Mexico: Harrison Gray Otis (*Los Angeles Times*) held 200,000 acres in Mexico in 1908, Thomas E. Gibbon (*Los Angeles Herald*) held more than 850,000 acres, and William Randolph Hearst (*Los Angeles Examiner*) had holdings in Mexico the size of Vermont.[27] In reaction, the Spanish-language press in the United States, as Nicolas Kanellos has argued, particularly during the first decades of the twentieth century, promoted the notion of a *México de afuera* (Mexico from the outside) to encourage readers to "maintain the Spanish language, keep the Catholic faith, and insulate their children from what community leaders perceived as low moral standards practices by Anglo-Americans."[28] Heeding this call, *El Heraldo de Mexico* was distributed in Los Angeles during this period, reporting on the Spanish-speaking world of Los Angeles entertainment and printing film and revista reviews as well as serialized short stories.[29]

Also in the downtown area, there was the neighborhood of Little Tokyo, believed to have been started in 1885 when a Japanese former seaman named Kame (Hamanosuke Shigeta) opened a restaurant near First Street. There were approximately twenty-five other Japanese living in the area at the time, but by 1907, the Japanese population had reached six thousand.[30] In 1907, Bankoku-za (the International Theater), established through a partnership between Bungoro Tani and Tadayoshi Isoyama and located at 228 East First Street, became the first Japanese-owned movie theater in the United States.[31] *Rafu Shimpo*, a mimeographed tabloid written in English and Japanese, was launched in 1903 to report on Japanese American cultural life in Los Angeles; by the end of the decade, it was dedicated to covering the emerging cinephile culture of Japanese immigrants.[32] With the onset of U.S. involvement in World War II, many of Little Tokyo's venues, including other Japanese American–run cinemas, such as the Fuji-kan at 324 East First Street, were closed.[33]

As film journalism shaped public perception of Hollywood during the 1910s, historical texts on motion picture history began to emerge that directly addressed the growth of the movie industry in the Los Angeles area. Robert E. Welsh's *A-B-C of Motion Pictures* (1916) begins with a brief history of American film that emphasizes the importance of Southern California as a location for the film industry: "Los Angeles and New York, and the territory around these cities share the honors as picture producing centers in the United States. . . . But Southern California, with almost continuous sunshine has become the picture mecca, and it is estimated that over one half of the world picture supply is made there." Here, the "300 Days of Sunshine" slogan, the product of booster rhetoric, plays a critical role in the writing of the region's motion picture history. In Los Angeles, Welsh continues, several of the film companies "own estates covering many hundreds of acres, and it is seldom necessary to go off the company's property to take any scene desired"—a testimony the region's reputation for visualization and place substitution. "Dotting the estates, you will find village streets that would be transplanted from the four corners of the globe," and "well-stocked zoos [a reference to the Selig Zoo] that would be the prize possession of many a municipality are a unique feature of some of these studios."[34]

Another notable entry was Lee Royal's *The Romance of Motion Picture Production* (1920), written with the help of industry professionals. Starting with Edison's "novelty," Royal's text positions "Colonel William H. Selig and his Selig Polyscope Company" as the "real pioneers of this great industry."[35] What is curious is Royal's use of the term *pioneers* throughout the book, linking early motion picture history with the end of the American frontier era. Selig is cast in Royal's story of movie-made Los Angeles as one of the primary movers and shakers behind a historical moment when the West was both conquered and preserved through American film and its primary host city. This framing of Hollywood history also advances the early-filmmakers-as-outlaws narrative, also explored by McWilliams in *An Island on Land*, that contemporary scholarship has debunked as a fantastical creation myth.

A Million and One Nights: A History of the Motion Picture, written by former industry worker Terry Ramsaye in 1926, also capitalizes on a popular Los Angeles social imaginary created through visual culture and early American cinema. The opening pages proclaim that "Ramsaye, once aligned with the motion picture industry, freed himself of these alliances to write this history." Also appointed to write the first entry on motion pictures for *Encyclopedia Britannica*, Ramsaye begins his book with chapters titled "Pictorial Efforts of the Ancients" and "Leonardo Da Vinci," eventually working his way to chapters on Muybridge's experiments and Edison, finally culminating in chapter 53 on filmmaking in Los Angeles. In the chapter "The Discovery of California," Ramsey remarks that "the crab-apple of Eden and the orange of Hollywood are undoubtably fruit of the same tree," and later casts Selig as the art form's "savior" amid the conflict that ensued between early filmmakers, resolved through moving operations to Los Angeles.[36] In Ramsaye's, Royal's, and Welsh's books, we see elements of California visual booster iconography repurposed and embellished into propagandistic visions of Hollywood's origin story.

While some histories were written under the supervision of motion picture studios, others penned directly by the studios, seizing an opportunity to play a crucial role in how their work and legacy would be crafted. *The Story of Famous Players Lasky* (1919) chronicled the studio's origins on the East Coast and its eventual migration to Los Angeles. The idealized Southern California climate—the "setting and locations used in these pictures"—is again credited in a section that details the reasons for selecting California as an ideal location to build a studio, citing Cecil B. DeMille's *The Admirable Crichton* (1919) as a notable example.[37] Additionally, theater trades like *Motion Picture Mail*, for example, would feature specific instructions from Famous Players–Lasky on the correct way to advertise a film—which celebrities to emphasize and what story themes to accentuate. Other industry histories were written in conjunction with fan culture and an industry of celebrity news that rose in Los Angeles during the rise of the film industry. The life of actor Rudolph Valentino, for example, is detailed in *Rudolph Valentino: His Romantic Life and Death* (1926) by Hollywood screenwriter Ben Allah in coordination with Angelina Coppola. The growth of this industry of film cultural writing and celebrity histories contributed to the development of key literary institutions throughout the 1930s and beyond. Crucial locations include literary agent Stanley Rose's bookshop at 6661 Hollywood Boulevard, next to Musso and Frank's Grill—with notable associates being William Saroyan (author of *The Human Comedy*), *Day of the Locust* author Nathaniel West, F. Scott Fitzgerald, Dorothy Parker, Aldous Huxley, and Raymond Chandler; actors like Marlene Dietrich, Jean Harlow, Charlie Chaplin, and Edward G. Robinson were also known to frequent the shop.

Another industry hotspot energized by this culture of industry history writing was Garden of Allah in West Hollywood, built in 1913 as a private residence before being developed into a residential hotel in 1926. The hotel was a meeting spot and salon for writers throughout the late 1920s and 1930s (in 1936 Marlene Dietrich starred in an adaptation of the 1905 novel for which the hotel was named).

"Great fortunes were made and lost in this speculative endeavor, so dependent on the whims of public acceptance of the product," remembers cinematographer Charles G. Clarke in *Early Film Making in Los Angeles*, an account of the early Los Angeles movie colonies and their rise to form the Hollywood studio network from approximately 1908 to the mid-1920s.[38] The writing of Hollywood history during this period was also an industry of mythmaking, contributing to the construction of a Los Angeles/Hollywood social imaginary. The popular creation myth of Los Angeles—the easy escape route to Mexico to escape Edison patent agents narrative—was perpetuated by the motion picture industry literature that emerged in the 1920s and 1930s—reflected especially in Maurice Bardèche's *History of the Motion Pictures* (1938), and later echoed in Kenneth MacGowan's *Behind the Screen: The History and Techniques of the Motion Picture* (1965). There were eight motion picture companies in the Los Angeles area by 1911, about half of which where Motion Picture Patents Company members (including Bison, Biography, and Polyscope) and so had no need to circumvent any patent restrictions. An early attempt to set the record straight came from Clarke's 1976 *Early Film Making in Los Angeles*. Motion picture companies "were not drawn to Los Angeles because the Mexican border might provide a quick escape," notes one reviewer, adding that "the author never heard of such a case but admits it's a good legend."[39] "It is no wonder," Clarke remarked, "that by many of the more conservative residents of Los Angeles the movie workers were sometimes considered as a here-today-gone-tomorrow class of gypsies."[40] Clarke's book is an expansion of two talks he had given the year before: one to the Zamorano Club of Los Angeles and another to the Los Angeles Corral of Westerners.[41] Clarke entered the motion picture business in Los Angeles in 1915 and by the 1940s, as an avid collector of cinema memorabilia ("books, papers, photographs, equipment"), he was regarded by many in the Hollywood community as an authority on film history's early years in Los Angeles.[42] Later in his life, he was significantly involved in historical preservation work through the Academy of Motion Picture Arts and Sciences, alongside other notable figures like Margaret Herrick, after whom the academy's research library and archive is named. While *Early Film Making in Los Angeles* provides a detailed overview of the art form's rise from the "movie camps" to Hollywood as both a place and state of mind, tracing the "embryo motion picture companies of Los Angeles . . . to the days of larger studios and super epics," Clarke's account is also a reminder that the histories produced by the successors of pioneers like Selig, Sennett, the Horsleys, Christie, and others were motivated by interests in preserving an image of industry and the city that fostered its growth.[43] This can be read as a form of paratextual control of reception, like the movie studio tour films explored below, influencing public perception not only of the films that studios produced but also of the city that nurtured their production conditions. In a sense, the interwoven relationship between the city of Los Angeles and its film industry is a continuation of the boosterism described by Mike Davis and other scholars of Los Angeles history—especially when one considers both how the movies took over as the most effective form of city boosterism by the 1920s and, as Allen J. Scott notes, the transformation of "a loose and rather chaotic collection of motion picture activities" into a "dense interlocking system of production companies, anchored in a geographic space by its own virtual circle of endogenous growth."[44]

Francis Boggs wrote in a letter to William Selig on August 16, 1909, "I know we have got the American firms beaten for productions, and if we can catch the Biograph on acting, we will have them." In addition to notifying his boss that their new Los Angeles operation was in good shape, Boggs's message to Selig was also an early indication of the studio rivalry that would shape Hollywood as an imagined community during its early years. At the same time, this imagined community was solidified through a local Los Angeles industry built around cultivating partnerships between motion picture artists and the local businesses that serviced them, often in partnership with the press and local publishers. *Photoplayers Club of Los Angeles*, for example, was a booklet created in 1913 to be distributed at the organization's inaugural ball on St. Valentine's night, 1913 at the Shrine Auditorium.[45] This edition, the first of three annual publications, contained advertisements for local business that were created to directly service the growing film industry. The Kinemacolor Company of America (located at 4500 Sunset Boulevard, Hollywood), for example, marketed itself with the slogan "nature itself reproduced," while other companies, such as the Benham Company (808 South Broadway) dealt in "genuine Indian, trapper, or Western costumes and properties for sale or rent" (their slogan: "If it's Indian, we have it"). The Big Otto Company, run by Otto Breitkreutz, advertised its services in *Photoplayers Club of Los Angeles* and elsewhere, stating proudly, "We are responsible for Selig's animal pictures." Advertisements for lumber, hardware, refrigeration and cooling, tinware, china, and glassware also featured in *Photoplayers Club of Los Angeles*, helping to build a relationship between the city and the motion picture industry that, by 1930, was contributing to Hollywood's annual earnings of nearly $129.3 million.[46]

Hollywood also began publishing its own journals during the 1910s that were aimed at keeping industry professionals informed of current events and the latest developments in filmmaking techniques and motion picture technology. Some publications, such as *Static Flashes*, were newspapers "devoted to the men who make the movies," whereas others, like *Carl Laemmle Presents Universal's Great Move Lists* (which ran annually throughout the 1920s as a review of the year for Universal Pictures), directly reported on specific studios. The *Film Daily* provides some very illuminating examples of a trade paper written by and for Los Angeles industry professionals. Founded in 1913, *Film Daily* was a film journal that started publishing an annual "Directors Annual and Production Guide" in 1919.[47] It was run out of New York City but had a Hollywood office (6425 Hollywood Boulevard) and catered directly to the Los Angeles film studio community. Issues contained advertisements for film stock and equipment: Kodak Eastman film stock, Deluxe trailers for off-site location shooting, and Alfred E. Fiegel's poster printing service, for example. The journal also featured "The Critic's Forum," an analysis of the state of the industry and audience survey statistics, as well as op-eds on the latest production trends. As the journal progressed into the 1920s, annual reports targeting specific aspects of filmmaking began to appear, notably "The Year in Cinematography," written by John Arnold, president of the American Society for Cinematographers. Other sections included short opinion pieces by directors, director's profiles that included brief biographies and credits from the previous two years,

novels and plays available for optioning, and "The Independent Outlook," an overview of recent trends in the world of independent filmmaking. Incidentally, the founder of *Film Daily*, Wid Gunning, would
apply this "independent outlook" to *Wid's* during the 1920s.

Early motion picture producers in Los Angeles had an invested
interest in growing the film industry press in the city because the way
film journalists operated inevitably affected their promotional strategies.
Kia Afra identifies several motivations behind the way that studios cul-
tivated their relationship with the press. For starters, the studios were
interested in affecting the site of reception by managing their brand
reputations and stars personas.[48] From the very beginning, Hollywood
used its marketers to mobilize paratexts in order to offer "proper interpretations" of films as "ongoing and open texts" and of filmmakers as
the providers of these texts.[49] Forging a relationship with the press as a
means for mobilizing paratexts was considered essential for a studio's
ability to remain competitive in Los Angeles. Selig Polyscope, for example, controlled reception through the studio's in-house journal, *Paste-Pot
and Shears (PPandS)*. This weekly publication provided cost-free, ready-
made clipped materials for newspapers on stars, industry and studio
news, and film reviews. *PPandS* not only acted as Polyscope's press arm,
it also provided Selig with the leverage needed to counter the advantages
afforded to larger and more successful films from other studios.[50] The
studios were forced to pay for advertising because most exhibitors were
not willing to do so, and having a solid studio-press relationship was seen
as a means of drumming up publicity outside of other avenues of visual
marketing. As film fan culture presented studios with a built-in audience,
press releases with the studio's own visual and written promotional material through publication relations arms such as *PPandS* could potentially marshal a strong box office draw. Film producers did not trust the
way that exhibitors advertised films; exhibitors, left to their own devices,
advertised films for their immediate needs.[51]

As the story of Selig Polyscope reveals, a studio during this period
could expand its control of reception and image through its connections
with the press industry, especially when a particular news outlet had
as broad a reach as that of the Hearst press. In 1913, Polyscope and the
Hearst organization entered into an alliance when Edgar B. Hatrick,
the head of photographic services at the Hearst organization, negotiating

with William Selig to co-produce a newsreel series that would rely on Hearst's press corps and Selig's motion picture resources and relationship with film venues in Los Angeles and across the country. The partnership resulted in *The Hearst-Selig News Pictorial*, which premiered on February 28, 1914, in Los Angeles. Selig's association with Hearst lasted slightly less than two years, during which time "the term *newsreel* was coined for their twice-weekly, ten-minute cinematic tabloid."[52] A major highlight of *The Hearst-Selig News Pictorial* was when correspondents traveled to Europe in late 1914 to cover the onset of the Great War. By 1915, Selig edited together footage from World War 1 and its impact on European society to produce one of the first documentaries of the conflict: *The History of the World's Greatest War*, "made on gruesome European battlefields amid the dismal ruins of old-world cities."[53] Another contribution, one that played a crucial role in the growth of the Hollywood press, was *The Hearst-Selig News Pictorial*'s inclusion of film news and stories about celebrities, including coverage of motion picture figures who attended the Panama-Pacific Exposition in San Francisco in 1915.[54] When this partnership between Selig and Hearst ended (Hearst would pursue relationships with Pathé, MGM, and Universal in the years that followed), Selig formed another newsreel through a partnership with the *Chicago Tribune*, which resulted in the *Selig-Tribune*. Although this folded in 1917, it also strongly impacted the culture of film journalism through its subjects and global reach.

Collectables and ephemera comprised a significant component of early film fan culture, as well as situating Los Angeles in the minds of cinephiles nationwide as the city of dreams. The *Moving Picture Stars Art Stamp Album*, produced by New York's Wentz and Company in 1914, provides an interesting case in point. The album is divided by studio, each section containing pages with stamps of their most popular stars: Edison Studios, subtitled "American Stars," featured stamps of Norma Phillips, Kathie Fischer, Ed Coxen, Vivian Rich, and Jack Richardson; Majestic— Lillian Gish, Miriam Cooper, Billie West, and Mae Marsh; Keystone stars were Charlie Chaplin (referred to as "Chas Chaplin"), Roscoe Arbuckle, Shorty Hamilton, Mable Normand, Chester Conklin, and producer Mack Sennett. Other studios included Kalem, Reliance, Thanhouser, and Vitagraph. A significant feature of the album is that the stamps are set against a background of palm trees and South Pacific tiki mask designs (each studio's page a different color theme), a testimony to the enduring image of Southern California as the "semi-tropical" location depicted in H. T. Payne's stereoscopic album.

A by-product of this industry and citywide crafting of Los Angeles film history, one that still resonates in popular culture today, is a wave of memorialization of the symbiotic history of Los Angeles and the film industry that started during the 1940s. On September 22, 1940, the Los Angeles Chamber of Commerce unveiled a bronze memorial at Sunset and Gower to commemorate the founding of Nestor Studios by Al Christie and the Horsley brothers. The chamber of commerce also published *Los Angeles, Hollywood, and the Southland at a Glance* in 1943, with the support of major studios, aircraft manufacturers, and banks. Last, the death of William Selig in July 1948 prompted an even larger retrospective, as Selig had been presented with a special Academy Award the year before for his contributions to building an enduring relationship between Hollywood and its host city.[55]

"HOW THEY PHOTOGRAPHED US"

Jonathan Gray notes that Hollywood and its marketers mobilize "paratexts to offer 'proper interpretations'" of films as "ongoing and open texts," of filmmakers as the providers of these texts, and of the cinema-going experience writ large.[56] Behind-the-scenes footage and studio tour films of the 1910s and the 1920s can be read as early examples of this mobilization. Consider first this behind-the-scenes footage shot shortly after the opening of Chaplin Studios. The construction of the studio itself, which I will return to in chapter 6, was stylistically calculated, both architecturally and horticulturally, to construct an identity of respectability—what Barbara Klinger describes as a defining feature of the history of the Hollywood studios.[57] In this behind-the-scenes footage, Chaplin demonstrates for visiting general Hunter Liggett the process for transforming into the iconic Tramp character—donning the costume and applying the makeup. In moments such as this, the film collapses the distance between entertainer and spectator, inviting the viewer to participate in the studio's filmmaking process and proposing a new form of cinephilia.

Figure 5.1. "A visit from General Hunter Liggett": behind-the-scenes footage from Chaplin Studios, 1917. (*Charlie Chaplin: The First National Collection.* CBS/FOX Home Video, 2000.)

The *Christie Studios Film* (1916) opens with a panoramic view of the front of the studio at the corner of Sunset and Gower. The frame is filled with details that contribute to the film's function as a press kit: palm trees indicate an idyllic climate, and automobiles and open-air double-decker buses signal Los Angeles as an advanced and forward-thinking city, despite its location at the end of a frontier. *Behind the Scenes, Mack Sennett Studios* (1917) treats the viewer to several panorama views of Edendale (or what is now Echo Park, Silver Lake, and Los Feliz): a left–to-right sweeping shot across Glendale Boulevard, over the tops of white buildings, eventually landing along the side of a rooftop with a sign that proclaims, "Mack Sennett Comedies." Even more striking examples can be found in *Universal Studios, Behind the Scenes* (1915), which features several panoramic shots of the main building with the Hollywood Hills in the background, panoramic shots from a nearby hillside showcasing the studio and the surrounding San Fernando

Valley, and even some panorama shots that showcase costumed actors and actresses (Victoria Ford, for example), artisans and craftspeople, and even elephants arriving to set. These sweeping panoramic shots of the California landscape are later echoed in moments from Richard Attenborough's biopic *Chaplin* (1992), as Charlie (Robert Downey Jr.) arrives in Southern California among a sea of orange trees to work with Sennett. By staging studios in the idyllic setting that, by 1915, was familiar through booster publications like Charles Fletcher Lummis's California art and culture magazines *Land of Sunshine* and *Out West* and the California photography that was being created at the time by people like Edward Weston, the interpretation conveyed was that of a film industry that drew from the rich array of settings "conveniently at hand in California's varied geography."[58] This varied geography would ensure the dominance of Hollywood, domestically and internationally, during this period, and by the late 1910s 75 percent to 80 percent of American films were made in Los Angeles.[59]

The *Thomas H. Ince Studios* film (1922)—directed by Hunt Stromberg (later the producer of the 1936 film *The Great Ziegfeld*) and photographed by Henry Sharp (*Duck Soup*, 1933)—features a scene with actor Douglas MacLean preparing for a "strenuous day at the stages." Over breakfast, MacLean sips his coffee, reads the newspaper, and smiles directly at the camera before departing, the film declaring: "Doug has a habit of reaching the studio on time." On his way to the Culver City studio location, a motorcycle police officer chases him. After being pulled over, MacLean asks: "How fast this morning, officer?" The officer responds: "Scuse me for chasing you, Mister MacLean, but I am quitting the force and want a job in your fill-ums." The two then shake hands, and MacLean escorts the officer to the studio. This scene is followed by two "making of" segments—one for "How we photographed that auto chase," and another for "How they photographed us." The first shows the scene being filmed by a camera operator and director on a platform attached to the front of a moving car, while the second segment reveals another cameraman filming with a handheld shot from a moving convertible.

The film also shows the viewer construction of sets and the arrangement of electrical lighting effects, with a title card proclaiming that the "decoration of the interior sets demands a force of the country's highest salaried artisans." A violin player (James Kirkwood) and a piano player (Louise Glaum) are shown performing off camera to establish the mood of a scene: "Music hath its charms when Louise Glaum and James Kirkwood register pathos." "A mammoth carpenter plant" is shown teaming with "hundreds of skilled experts [building] interior sets from blueprints designed by the finest [draftsmen]." "Enid Bennett does need an alarm clock to 'rouse her" from her sleep in her Beverly Hills Tudor house. Lloyd Hughes, "newest of Ince's discoveries," plays catch in his front yard with his brother Earl, Hobart Bosworth receives fan letters ("well perfumed envelopes" and clothing from Japan), and the Ince Private Fire Department performs its daily drill at 5 p.m. each day. Last, Ince himself appears as the "maker of stars," starting his morning exercises with a "professional trainer who keeps the producer trim."

The Ince film reveals that the early Los Angeles studios were committed to revealing a human apparatus at the center of a newly formed dream factory, populated by figures with recognizable emotions and interior lives. Universal's 1915 studio tour films foreshadow this by presenting a familial quality to Carl Laemmle and the performers, who dine together at the studio café. Actors mug for the camera, trying on fake beards and wigs, Scottish Highland outfits, and sailor costumes in the *Christie Studios Film* (circa 1916), shot at 6101 Sunset among a street lined with palms. Mack Sennett is shown as a family man and animal lover in his studio tour film of 1917. Tom Mix introduces viewers to his horse Tony for a William Fox Studio film the same year. While images of the Los Angeles area before the arrival of the movies were sold to the country to present a place where tourism could be defined as an immersive experience, filmmakers like Selig and his troops (and the L.A. studios that followed) sold Hollywood cinema as another form of immersive experience and Los Angeles as an environment conducive to this new form of entertainer-spectator relationship.

In looking at the aspect of Hollywood's ascendancy, these studio tour films exhibit qualities of Progressive Era visual culture that serve as a scholarly retrieval of L.A. palimpsest layers, as well as contributing to the study of how reception is controlled through paratexts. What is also interesting about *all* of these early Hollywood paratexts explored in this chapter, when taken collectively, is the way they connect with the legacy of Southern California tourism, through what Reyner Banham describes as "showing the plant visitors as [an] attraction." Whether the attraction is a studio tour film with sweeping panoramic vistas of Los Angeles or the contemporary theme parks of Disneyland or Universal Studios, Hollywood and Los Angeles are conflated: the "identifiable ingredients" of the two locations dissolve into an "environmental phantasmagoria." The city at the end of the frontier is repackaged and sold as a "compact set of habitable fantasies," mobilized by Hollywood writing its own history in a way that echoes Lummis and the Arroyo group's visual marketing of the region as a transformative anywhere space.[60] Following on this idea, the next chapter will explore the Los Angeles architecture that emerged at the end of the Progressive Era as both a pinnacle of the period's visual culture and as a literal construction of "habitable fantasies" that were highly cinematic in their construction.

6

Sunshine Modernism

"One of the glories of Los Angeles is its modernist residential architecture," notes Thom Andersen in *Los Angeles Plays Itself*, "but Hollywood movies have almost systematically denigrated this heritage by casting many of these houses as the residences of movie villains." A modernist home in the Hollywood Hills is held hostage by a gang of kidnappers led by John Cassavetes in *The Night Holds Terror* (fig. 6.1). Frank Lloyd Wright's Ennis House (also in the Hollywood Hills) has frequently been cast as the home of "some gangster chieftain," and one of the most famous homes designed by Wright's protégé, Richard Neutra's Lovell

Figure 6.1. *The Night Holds Terror* (Andrew L. Stone, Columbia Pictures, 1955).

Health House, is the home of pornographer and pimp Pierce Patchett (David Strathairn) in *L.A. Confidential* (Curtis Hanson, 1997). Pierre Koenig's Stahl House is let off lightly, according to Andersen, probably because of Koenig's knack for "turning steel and glass cubes into Hollywood regency style mini-mansions." John Lautner, by contrast, is the architect "Hollywood most loves to hate," his work appearing in films such as *The Big Lebowski* (Joel and Ethan Coen, 1998; as Jackie Treehorn's Malibu mansion) and *Lethal Weapon* (Richard Donner, 1987; Lautner's Chemosphere). As Donald Albrecht notes, "No vehicle provided as effective and widespread an exposure of architectural imagery as the medium of the movies," and as Andersen's film illuminates, California modern architecture is interwoven with Los Angeles cinema, even if it is often encoded in these films in ways that run counter to the philosophies of their original designers.[1]

Architecture in Southern California has a complex relationship with the history of regional visual culture and Hollywood's ascendancy in Los Angeles. On the one hand, there are styles and architectural practices that can be read as a continuation of the visual boosterism manifest in photography, painting, and tourism attractions. The California look and feel is exhibited strongly in historical period revival architecture, not just the obvious connection in the Spanish Colonial Revival style but also styles like Tudor, Moorish, and Châteauesque, as each refers to an imagined past and highlight Los Angeles's reputation as an "anywhere space." Furthermore, period revival is wedded to a familiarity with movie production design and a literacy in film language that was growing rapidly during the late 1910s and early 1920s. This overlap between film set design and residential architecture highlights what David E. James identifies as a doubling that has defined Los Angeles throughout much of the twentieth century, in which "the city [is] a nostalgic simulacrum of its own imaginings."[2] On the other hand, modern architecture initially sought to assert itself in Southern California in stark contrast to period revival architecture. Modernists saw their task as popularizing a different style of home design, and indeed a radically different philosophy of living, in a city that was being defined by Craftsman bungalows and Mission Legend nostalgia. Richard Neutra, for example, blamed motion pictures for confusing architectural tastes in Los Angeles, and saw his central goal as moving architecture away from evocations of the past toward a future of space, functionality, and natural living.[3] Neutra's mentor, Frank Lloyd Wright, described Mission Revival architecture as "flatulent and fraudulent, with a cheap opulent taste for the tawdry," and blamed Hollywood for "confusing architectural tastes through historical revival styles."[4] At the same time, however, modern architecture and the motion picture industry developed a mutually beneficial relationship, starting in the late 1920s and enduring throughout much of the twentieth century. Modernism, as film art and production designers discovered, is very cinematic in its design, as it is largely concerned with manipulating procession, how light affects the way that objects look, and spatial relations. By the early 1930s, modernism had become absorbed by Hollywood as useful tool for set designers and a symbol of affluence. Hollywood executives, stars, and craftspeople adopted modernism into both their personal and professional lives, further entrenching the style in the Los Angeles cultural landscape.

This chapter considers how early Hollywood studio practices contributed to the growth of Los Angeles through a variety of architectural trends, culminating at the end of the Progressive Era with modernism. First, I explore period revival architecture as part of a larger phenomenon of architecture that Paul J. Karlstrom terms "California Eclecticism": the "random grazing among historical styles" that points the growing interplay between film architecture and locale architecture during the 1920s.[5] From there, I look at the ways that modernism in Southern California toward the end of the Progressive Era, what I refer to as "sunshine modernism," advanced booster notions of "Californianess" and California lifestyle, while at the same time comingling with the developing visual practices of a film industry that had assumed the mantle of chief regional booster. Despite initial criticisms of the motion picture industry by modernists, the style and the Hollywood studio system overlapped in many striking ways, especially toward the end of the 1920s and into the early 1930s as sound film technology brought Los Angeles films indoors, where soundstages could control this new way of seeing *and* hearing.

"A WHIMSICAL TYPE OF ARCHITECTURE"

Early in Nathaniel West's novel *The Day of the Locust* (1939), Tod Hackett, artist and movie studio set painter, walks through Hollywood at sunset toward Beachwood Canyon beneath the Hollywood sign (referred to as "Pinyon Canyon" in the novel). "The edges of the trees burned with a pale violet light at their centers," but not even the "soft wash of the dusk could help against the houses"—"Mexican Ranch houses, Samoan huts, Mediterranean villas, Egyptian and Japanese temples, Swiss chalets, Tudor cottages, and every possible combination of these styles."[6] The "Mexican Ranch houses" and "Mediterranean villas" are, of course, a testimony to the endurance of the Mission Legend. Any building design that "actively engages with the ecology and psychological facts of life in the area has a tendency to emerge with a Spanish colonial revival air," writes Reyner Banham, noting that this style is expressed through a Southern California subconscious.[7] Spanish Colonial homes generally consisted of a series of rooms in single row or an L configuration, with a courtyard plan where, as Charles Fletcher Lummis described in an article for *Land of Sunshine*, "every room opens up on it" and "every member of the family is joyed and benefited by it."[8] Considered alongside the other styles, West describes a style of residential design that rose in direct response to the motion picture industry and its tendency toward world building and simulated environments.

Hollywood's origins as a place-substitution and world-building enterprise, inherited from the tourist industry and its attendant visual culture, is coded into the design of the film studios constructed in Los Angeles during the 1910s. The earliest film studios in Los Angeles responded to "dual demands for operational efficiency and corporate prestige" through creating "hybrid structures and functional interiors hidden behind spectacular facades," as Brian Jacobson observes.[9] This is evidenced by the construction of the First National Studio and Selig Polyscope Pacific Coast Studio in a recognizable Spanish Colonial style, linking the burgeoning film industry with the visual grammar of regional boosterism. Jacobson further describes the "visual character" of these early Hollywood studios as one of "fantastic functionality," responding to a demand that movie factories be not only "hives of efficient production . . . [but also] visually pleasing."[10] Jacobson points to the attractiveness of Chaplin's studios at Sunset and La Brea, built in an English Tudor style and emphasizing the property's orange groves, as means a for constructing a "corporate identity" and developing a relationship with the public.[11] Just as the early studio tour films and Hollywood's crafting of its history through the film press industry were intended to control public perception and reception of the films they produced, the architectural design of the studios themselves, whether the Chaplin studios or the adobe First National or Selig Polyscope studios, would become another paratext to infuse their products and image with respectability and cultural sophistication. Chaplin's Tudor-style studio is now a tourist attraction as the Jim Henson studio, preserving a palimpsest layer of Los Angeles history (in a slightly oblique manner) and acting as a physical example of Norman Klein's conception of Los Angeles imagos and social imaginary.

This desire for "spectacular facades" and "visual character" of early studio facilities intersected with design trends that had been steadily growing in Los Angeles since before the arrival of motion pictures. From roughly 1900 to 1917, the California bungalow, popularized by the *Craftsman* magazine, dominated new buildings in Los Angeles.[12] California bungalows were often used in promotions that bridged connections between the state's "physical qualities and opportunities for individual achievement," as advertisers depicted a "lush and culturally advanced lifestyle" that drew analogies with ancient Mediterranean themes. For example, the label for Suburban Brand oranges in 1915 "illustrated a Craftsman-style bungalow flanking an abundant orchard, presumably a dwelling for a typical California grower."[13] The California look and feel from photographs and paintings—a sense of freedom augmented by vast and open surroundings—was reinforced by these bungalows' structures and building plans. The patios associated with these homes had also become, as Paul Adamson describes, a "symbol of family life and a common feature of prototypical California house designs."[14] By the end of the 1910s, however, there was a shift in the popularity of the Southern California Craftsman bungalow toward historical period architecture. Historians attribute this to several factors: the lingering effects of World War I, the influence of world's fairs, an interest in historicism stimulated by high-profile restoration projects, architectural promotional publications and house plan books, and the association of mansions with the rich and famous.[15]

In sharp contrast to the bungalow—which was not about "pretense, borrowed style, or manipulated scale"—historical revival architecture in Los Angeles, according to Merry Ovnick, was a by-product of the symbiotic relationship between Los Angeles and filmmaking.[16] "Early motion pictures affected a revolution in *seeing* and the development of culture," according to Ovnick, with Los Angeles's "stars and imagery . . . an integral part of what [the city] means to outsiders and to its residents."[17] By the 1920s, Angelenos were familiar with visual cultural forms with discernable messages, a response conditioned over the course of several decades. Yet cinema, as L.A. residents would discover, provided a unifying language with which to read visual messages with a greater level of sophistication, which explains in large part why film assumed the role of primary booster at this stage. Los Angeles produced 84 percent of American films by 1922, and by 1925, there were, on average, 5 million daily movie admissions nationally.[18] Just as other Southern California visual culture forms contributed to previous population booms, the population of Los Angeles doubled from 1920 to 1925, with new residents who were now versed in moviegoing. Home designers recognized this new population's ability to understand visual references with greater sophistication than the previous generation, and in Los Angeles a taste for "historical revival and fantasy styles on screen" reinforced the transformation of the city on the ground into its alter ego, Hollywood.[19]

Films set in distinguishable historical pasts, which had become increasingly popular, played a key role in inspiring California eclecticism, as art directors prioritized exaggeration and emotional effect over authenticity. Ovnick identifies three movie set design techniques that informed this transformation on the ground into California eclectic home design. First, there was a strong attention to texture and value contrast. Contrast and texture, in both home design and set design, stemmed from an attention to the way surfaces interacted with light, whether outdoor natural light or the artificial light of interior space. Second, the crowded style references and miniaturized scale of these homes were key to their popularity and reproducibility throughout the Los Angeles area. The Spanish Colonial Revival style, for example, had an established presence in Los Angeles through cultural heritage and the ways that the Mission Legend, through visual boosterism, shaped the cultural landscape. Additionally, productions of films that used Old California as a recognizable setting further popularized the style. By the 1920s, the style evolved into a design process in which Old California can be reduced endlessly in a miniature package. Third, the fragmentation of forms created a dynamic relation between receding and advancing planes.[20] The Spadena House (also known as the Witch House) in Beverly Hills at the corner of Walden Drive and Carmelita

Avenue highlights the ways that each of these three set design techniques were adapted into home design. The house was built in 1921 by Hollywood art designer Harry Oliver, who would later go on to design the silent Fred Niblo–directed epic *Ben Hur: A Tale of Christ* (1925) and Howard Hawks's gangster classic *Scarface* (1932). Reyner Banham describes the house as a home with "domestic functions repackaged in a Hansel and Gretel image."[21] This fifteen-hundred-square-foot cottage provides "an attention to texture and value contrast" through the material and color differences of its façade (contrasting the wall to its windows and roofing), "crowded style references and miniaturized scale" supplied by the Storybook style of both the exterior and interior (a "whimsical type of architecture that emerged in Los Angeles with the burgeoning movie industry of the 1920s"), and the structure's "lopsided roof, tiny windows, and . . . stucco with a distressed paint job" exemplifying "the fragmentation of forms, creating a dynamic relation between receding and advancing planes."[22]

Harry Oliver was not the only art designer to participate in residential home design throughout the 1920s and 1930s. Louis B. Mayer's Santa Monica beach home, a Spanish Colonial–style home constructed in 1926 by art director Cedric Gibbons, embodied these principles of California eclectic through its twenty rooms insulated by walls a foot thick and the sharp value contrasts of interior and exterior.[23] Designer Gibbons would later remark that set design was more complicated than architecture because the motion picture architect had to understand not only design and construction but also "light, color, and human figures as they would appear when filmed by a camera."[24] From the early days of Hollywood production design, the art of film set design and the art of architecture were not seen as mutually exclusive. For example, in *The Story of Famous Players Lasky*, mentioned in chapter 5, art director Wilfred Buckland is described as an "architect and decorator of twenty-years-experience."[25] In 1924, Louis B. Mayer hired Russian-born designer Romain de Tirtoff, commonly known as Erté, who had made a name for himself in America since 1915 for interior design and cover illustrations for *Harper's Bazaar*. Inspired to design for motion pictures by *The Cabinet of Dr. Caligari* (1919), Erté crafted film interiors and "decorative accessories" for Mayer that were described as "flat, abstract planes" that "divided into sharply defined rectangles."[26] Eventually frustrated with Erté's designs, as well as his frosty relationships with actors and crew members, Mayer replaced him with Cedric Gibbons, who had studied under artist and filmmaker Hugo Ballin during the 1910s. Gibbons was the head of MGM's art department from 1924 to 1956, and from the outset, he called his department the "architecture and engineering department" (the term "environmental arts" was also commonly used).[27] Modern design would eventually carry over from Gibbons's film work into his personal life when, in 1928, he built a home in Santa Monica Canyon overlooking the Pacific Ocean in the modern fashion—a house that anticipated the innovative sets that would become MGM's signature style from the early to mid-1930s.[28]

California eclectic has appeared in cinema produced in the second half of the twentieth century and onward, both in films set in Los Angeles and those set largely elsewhere. The use of this design is wedded to a cultural memory of early filmmaking in Los Angeles and the close relationship between the city's visual culture and its film industry. In *The Godfather* (1972), though it is not a film set in Los Angeles, film producer Jack Woltz (John Marley) represents the Old Hollywood establishment through his Roman villa–style mansion, adorned with hedgerows and columns (the Beverly Hills home of William Randolph Hearst provided the location). A few years later, the California eclectic remnants of the silent era would provide locations for *Chinatown* and the insular imagined community of *Day of the Locust*, and the High Tower built in 1920 in a Bolognese campanile style would be the apartment of Philip Marlow (Elliot Gould) in *The Long Goodbye* (Robert Altman, 1973), an ideal location for a detective trapped between an older noir world and a new world of the L.A. counterculture scene. The mansion of Daniel Plainview toward the end of Paul Thomas Anderson's *There Will Be Blood* (2007) is built in a Tudor style, conflating the megalomaniac oil baron with the sinister figures of Hollywood royalty familiar through previous works of Los Angeles cinema. Employing California eclectic draws on the memory of its use in Los Angeles cinema during the classic Hollywood era, often finding its way into film noir as flashy exteriors that conceal dark secrets within. In *Double Indemnity* (Billy Wilder, 1944), the home of Phyllis Dietrichson (Barbara Stanwyck) near Los Feliz Boulevard is, according to Walter Neff (Fred MacMurray), "one of those Southern California Spanish houses that everyone was nuts about ten or fifteen years ago." In *Sunset Boulevard* (Billy Wilder, 1950), the home of Norma Desmond (Gloria Swanson) is a mansion built between 1919 and 1924 by William O. Jenkins that had earlier been the home of J. Paul Getty. Though the depiction of modern-style homes in Los Angeles cinema has often been in stark contrast to the philosophies of modern living that produced them, the use of California eclectic in Los Angeles cinema has generally been to evoke the ideas of Davis's Noirs and Debunkers in contrast to the dreams-for-sale ethos that sold the homes to a newly arrived and expanding population in Los Angeles during Hollywood's early years.

Reyner Banham describes California eclectic as "fantastic architecture"—Los Angeles architecture where "fantasy lords over function" in the form of "symbolic packaging"—and identifies several examples in *Los Angeles: The Architecture of Four Ecologies*.[29] In the suburban flatlands, Banham finds restaurants like the Brown Derby (Wilshire Boulevard), ice cream stands, and hot dog joints elevated to the level of pop fantasy and gestalt, but a landmark Banham views as an exceptional example of L.A. fantasy architecture is Grauman's Chinese Theatre, opened in 1927. As a shrine to the movies, Grauman's is fantasy-as-fact, much in the way other works of California eclectic (past and present) may be read; the fantasy, according to Banham, survive one movie to live again in another—and another and others still to come.[30] Here, Banham suggests that Grauman's, and by extension other still-standing legacies of California eclectic, are monuments to Los Angeles's origins as a land of place substitution and a transformative anywhere space, first proposed through Progressive Era visual culture and advanced through motion picture worlds.

"A MANIFESTO FOR NATURAL LIVING"

> Imagine an architectural space that inspires an engaged discussion of radical cultural and social issues. Imagine a place where fundamental architectural ideas are crafted in a novel way through the honest use of materials and a new programmatic order of living that conspire to envelop and seduce a new generation of Southern Californians.
>
> —Mark Mack, introduction to *Schindler, Kings Road, and Southern California Modernism*

As part of a broader Southern California visual culture, modern architecture had a paradoxical relationship with booster ideology. On the one hand, the style embraces the call for natural living that echoed through the pages of Nordhoff, Lummis, and McGroarty with its attempts to blend built environments and the natural environment seamlessly. Added to this, sunshine modernism placed an emphasis on spatial relations in a region that was marketed to the rest of the country as a location of vastness where the lines between nature and domesticity were often porous. Modern architecture in Los Angeles, according to Reyner Banham, "started with the useful advantage that the difference between indoors and outdoors was never clearly defined there," and the same quality can be found in images of California produced through stereoscopic and panoramic views, as well as through a tourism industry that emphasized Southern California's end-of-the-frontier status.[31] This echo of booster promises in modern design—or, alternatively, the idea that modernists traveled to California intrigued by this notion—calls into question the assertion that modernism developed in California "with little historical precedent," as some have argued.[32] On the other hand, modernism attempted to create an architectural iconography associated with progressivism, embracing values that may have been out of step with the booster class of Harry Chandler and authors of All-Year-Round Club publications.[33] For example, throughout the early 1930s, the Lovell House was a "center for radical left wing political meetings" in conjunction with its design as a "manifesto for natural living."[34] In sharp contrast to California eclectic, modernism's central goal was to move away from "evocations of the past" toward Le Corbusier's notions of a "non-elitist art," all the more relevant in the Southern California context when Los Angeles was sold as a city that "departs from civilized living."[35] These contradictions, however, converge in the way modernism impacted the design thinking of the Hollywood film industry at the end of the Progressive Era, and the industry, in turn, promoted the modern style to the public through the style's visible presence in motion pictures.

Studying the overlap between modernism and narrative cinema, whether in L.A. cinema or films set outside of L.A., reveals a process that Jacques Rancière referred to as an "archeo-modern turn."[36] This cinematic recovery of earlier modern aspirations is "deployed as both an obstacle to change and a paradoxical source of renewal."[37] The connection between

modern planning and cinematic design thinking can also be seen beyond
the history of Hollywood studio ascendancy, through the postwar years
and even into contemporary cinema. Modernism, in this sense, should
not be looked at as a historical concept but rather as a contemporary
and futuristic one. In this book's final chapter, I explore how this idea
continues to play out in contemporary Los Angeles–set films, but here
I would like to look at the origins of this design thinking in early studio
design through the work of some of its most notable late Progressive
Era practitioners.

First, let us set the stage for modernism before the arrival of Frank
Lloyd Wright, Richard Neutra, and Rudolph Schindler—three-quarters
of a veritable Mount Rushmore of modernism's pre–World War II legacy
in Southern California. The Walter L. Dodge House, designed by architect Irving Gill, was constructed from 1914 to 1916 at 950 North Kings
Road between Melrose Avenue and Santa Monica Boulevard. Described
by the *Los Angeles Times* as a sixty-five-hundred-square-foot, reinforced
concrete mansion ("extraordinarily modern in concept and materials"),
Gill's Dodge House was what Esther McCoy would dub the first truly
modern house in the American West in her book *Five California Architects* (1960).[38] The Dodge House was a mecca for students of architecture
and design until it was demolished in 1970s despite preservation efforts
by the Southern California chapter of the American Institute of Architects, Los Angeles Beautiful, the Cultural Heritage Board of Los Angeles, the
Los Angeles County Museum of Art, and impassioned pleas from Esther
McCoy and Richard Neutra. The work of Irving Gill, and similar residential architects like Charles and Henry Greene, during the 1910s was also
made visible through the silent slapstick films that helped to map Los
Angeles at a ground level, such as the Keystone films discussed in chapter 1. The façades and front yards of these suburban homes, pictorialized
in Sennett's Edendale films, transformed them, according to Mark Shiel,
into "performance spaces akin to traditional stages."[39] These homes and
their use in early Los Angeles cinema provide an early example of the relationship between modern design and narrative filmmaking. What is also
striking is that the silent era in Los Angeles would conclude with a construction technique introduced by Gill to the region in 1912: the "tilt-up"
technique was a construction method "in which pre-cast concrete panels
were simply tilted up from the ground and fitted into an awaiting steel

frame," a practice that lent itself effectively to the construction of sound-stages on studio lots during the late 1920s and early 1930s.[40]

Though modernism would overtake eclectic as the defining architecture form of the Los Angeles social imaginary over the next few decades, it is worth noting that the modern style was foreshadowed by studio construction in the 1910s just as much as historical revival architecture. During the first decade of the twentieth century, studio architects used materials and designs that would "come to define modern architecture's well-tempered environments [as] the basis for early studio film production."[41] Vitagraph's studio constructed in Brooklyn in 1905, for example, was an early example of the relationship between studio design and modern architecture, as the studio was transformed "from the iron, brick, and wood that defined the nineteenth century factories into the reinforced concrete steel that would define early twentieth century modernism."[42] If the early studios were constructed to "reproduce features of natural environments," even with the availability of location shooting around Los Angeles, then the blurring of boundaries between indoor and outdoor shooting spaces (and the development of simulated environments discussed in chapter 3) can be read as a harbinger of modernist design thinking's impact on the film form.[43]

In 1923, Austrian-born architect Richard Neutra arrived in Los Angeles to join his former University of Vienna colleague Rudolph Schindler and the famous pioneer of modern architecture Frank Lloyd Wright. Wright's California homes, according to Paul J. Karlstrom, were some of the most theatrical of his career, the Barnsdale Park Hollyhock House (1922) and the Ennis House (1924) notable examples.[44] What drew the three to Los Angeles, ultimately, was the region's openness to "the imaginary of the new" as well as the opportunity to advance the promises of a future-oriented style in a nostalgic and increasingly movie-made Los Angeles. Wright, Neutra, and Schindler's design philosophy overlaps with both Southern California's climate and its visual culture through an emphasis on space.[45] Schindler, crafting his design strategies around the demands of the region, defined his architectural philosophy as "space architecture," directly opposed to the ideas of cubism that had been in vogue. The basic principle behind this space architecture was that the solution to an architectural problem lay in its function: "The architect has finally discovered the medium of his art: Space," wrote Schindler in his manifesto.[46]

Figure 6.2. Frank Lloyd Wright's Ennis House, present day. (Image provided by the author.)

Among Schindler's many designer homes that dot the Los Angeles and San Diego landscape to this very day, a notable creation was the Kings Road House (Schindler House), built in 1922. It is currently open for public viewing as part of Los Angeles's MAK Center for Art and Architecture in West Hollywood. Situated between Santa Monica Boulevard and Melrose Avenue, Schindler's Kings Road House can be seen during the motorcycle chase sequence in Buster Keaton's *Sherlock Jr.* (1924), an L.A. palimpsest layer preserved in celluloid and another example of early silent comedy mapping the city cinematically from ground level. Initially, the Schindler family wanted to settle in Pasadena, as they didn't like Hollywood (except for a "little of the canyons"), and they were drawn to the bohemian legacy of the Arroyo group and its hold on the allure of Los Angeles and the projection of its image.[47] Eventually they settled in Hollywood anyway, "for reasons of professional advertising," and Schindler constructed the Kings Road House in 1921–22. Not long after opening, the Kings Road House became an intellectual salon, with guests such as Edward Weston frequently visiting. Toward the end of the 1920s, Sadakichi Hartmann, art and photography critic, was a regular visitor, hosting poetry readings.[48] By the 1930s, the Kings Road House was hosting regular painting circles, poetry readings and, by December 1936, the Regional Council of Western Writers Congress, which had been organized by Carey McWilliams. Despite Schindler's anti-booster affiliations, he described the California conditions that informed his architectural approach in the region in a way that echoes the notion of California as the ideal anywhere space:

> Southern California is a completely unique corner of the U.S.A. Although in a tropical latitude, its climate is definitely not tropical. Its flora is not tropical nor has it real desert characteristics. Its slight seasonal variations lead to a relaxed outdoor life of especial ease. Although its sun is strong, it is controlled by morning fogs. The resulting character of light and color are unique. Instead of the opaque material coloring of the east, we have here subtle transparent shades, created by the light on grayish backgrounds.[49]

Writing about Los Angeles, Richard Neutra asked, "Was this metropolis a paradise, or did there exist here a type of blight which fitted none of the classical descriptions?"[50] The designs of Neutra's houses appear to suggest the city was both, and the Lovell Health House, in some respects, anticipates this view. Constructed between 1927 and 1929 for physician Philip Lovell, the project highlights the enduring legacy of the health-seeking migration to Southern California exemplified by Charles Nordhoff's *California for Health, Pleasure, and Residence* (1873) and the works of "Don Carlos" Lummis. The Lovell House solidified Neutra's reputation as one of the West Coast's leading modernist architects, with over fifteen thousand Angelinos pouring through it over the course of four consecutive open-house Sundays. This "photogenic" steel-framed home fuses the "hard sciences of building technology" with the "softer worlds of sociology and psychology," architecture used to articulate a form of humanism through a domestic design context.[51] With a view from Dundee Drive above Los Feliz, the Lovell House harkens back to the panoramic vision that helped build Los Angeles during the nineteenth century, while at the same time providing a sense of containment and security (a conflict between the wild and the domestic exhibited across other visual culture forms). The popularity of the Lovell House and Neutra's other designs were highlighted at an exhibition on modernism in New York in 1932 organized by Henry-Russell Hitchcock, who solidified Neutra's reputation as a leading West Coast modernist and praised sunshine modernism's "commitment to improving society through architecture."[52]

Yet, as we have seen with painters in chapter 2, the financial crisis of the 1930s brought a series of challenges to Neutra and other prominent architects in Los Angeles. The Los Angeles construction industry went into a decline during the first half of the 1930s, temporarily slowing down the spread of sunshine modernism until it picked up again around 1935.[53] Fortunately, Neutra's immigrant status provided him with a reliable network of fellow immigrants to keep him gainfully employed during the early years of the Great Depression in California. During this period, Neutra designed offices for German immigrant and Universal head Carl Laemmle, the Universal International Pictures Building at Hollywood and Vine (constructed 1931–32). Shortly thereafter, he designed houses for movie stars like Anna Sten and directors like Josef von Sternberg. Rudolph Schindler also would design homes for people affiliated with the film industry in Silverlake, Studio City, and Baldwin Hills throughout the 1940s, while other architects, like Pierre Koenig and John Lautner, designed similar homes in the Los Angeles foothills for the Hollywood elite. The distinct presence of these homes in motion pictures throughout history, not just in the 1930s and 1940s, further entrenched the social imaginary of Banham's foothill ecology as a land of "heart-breaking picture-postcard splendor" and an affluent lifestyle known around the world.[54] The contradictions woven into the story of sunshine modernism also became more pronounced in the foothills, an L.A. environ organized around the idea that the higher the elevation the wealthier the bracket. The style's association with, and projection of, affluence is exhibited strongly in post–Progressive Era visual culture and by Hollywood production designers who would use the style inside and outside of the studio.

The *Case Study Houses* books produced from the mid-1940 to approximately the mid-1960s demonstrate the enduring legacy of Southern California visual culture beyond Hollywood and the silver screen.[55] A defining feature of these books is the photography of Julius Schulman, which sold this vision of modern living through his use of deep focus,

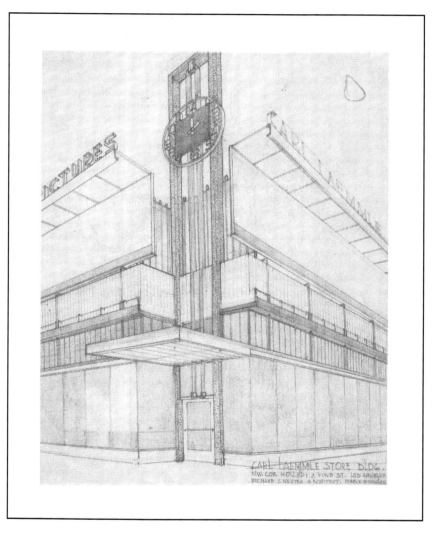

Figure 6.3. Richard Neutra's design for Carl Laemmle's Universal office, circa 1932. (Richard and Dion Neutra Papers, UCLA Library Special Collection, Los Angeles, CA.)

popularized by John Ford's *Stagecoach* (1939) and Orson Welles's *Citizen Kane* (1941). Homes like the Loggia House (designed by Whitney R. Smith and ultimately dismantled) are described as emphasizing "the primacy of outdoor living" and considered the most "native Californian" of all the *Case Study Houses* due to their "unusual plan and unconventional choice of materials."[56] Architects William Wurster and Theodore Barnardi specified "a color scheme that was based on the hues of native planting surrounding the site" for the Chalon Road House in Mandeville Canyon, a description that resembles the creative collaboration between an art director and a cinematographer.[57] While some homes, like the Bass House in Altadena, "reveal a closer association with the heritage of the Craftsman style" (common for homes in Pasadena even by midcentury), others, like Rodney Walker's Beverly Grove Drive home (built 1946–47) featured a "skylit entrance," reminiscent of cinematic lighting techniques and the principles of plein air painting.[58] What is curious about the *Case Study Houses* books is the recurrence of the phrase "a common vocabulary of materials," suggesting a cohesion among Southern California home planners' visual strategies, which were wedded to a memory of Southern California visual culture and Hollywood as an extension of that culture. If California eclectic during the 1920s sold the Los Angeles environment as a fantasy, an otherworldly place that was becoming indistinguishable from Hollywood's fairy tales, then sunshine modernism responded to clients' specific needs through an overlap between architecture and the principles of cinematic mise-en-scène—in sharp contrast to California eclectic as a form of architectural montage.

By the late 1920s, practically every facet of the Hollywood feature film was impacted by the "modern look," from "production values to advertising layouts to movie designs."[59] In the 1930s, Hollywood cinema had a two-tier system of production design that was a direct by-product, according to Donald Albrecht, of modern design: "divided responsibility between a supervising art director, who established the set's tone and concept, and a unit art director who carried out the design and oversaw its construction."[60] RKO and MGM were especially receptive to modernism, as the style lent itself so effectively to the genres they specialized in: "Modern décor was a particularly appropriate backdrop for their society comedies and dramas and lavish fairy-tale musicals."[61] MGM in particular made extensive use of open planning in its set design for these genres, drawing upon the work of Frank Lloyd Wright—in radical opposition to the architectural forms produced by fantasy-world building, such as the Storybook architecture of the Spandena House. By featuring modernism on film, particularly in the films of MGM, Hollywood cinema promoted the modern style to the public and created a new architectural iconography that became associated with affluence and progressivism, as well as providing a value system and style by which to promote its stars—affiliating this style with Greta Garbo and Clark Gable, for example. To replicate modernist symbolic affluence and progressivism, Hollywood executives, stars, and craftspeople adopted modernism in both their personal and professional lives, further entrenching the style in the Los Angeles cultural landscape. For example, like Gibbons, William Cameron Menzies also designed a home for himself in the modern style. In this regard, we can view sunshine modernism as another example of Southern California visual culture providing early Hollywood with a paratext for promoting a studio's image and for controlling reception of film texts and their affiliated celebrities.

Asked about the design of the modern home used in the finale of Hitchcock's *North by Northwest* (1959), production designer Robert Boyle noted that "every architect is influenced by Frank Lloyd Wright," and that the "horizonal, striated stonework" of Wright's Fallingwater House in Pennsylvania provided the inspiration.[62] Regarding his design process, Boyle said that, when first reading a script, he would ask: "Where do the people move, do they come in, and in what manner do they come in? Is this for suspense reasons or are we just being objective and introducing people to a particular place? Then I can begin to do my plot of how people move in the space, because their movement is the space and the image size is important."[63] Here Boyle, who had trained under frequent Lubitsch and von Sternberg collaborator Hans Drier, is describing an overlap between modern design principles centered on movement—a moving image's incorporation of a style and an architectural philosophy based around moving people, moving light, and stationary objects. We can see the same overlap of architecture and cinematic design thinking in contemporary Los Angeles cinema as well as the endurance of the idea that modernism has always been futuristic in its orientation.

1

Movie-Made Los Angeles . . .

Thom Andersen comments in *Los Angeles Plays Itself,* "If we can appreciate documentaries for their fictional qualities, then perhaps we can appreciate fictional films for their documentary revelations." Consider one such documentary revelation in a scene from Antoine Fuqua's L.A. neo-noir film *Training Day* (2001). Rogue narcotics detective Alonzo Harris (Denzel Washington) and his trainee Jake Hoyt (Ethan Hawke) embark on a training day in Los Angeles's roughest neighborhoods, beginning their journey in the downtown area. Alonzo's car is a black 1979 Monte Carlo. The song playing on the stereo is "Still D.R.E." by Dr. Dre and Snoop Dogg (released in 1999). Art deco buildings constructed in the 1920s can be seen from the driver's side window. In short, the 1990s, 1970s, and 1920s comingle in the same frame, and yet this fusion does not feel out of place. There is also no need for Fuqua to deliberately call attention to it. It is a naturally occurring fact of L.A. life that viewers have been conditioned to accept through their experience with other films set in L.A. Though *Training Day* is absent from *Los Angeles Plays Itself,* this patterning of period artifacts is echoed in Andersen's view of *L.A. Confidential* (1997), a film set during the 1950s (and notably featuring Neutra's Lovell Health House) that acknowledges that "we live in the past" and that "the world that surrounds us is not new . . . [but] an amalgam of many earlier times."[1] This layering of historical styles and art objects within both films (and countless other works of Los Angeles cinema) is also a reminder of David E. James's characterization of Los Angeles as a film setting (in both mainstream cinema and works operating at the margins) exhibiting a form of doubling "that makes the city a nostalgic simulacrum of its own imaginings."[2]

Los Angeles's "own imaginings" stem from the visual culture forms that, apart from constructing a social imaginary of Southern California in the late nineteenth century, anticipated the advent of cinema. The art deco buildings of downtown, seen in *Training Day* point to a legacy of L.A. architecture design and the growth of the downtown area fueled by regional photography and a culture of stage/moving image theater (with both Anglo and Hispanic roots). Yet there is a key moment in Andersen's film that points to a Los Angeles state of mind (or stadtbild) cemented into the public consciousness by each of the visual forms discussed in previous chapters—an L.A. look and feel advanced by moving pictures. New York City, argues Andersen, almost always plays itself. "New York seems immediately accessible to the camera. Any image from almost every corner of the city is immediately recognizable as a piece of New York." Conversely, in Los Angeles "everything dissolves into the distance, and even stuff that's close up seems far off." This comparison between the two cities underscores L.A.'s "own imaginings" as an anywhere space and nowhere space. The legacy of tourism and regional plein air, an industry of nostalgic simulacra, is brought to bear in movie-made Los Angeles's continued life as a land of place substitution.

It is impossible to talk about the City of Angels without talking about its movie business. The history of American cinema is so intertwined with Los Angeles that the term "Hollywood" is used interchangeably with "American film" worldwide. The city of Los Angeles, as we have seen, grew out of a vibrant culture of visualization before the movies arrived. This was an industry of land promotion in conjunction with journalism, advertising, tourism, and transportation, accompanied by a regional mythology that informed the ways that painters and photographers visualized the state. As a conclusion to this book, I would like to offer a brief sketch of how the visual culture forms explored in previous chapters have had a distinct presence in Los Angeles–set cinema at various stages of film history. This overview is by no means a thorough investigation into this topic; rather, it is intended as an invitation to future scholars wishing to further explore this symbiotic relationship between the city and its visual culture industry.

PHOTOGRAPHING URBAN HELL

The Edison actualities of Los Angeles toward the end of the nineteenth century offered audiences the first glimpse of L.A.'s stadtbild in motion and would also serve as a prototype for the popular 1920s nonnarrative film genre of city symphony: day-in-the-life films that celebrated the splendor of modernity and city life.[3] Dziga Vertov's *Man with a Movie Camera* (1929) is perhaps the most famous example of city symphony, but *Los Angeles, ca. 1920* (discussed in chapter 1) is an example that not only foreshadows Vertov's civic poetry but also advances the vision of L.A.'s new urbanity found in the 1870s and 1880s photographic albums of H. T. Payne. We can see the legacy of the city symphony in a variety of places throughout the history of Los Angeles cinema, but two sites in particular strongly exhibit aspects of L.A. photographic history: the influence of art photography on the one hand, and L.A. noir and neo-noir films, anti–city symphonies cloaked in shadows, on the other.

First, the influence of art photography on L.A. cultural history has contributed to various expressions of the city symphony genre, both in still and motion picture form. As discussed in chapter 1, Hollywood emerged as a dominant force behind the Los Angeles cultural economy around the same time as did Southern California pictorialism and other forms of regional art photography. Weston and other members of the art photography community at the time can also be seen as part of a larger constellation of artists radically opposed to booster ideology and rhetoric, collectively referred to as the "Debunkers" by Mike Davis. As a "united front of the New Form," the Debunkers increasingly found themselves in a paradoxical relationship with Hollywood as it emerged as the region's most effective booster around 1917; though photographers like Weston, painters like Boris Deutsch, writers like Upton Sinclair, and architects like Frank Lloyd Wright are often considered part of modernist traditions that are defined in contrast to the motion picture industry, this bohemian community of Debunkers in Los Angeles during the 1910s and 1920s found inspiration in the movies and exerted a reciprocal influence upon the development of Hollywood practices.

Photographic pictorialism, cartographic photography, and the Los Angeles stadtbild in still form can be seen in the work of Los Angeles pop artist Ed Ruscha, crystallizing the varying legacies of Progressive

Era photography. The photographic book *Some Los Angeles Apartments* (1965), for example, features thirty-eight façades of apartments from various places and ecologies of Los Angeles, accompanied by essays citing the influence of photographers such as Carleton Watkins. His follow-up book, *Every Building on the Sunset Strip* (1966), also taps into the essence of early California photography in a variety of striking ways. The title of the book could not be a more accurate description of its contents: it is an accordion folio book, like the ones used to publicly distribute Muybridge's San Francisco panoramas, featuring two continuous photographic views of Sunset Strip. The top photos, right side up, display one side of the street, and the other side is featured, upside down, on the bottom of the page. The book provides a city symphony of sorts, or perhaps a city symphony movement that showcases a portion of the city that was the epicenter of the L.A. rock and roll scene the year it was released. A year later, Roger Croman would shoot sequences of his psychedelic B-movie/exploitation film *The Trip* (1967) at the same locations, as Peter Fonda on LSD wanders through a city symphony conjured by his own imagination. The successive photographic experiments of Étienne-Jules Marey and Eadweard Muybridge spring to mind when looking at Ruscha's successive photography process in this book, but the work of Muybridge, and by extension Carleton Watkins, can especially be felt here when one considers Ruscha's city symphony as a succession of plates. Also similar to Muybridge's panoramas, Ruscha's L.A. panorama has a slight time-lapse quality that communicates a day-in-the-life aspect to the city. There are certain portions of Ruscha's panoramas that feel seamless until there is a mismatch. Typical of Los Angeles imagery, this mismatch is revealed through different colored vehicles entering or exiting the frame between plates, a reminder of the role that automobile culture plays in Los Angeles's moving-image mapping impulses. Last, the stadtbild of vastness and openness felt in the albums of H. T. Payne and the Historical Society of Southern California, the All-Year-Round Club's *Southern California through the Camera* photos, and in the Edison Spring Street actuality can be felt through Ruscha's images. In this sense, the Sunset Strip of 1966 is treated less like an urban space and more like the frontier.

By contrast, the city symphony as a form of debunking is embodied strongly by film noir, or what Thom Andersen would describe as the ultimate metaphor for L.A. In noir cinema, the visual conventions of the city symphony are turned toward exposing how boosterism's American promise and middle-class dream had become a nightmare. For Mike Davis, writers like James M. Cain and Raymond Chandler "reworked the metaphorical figure of the city" and repainted the "image of Los Angeles as a deracinated urban hell."[4] Cinematically, Los Angeles provided the ideal conditions for noir to flourish, largely through four reasons identified by Tina Olson Lent. First, Los Angeles was a new city, situated on what had previously been viewed as the American frontier—symbolizing American promise in 1920 and its failure during the Great Depression of the 1930s. This end-of-the-frontier status contributed to the region's development as a land of place substitution, a crux on which the migration of studios to the West Coast hinged. At the same time, Los Angeles's place at the end of the frontier also framed an image of the city as a bastion of lawlessness, existing at great distance from the democratic institutions and long arm of the federal government on the East Coast. Second, the area now known as downtown Los Angeles was structured in the form of a classic American city, in contrast to the rest of the city's sprawl, and it embodied the problems of other major American cities. Third, Southern California's automobile culture and urban sprawl set the tone for other American cities. As mentioned earlier, Greg Hise notes that this quality of Los Angeles allowed the city to set the tone for the development of other major American cities (and indeed other global cities) throughout the twentieth century: multi-centered, dispersed, and less concerned with "city" than with "region."[5] Finally, since Los Angeles was the home of the film industry, it was an attractive location for writers who would use the city as a character. If L.A. noirs like *In a Lonely Place* (Nicholas Ray, 1950), *Sunset Boulevard* (Billy Wilder, 1950), *Kiss Me Deadly* (Robert Aldrich, 1955), and even 1970s throwbacks like *The Long Goodbye* (Robert Altman, 1973) position the genre and its visual and thematic stylings as the ultimate metaphor for Los Angeles, then L.A. noir revises the city's stadtbild, encoded into the social imaginary through Southern California photography, actuality films, and city symphonies, as a "dialectic between the promise of freedom and the price of this freedom."[6]

A key component film noir's flowering in Los Angeles is Lent's third reason: Southern California's automobile culture and the crucial role it played in both noir narrative strategies and in informing the civic planning of the Los Angeles residential and commercial landscape. As the "imaginative mappings" of L.A. started to take shape in the 1910s and 1920s, the city itself was being shaped through civic projects like the 1922 "Los Angeles Plan," sponsored by the City of Los Angeles with the advertised aim of historical conservation celebrating "the wonder city of the world . . . a city of splendid industrial structures and beautiful homes . . . the capitol of the film world and as such . . . the best advertised city on earth."[7] The real aims, however, were to improve the city for motorists, find solutions for "constantly increasing traffic congestion problems," and curb reckless driving and dangerous grade crossing. Automotive concerns, therefore, would trump historical and cultural preservation, cementing a recurring theme in L.A. history and L.A. cinema. If Los Angeles was constructed on the "sheer vastness of movement patterns," as Reyner Banham argues, then the cinematic mapping of the city through silent movies anticipated how these patterns would shape a variety of Angeleno identities.[8]

The centrality of automobile travel in L.A. noir can be seen in the way the anti-heroes of film noir and their neo-noir successors perform cinematic cartography in service of debunker critics. Aldrich's *Kiss Me Deadly*, for example, sees its central character, private eye Mike Hammer (Ralph Meeker), living at a real apartment building address (1041 Wilshire Boulevard) and visiting real locations in Malibu and Bunker Hill, including sites that would be demolished a decade later (rendering the film something of a palimpsest layer recorded in a time capsule). The film maps Los Angeles for the viewer in scenes of Hammer driving from location to location in a Jaguar XK120, an MG-TD, and a 1954 Chevrolet Corvette. By contrast, the loss of a vehicle in films like *Sunset Boulevard* or *Chinatown* (Roman Polanski, 1974) destabilizes the viewer's capacity for mentally mapping the city through the eyes of the central character. The loss of a vehicle becomes not only a form of castration in L.A. cinema, as Andersen discusses at great length in *Los Angeles Plays Itself*, it also rewrites the pathos formula of the moving-city panorama in which the spectator is overwhelmed by the spectacle that is Los Angeles, rather than being able to navigate its chaos from a distance.

When we look at contemporary Los Angeles films, we see that this mapping impulse not only remains a vital component of Los Angeles cinema but also layers Banham's four L.A. ecologies with temporal dimensions and political implications. *Drive* opens with a map of Los Angeles showing handwritten notations from its central anti-hero, the Driver (Ryan Gosling), signaling straightaway that the film's relationship with the tradition of cinematic mapping in Los Angeles cinema. "There's a hundred thousand streets in this city," the Driver tells his client on a disposable mobile phone, "You don't need to know the route. You give me a time and a place. I give you a five-minute window. Anything happens in that five minutes, and I'm yours. No matter what. Anything happens a minute either side of that, and you're on your own." In this pre-credit sequence, the Driver provides the getaway vehicle for a heist near downtown (421 South Alameda)—taking an escape route over the Sixth Street Bridge and eventually ending at the Staples Center as a Clippers' basketball game ends. A police scanner in the Driver's vehicle provides the audience with both a form of narration on his movements and a mental map of the city for the viewer ("suspect last seen near Seventh Street and Santa Fe"). *Nightcrawler* (Dan Gilroy, 2014) also taps into this Los Angeles cinematic mapping impulse in similar ways. Louis "Lou" Bloom (Jake Gyllenhaal), the film's anti-hero, is a stinger: a freelance videographer who captures footage of crime scenes and accidents to sell to local news networks. The film is an exemplar of contemporary L.A. neo-noir stylistically (the film was photographed by Paul Thomas Anderson collaborator Robert Elswit) and thematically: a uniquely Los Angeles style of open-all-night capitalism, "a jungle in which it is acceptable for the weak to perish at the hands of the strong," is placed front and center in the film's narrative.[9] *Nightcrawler* also features all four of Banham's L.A. ecologies in service of Gilroy's critique of the city: Venice Beach is portrayed as a space for meditation and opportunistic bike theft; a triple murder in Granada Hills reveals the corruption at the heart of the foothills' affluent class while at the same time providing another excuse for the media to render L.A.'s less fortunate even more invisible; Lou's low-end apartment exemplifies the foothills' attitude toward flatland life; and the L.A. streets are well mapped throughout Gilroy's film, though more often the surface streets rather than the freeway system.

As Levi Bryant notes, the "ecologies of many worlds contain elements of both content and expression [contributing to] the investigation of social and political assemblage."[10] Expanding further on how L.A. noir provides L.A. ecologies with political implications, Paul Thomas Anderson's 2014 adaptation of Thomas Pynchon's novel *Inherent Vice* reminds the viewer that early L.A. cinematic mappings were "ideologically biased by gender, race, and class" and that these biases "decisively shaped the city's rapid expansion" through real-life civic projects.[11] In other words, noir plots of city domination through shady land-development deals—as seen in Anderson's film, *Chinatown*, *L.A. Confidential* (Curtis Hanson, 1997) and, satirically, in *Who Framed Roger Rabbit?* (Robert Zemeckis, 1988)—expose the L.A. stadtbild (one centered on freedom of movement) as something engineered by the city's capitalist overlord class and propped up by the dominating role that motion pictures play in manufacturing public consciousness. For example, *Inherent Vice* features a scene in which the stoner detective protagonist Larry "Doc" Sportello (Joaquin Phoenix) drives with friend and confidante Sortilège (Joanna Newsom) to investigate a lead regarding a missing real estate developer. The two speak of a history of displaced people: "Mexican families bounced out of Chavez Ravine to build Dodger Stadium, American Indians swept out of Bunker Hill for the Music Center, and now [South Central] bulldozed aside for Channel View Estates." During this conversation, the film partially dissolves to a map of Los Angeles (bordered by the 405, 91, and 105 Freeways). This phantasmagoric mapping in the

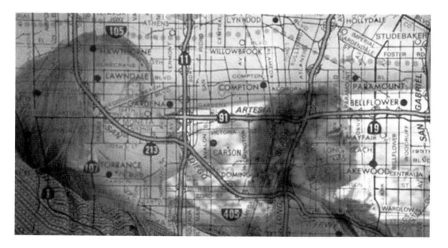

Figure 7.1. *Inherent Vice* (Paul Thomas Anderson, Warner Bros., 2014).

film (fig. 7.1) suggests an awareness in L.A. cinema of the established tradition of cinematic mapping, which can be traced back to the visualization practices that transformed Los Angeles from a small city into major economic center. Like *L.A. Confidential* and the *L.A. Quartet* novels of James Ellroy, *Inherent Vice* acts as a "postmodern historical metafiction" that deliberately engages with the audience's understanding of the centrality of race and class conflict to the L.A. story, as well as a cultural memory of L.A. cinema.[12]

From a radically different perspective, Kent Mackenzie's *The Exiles* (1961), a documentary/neorealist film about the "American Indians swept out of Bunker Hill for the Music Center," performs a cinematic debunking of L.A. boosterism through providing a counternarrative to a "popular understanding of [Bunker Hill's] social identity" and defying "urban planners' vision of a lucrative downtown."[13] Following the lives of Native Americans from Arizona and the conflict between tradition and modernism, Mackenzie's film addresses the legacy of all key functions of Progressive Era photography through a city symphony that directly confronts the Anglo American Eden visions of Progressive Era boosterism as well as the perceived anti-humanism of film noir's cold detachment. As the film's characters congregate on top of Chavez Ravine (known in the film as Hill X) to sing and dance to traditional tribal songs, Los Angeles is remapped in a way that reimagines the city through Viola Fay Cordova's conception of "bounded space"; in overlooking the city from Hill X's panoramic vista, L.A. is recast as a territory that people belong to rather than as a part of an Anglo American destiny prophesied by the Wheeler Expedition photographs or plein air painting. The Los Angeles stadtbild is also renegotiated through turning the lens on people marginalized by gentrification. As the camera follows Yvonne Williams through downtown sidewalks at night, the viewer is invited to reflect with her on how economic hardship has demolished any faith that L.A.'s booster aspirations apply to her. Last, the film offers a revised take on photography as an art form and the way this function informs the city symphony genre. Inspired by the film theories of Paul Rotha and global new wave movements (in France and Japan especially), Mackenzie overlapped natural settings and wardrobe with soundstage-recorded dialogue, artificial lighting, and thirty-five-millimeter Ariflex photography.[14] Through repurposing these three photographic functions, *The Exiles* is an L.A.

anti-myth set against a sea of city lights that would forever be associated with the sublime elements of L.A. neo-noir cinema and booster vision offered by the panorama views of *Southern California through the Camera.*

A SEA OF LIGHTS

"In Fiji, they have these iridescent algae that come out once a year in the water," says master thief Neil McCauley (Robert De Niro) in Michael Mann's L.A. crime epic *Heat* (1995). "That's what it looks like out there," he goes on as he gestures toward a panoramic view of the city lights at night from a Hollywood Hills home (fig. 7.2). At first glance, this vista recalls the panoramic scope of the Spence Airplane photography in *Southern California through the Camera*. The colors of L.A. at night, however, bring the influence of painted forms into cinematographer Dante Spinotti's anamorphic wide-angle shots. Years later, Mann would describe these nighttime light and color patterns while shooting another L.A. crime film, *Collateral* (2004): "When its humid, the sodium vapor from the streetlights in this megalopolis of 17 million people bounces up onto the bottom of the cloud layer and it becomes diffused light. You see this wondrous, abandoned landscape with hills and trees and strange lighting patterns."[15] In *Collateral*, there is a moment when diffused light and a "wondrous, abandoned landscape" elevates ground-level L.A. to a sublime space: a coyote runs out in front of Max's (Jamie

Figure 7.2. *Heat* (Michael Mann, Warner Bros., 1995).

Foxx) taxicab. Max has spent the evening driving around a hitman, Vincent (Tom Cruise), and for a moment the two men forget the horrible things they have done and recognize something oddly beautiful in this moment—familiar yet strange. In the background, colors twinkle in soft focus, while a yellow glow provides the image with an otherworldly feeling. In both *Heat* and *Collateral*, there is a recognition that color is something changes and moves, and that atmosphere color can be manipulated to create a broader range of storytelling and emotions. Hues of yellow bouncing off sodium vapor fog defamiliarize the "Golden State" and contribute to a form of L.A. noir that D. K. Holm refers to as *film soleil*: distinct from the broader term *neo-noir*, this is the use of Los Angeles's (and Southern California's generally) colorful vibrancy to convey, paradoxically, a "bright and guilty place."[16]

Holm's term suggests a paradoxical relationship between turn-of-the-century California boosterism and the anti-mythology of Mike Davis's Debunker class, centered around color and its significance for visualizing Los Angeles. On the one hand, film soleil uses color and light patterns to bring the city's subconscious, shadow side into relief and to visualize the folly of booster promises. A film soleil, in this sense, is a city symphony where color infuses the narrative with a feeling that David Batchelor refers to as chromophobia: a fear of corruption or contamination through color. For Batchelor, this fear arises from "something that is unknown or appears unknowable," usually through making color "out to be the property of some foreign body—usually the feminine, the oriental, the primitive, the infantile, the vulgar, the queer, or the pathological" or by relegating color to the "realm of the superficial, the supplementary, the inessential, or cosmetic."[17] On the other hand, film soleil employs approaches to light and color that have a lineage to an art movement whose history is heavily intertwined with boosterism. From roughly the early 1890s to the late 1920s, California impressionism (or California plein air painting) evoked a sense of nostalgia and escapism while emphasizing the state's natural beauty, techniques that anticipated Hollywood practices of place substitution.

Roman Polanski noted that Los Angeles is one of the most beautiful cities in the world, "provided that it's seen at night and from a distance."[18] In Los Angeles cinema, nighttime cityscapes evoke the sublime, as Neil McCauley observes in *Heat*, while at the same time, the colors of L.A.

night life have been encoded into film as recognizable signs through which viewers can read the city. When analyzing the use of colors in Los Angeles cinema, it becomes useful to contrast this L.A. film grammar with early twentieth-century Southern California impressionism, as one of the key features of this art movement was that it reinforced the state's emblematic colors, notably shades of gold and purple.[19] L.A. neo-noirs of the 1980s and 1990s, such as *To Live and Die in L.A.* (William Friedkin, 1985) and *Heat*, feature a spectrum of night colors that would provide the basis for the look of twenty-first century L.A. noirs shot on digital, notably Michael Mann's *Collateral*, Nicolas Winding Refn's *Drive*, and Dan Gilroy's *Nightcrawler*. What sets these films apart from night scenes shot elsewhere—New York or Tokyo crime thrillers, for example—is the vastness and horizontality of the city, in stark contrast to the densely vertical nature of other cities, a quality captured by California Scene Painting. Additionally, L.A. night colors are used in film to defamiliarize the city, providing L.A. with an almost Freudian uncanny feeling.

Consider a moment from Michael Mann's made-for-television film *L.A. Takedown* (1989), a scene that was not repurposed for the remake *Heat*: a montage early in the film in which LAPD detective Vincent Hannah (Scott Plank) and his team cruise around Los Angeles at night, hitting up their contacts and informants on the streets, hoping to generate a lead on the robbery of an armored car earlier that day. The music playing over the montage is Billy Idol's cover of the Doors' "L.A. Woman."[20] On a phantom ride, the camera whizzes down Sunset Strip and Hollywood Boulevard, the blurred lights creating an expressionist portrait of the city; helicopter shots pass over downtown's buildings, citadels of old power standing tall in the middle of suburban sprawl and vibrant murals on brick walls pronouncing a street history largely stricken from the official record; and the network of freeway systems looks like a sleeping giant's circulatory system. This scene functions as an updated city symphony, the colors infusing it with a sense of chromophobia—the nighttime colors familiar and understood through similar films set in L.A., but at the same time evoking a feeling of foreignness.

Another example of film soleil and the legacy of plein air's color palette can be seen in *Nightcrawler*, shot on thirty-five-millimeter film for daytime scenes but on an Alexa digital camera for nighttime scenes because of the medium's ability to reproduce such vibrant colors at night.

There was a beauty to L.A. at night that Gilroy and cinematographer Robert Elswit found in the neon glow and sodium vapor lights, noting that digital photography can pull in "lights from forty miles away—a candle would be seen." Gilroy further noted that he "wanted to show the functional side of the city . . . but hopefully we also wanted to catch some sort of physical beauty, that at night there is this clarity of light and you can see long distances. So, we used great depth of field in the shots rather than soft focus, and we tried to get wide angles as much as possible. Sometimes we were down to a 14mm lens to really make it wide angle, because in an equation sense, the character of Lou is like a nocturnal animal that comes out of the hills at night to feed."[21]

Turning away from plein air toward the filmic legacy of modern art forms, Los Angeles during the 1940s provides an interesting moment in history, as there was a noticeable convergence between the film industry and distinct features of California life. As Paul Karlstrom has observed, the role of the film industry in the local economy allowed popular culture to take on a greater significance than it would elsewhere, and through the cross-pollination between popular art and film, Los Angeles "had come to embody (physically and psychologically) change, freedom, and mobility."[22] Some important themes emerged from the L.A. modern art scene of the period, according to Karlstrom: a Hollywood-influenced preoccupation with light and movement, an openness to nontraditional forms and sources, a distance from the influence of the New York art scene (a defining feature of early twentieth-century California impressionism as well), and new ideas about color harmony.[23] Some artists recognized the expressiveness of "cinematic devices" through their art, such as Lorser Feitelson and Man Ray.[24] Other artists worked in the film industry, such as Jules Engel and Rico Lebrun, who worked for Disney and taught animators how to draw animals for *Bambi*, June Wayne (who operated a lithography business and founded the Los Angeles Women's Building in 1977), and Stanton MacDonald-Wright, who collaborated with ceramist and film special effects pioneer Albert King.[25] Although there is not a convenient set of styles and influences that binds the modern artists of 1940s Los Angeles, their overlap with Hollywood is significant, as the film industry was instrumental in distributing Southern California imagery to receptive international audiences.

During the 1950s through the 1970s, Los Angeles, according to William Hackman, was the center of gravity in America for modern art, and the role cinema would play in making the American counterculture visible would, in turn, raise the visibility of Los Angeles pop art.[26] Willard Huyck and Gloria Katz's horror film *Messiah of Evil* (1973), for example, takes place largely in Banham's surfburbia ecology, an environment that "other metropolises should envy in Los Angeles, more than any other aspect of the city," and where "the culture of the beach is in many ways a symbolic rejection of the values of the consumer society."[27] In *Messiah of Evil*, a "consumer society" literally consumes the film's characters against the backdrop of this idealized Southern California ecology. The film is the story of Arletty (Marianna Hill) and her search for her father, an artist living in Point Dune who mysteriously disappears. She soon discovers that the town's residents have been turned into flesh-eating ghouls, awaiting the return of their leader, a dark stranger and survivor of the Donner Party known as the Messiah of Evil. The film was shot around the Los Angeles and Orange County area over the course of two months in 1971 and released in May 1973. Arriving five years after George Romero's *Night of the Living Dead* (1968), *Messiah of Evil* is a film that Kim Newman describes as "strangely surreal . . . shot through with the pretensions one might expect from fresh film school graduates . . . but rich in narrative convolutions and peculiar atmospherics."[28] The movie is connected to a broader group of films set in and around the Los Angeles area during the late 1960s and early 1970s. The film's horror elements and social critique are underscored by the L.A. pop art–influenced production design of Joan Mocine and Jack Fisk (who would later collaborate with David Lynch on *Mulholland Drive* and with Paul Thomas Anderson on *There Will Be Blood* and *The Master*). The art of Andy Warhol, Ed Kienholz, Ed Ruscha, and other regulars at L.A.'s famed Ferus Gallery can be felt in Mocine and Fisk's visual design—a design that underscores the clash between counterculture and consumer culture at the heart of the film.

Asked what tourists should see in Los Angeles, Ed Ruscha responded: gas stations and "any kind of edifice that has to do with the car." Gas stations, according to Ruscha, are fascinating because "everything about them is streamlined," the fact that "they can put them together in three days or less" is truly remarkable.[29] An early scene in *Messiah of Evil* features a gas station that recalls the paintings in Ruscha's photobook

Figure 7.3. *Messiah of Evil* (Huyck and Katz, Bedford Entertainment, 1973).

Twentysix Gasoline Stations (1963). These paintings, according to Ken D. Allan, are "often characterized as having a deadpan quality that projects a kind of cool indifference towards the viewer," a reconfiguring of the everyday and mundane into something liberating in its absurdity.[30] Through evoking Ruscha in this manner, the gas station in the film taps into a Freudian sense of the uncanny similar to what we find in contemporary L.A. noir nighttime colors.

    Messiah of Evil coincided with the period that is generally referred to as New Hollywood, and many of the L.A.-set films of this era deliberately foreground pop art and other counterculture-influenced regional visual culture. Pop art is used in exceptional ways, however, by what Thom Anderson describes in *Los Angeles Plays Itself* as "high tourist" filmmakers: those not born in L.A. who appreciate Los Angeles in all its complexity. Andersen points to Roger Corman's psychedelic exploitation film *The Trip* (1967) and John Boorman's neo-noir classic *Point Blank* (1967) as notable examples. In the work of Agnes Varda and Jacques Demy, two filmmakers who became enamored with Southern California during the late 1960s, we can see "high tourists" explore Los Angeles through pop art in a way similar to the approach of longtime L.A. resident and co-director and writer of *Messiah of Evil* Gloria Katz: Demy, Varda, Katz, her partner and co-director Willard Huyck, and artist Ruscha use their art to address "the dynamic between the pictorial space, the mental space, and the actual space that structures our encounters with works of art as objects."[31] This dynamic comes through clearly in Varda's *Lions*

Love (. . . and Lies) (1969), a film featuring Warhol actress Viva (born Janet Susan Mary) that explores L.A.'s rivalry with the New York arts scene. Demy's *Model Shop* (1969), a film set largely inside the central character George's (Gary Lockwood) automobile, features pop art–influenced costuming and props, as well as several prominent uses of Standard Oil gas stations that directly recall the work of Ruscha. There are several ways of interpreting this trend in 1960s and 1970s L.A. films. For me, films like *Model Shop* and *Lions Love (. . . and Lies)* use pop art as a form of anti-establishment neo-boosterism—a counterculture rebuke to the conservatism of the original California boosterism that coincided with the rise of the American film industry during the early twentieth century. *Messiah of Evil* interacts with this neo-boosterism through its pop art–influenced design, but it does so in a way that reminds the viewer of the haunting qualities of California dreaming.

THE WILD WEST'S AFTERLIFE

L.A. noir can be read as a metaphor for the Wild West having an afterlife through the brutal logic of Los Angeles corruption and the city's inscrutable nature. Yet the city's end-of-the-frontier status, linked to Progressive Era practices of rewriting Southern California as a performative space, is found in other types of Los Angeles–set films. L.A. disaster films, which have been explored extensively by Andersen and Mike Davis, exhibit this pattern of Los Angeles as anyspace.[32] Davis in particular notes three key features of what he calls the "gleeful expendability of Los Angeles in the popular imagination."[33] First, Davis recognizes that there is a dramatic trend over time toward the "merging of all Los Angeles fiction with the disaster or survivalist narrative." In *Kiss Me Deadly*, for example, a suitcase bomb (or "the great whatsit") is interwoven into a noir tale of intrigue. By contrast, *Miracle Mile* (Steve De Jarnett, 1988) stages an apocalyptic disaster romance amid an identifiable L.A. location. Second, Los Angeles disaster fiction falls into one of two subgenres: "romantic disaster" or "magical dystopic." By alluding to magic realism and romantic art, Davis suggests a painterly inflection in these films through special effects and stylistic echoes of visual art in the disaster imagination. These subcategories also recall Frederic Jameson's description of magic realism as having a "strange seductiveness," which in the context of L.A. disaster films, points to works like *Earthquake* (1974) and *Independence Day* (1996), where there is a vicarious thrill to be had in L.A.'s destruction.[34] Third, Davis argues that the "abiding hysteria of Los Angeles disaster fiction, and perhaps all of disaster fiction—the urge to strike out and destroy, wipe out an entire city and untold thousands of its inhabitants—is rooted in racial anxiety."[35] This last point brings disaster narratives back to the origins of L.A.'s imaginings, in which Southern California was conceived of as a "sunny refuge of White Protestant America" by the Arroyo group.[36] The layering of *Ramona* myth over real history, or what Carey McWilliam's referred to as "the Indian in the closet," can be seen as a foreshadowing of contemporary L.A. racial politics played out metaphorically through L.A. cinema's disastrous imagination.[37] All three of these L.A. disaster film characteristics unite in *Blade Runner* (1982), which Davis refers to as L.A.'s official nightmare. Blade Runner is more than simply a sci-fi noir or future noir. The film is noir as the ultimate L.A. metaphor merging with disaster fiction, which Davis sees as the logical end point for any L.A. narrative. Though ugly and dystopian, the L.A. of *Blade Runner* is strangely sublime in the way it repurposes the L.A. panoramic vision and iconic architectural landmarks (such as Frank Lloyd Wright's Ennis House or downtown L.A.'s Bradbury Building, both of which have had numerous lives through film, television, and other media). Last, in addition to replicants exemplifying what Davis sees as disaster narratives' "racial anxiety," the film's "urge to . . . wipe out" Los Angeles is wedded to nostalgia for a city that never really existed, such as what was engendered by the California social imaginary promoted by pre-cinema photography, painting, and other visual culture forms.

Shifting away from disaster science fiction, independent L.A. cinema interacts with the city's history of place substitution and end-of-the-frontier status in a variety of ways that warrant further scholarly attention. Consider two trends outside of mainstream Hollywood that intersect with Banham's flatland ecology. Penelope Spheeris's punk rock film *Suburbia* (produced by Roger Corman, 1984) is set in L.A.'s flatland environment, or what Reyner Banham refers to as the "plains of id": a daunting sea of suburban houses in which "Los Angeles is least distinctly itself and . . . most like other cities."[38] In Spheeris's film, the flatlands are redrawn in almost apocalyptic terms to create a world that aims for what Guido Aristarco describes as "critical realism": when a film reveals "the dynamic causes of social change through exemplary situations and figures."[39] *Suburbia* is the story of runaway squatter punk kids, known collectively as the Rejected, living in an abandoned tract house. The film is largely set in what are now considered the cities of Norwalk and Downey, at the intersection of the 105 and the 605 Freeways. This is a neighborhood that fell into eminent domain during the late 1960s and remained a sea of vacant homes until they were demolished during the 1990s. The film begins with Evan leaving his suburban home, alcoholic single mother, and younger brother Ethan. As Evan sets out on foot during the opening title sequence, Alex Gibson's melancholy rock score kicks in with an almost spaghetti western tone. In this sense, the tract housing area that he will eventually live in can be viewed as something of a new age ghost town.

By contrast, in the neorealist films of the L.A. Rebellion filmmakers of the 1970s and 1980s, Los Angeles's status as the land of place substitution is challenged through engaging with Banham's flatland ecology in a very different way. During the late 1960s, a generation of African American film students at UCLA formed what would later be known as the L.A. Rebellion Movement (sometimes referred to as the UCLA Rebellion). Under the tutelage of professor and filmmaker Elyseo J. Taylor, a former U.S. Army major during World War II and a photographic journalist in the years that followed, the L.A. Rebellion embraced the humanity and radically different reckoning of time in the films of Yasujiro Ozu, the anticolonial spirit of Ousmane Sembéne's films, and the minimalism and raw immediacy of Italian neorealism. A key characteristic of the films produced by the L.A. Rebellion filmmakers, in stark contrast to their mainstream counterparts, was an "explicit political desire to deconstruct what they viewed as Hollywood's ideological prison house."[40] The primary challenge, according to Ntongela Masilela, was to find a film form unique to their historical situation and cultural experience that could not be "appropriated by Hollywood."[41] In films like *Killer of Sheep* (Charles Burnett, 1978), *Bush Mama* (Haile Gerima, 1979), and *Bless Their Little Hearts* (Billy Woodberry, 1984), the city of Watts is used to overcome this challenge and deconstruct "Hollywood's ideological prison house" through emphasizing this flatland community as an "area where Los Angeles is least distinctly itself."[42] As Banham notes, Watts began as "a strategically well-placed community to live in," a creation of the Pacific Electric route to the Long Beach–based manufacturing industries, but eventually became, by the 1960s, the most "strategically ill-placed" community when Pacific Electric terminated the Watts connection.[43] In the L.A. Rebellion films, as well as other neorealist-inspired presentations of Los Angeles that Thom Andersen advocates for in *Los Angeles Plays Itself*, Watt's ecology is simultaneously a place substitution for the African American experience in any major U.S. city and a locale that defies the place-substitution tendencies that have defined the Los Angeles area for well over a century. The L.A. Rebellion films and other L.A. neorealist films (such as Sean Baker's 2015 film *Tangerine*), in this regard, can be read as debunkers par excellence to the form of visual boosterism that enticed Selig to build his movie empire in Edendale at the height of the Progressive Era.

VISUAL FUTURISM

California eclectic has appeared in cinema produced in the second half of the twentieth century and later, both in Los Angeles cinema and in films set largely elsewhere, as part of established visual codes and narrative strategies that are wedded to a cultural memory of early filmmaking in Los Angeles and the close relationship between the city and its film industry. The California eclectic remnants of the silent era would provide locations for *Chinatown* and the insular imagined community of *Day of the Locust*, and the High Tower built in 1920 in a Bolognese campanile style would be the apartment of Philip Marlow (Elliot Gould) in *The Long Goodbye*, an ideal location for a detective trapped between an older noir world and a new world of the L.A. counterculture scene. The mansion of Daniel Plainview towards the end of Paul Thomas Anderson's *There Will Be Blood* (2007) is built in a Tudor style, conflating the megalomaniac oil baron with the sinister figures of Hollywood royalty familiar through previous works of Los Angeles cinema. This use of California eclectic draws on the memory of Los Angeles cinema during the classic Hollywood era, often finding its way into film noir as flashy exteriors that conceal dark secrets from within. In *Double Indemnity* (Billy Wilder, 1944), the home of Phyllis Dietrichson (Barbara Stanwyck) near Los Feliz

Boulevard is, according to Walter Neff (Fred MacMurray), "one of those Southern California Spanish houses that everyone was nuts about ten or fifteen years ago." In *Sunset Boulevard* (Billy Wilder, 1950), the home of Norma Desmond (Gloria Swanson) is a mansion built between 1919 and 1924 by William O. Jenkins and had been the home of J. Paul Getty prior to shooting. Though modern-style homes in Los Angeles cinema have often been in stark contrast to the philosophies of modern living that produced them, the use of California eclectic in Los Angeles cinema has generally been to evoke the ideas of Davis's Noirs and Debunkers in contrast to the dreams-for-sale ethos that sold the homes to a newly arrived and expanding population in Los Angeles during Hollywood's early years.

Blade Runner, according to Mike Davis, is Los Angeles's dystopic alter ego.[44] The film has provided writers with a shorthand for describing what amounts the "city's official nightmare," a story that takes the subgenre of future noir to what Vincent Brook calls metanarrative terminus.[45] Ironically, as Norman Klein points out, *Blade Runner* provided urban planners during the early 1990s with inspiration, with one member of the Community Redevelopment Agency, at a series of public lectures at the Pacific Design Center in February 1990, praising the logo atop the Interstate Savings and Loan building in downtown as "reminding him favorably of *Blade Runner*."[46] *Blade Runner*'s production designer Lawrence G. Paull notes that much of the concept art of the film was rooted in "visual futurism," a set of ideas championed by Wright, Schindler, and Neutra that called for a liberation from the nostalgia of past forms.[47] Before entering the film industry, Paull was trained as a city planner, and he characterized his approach to production design for motion pictures in the same way: "I started out in the old studio system at 20th Century-Fox as a set designer, which was basically like an architectural draftsman."[48] What is also interesting is that, as Paull observes, the city was never identified as Los Angeles in the original script; the eventual decision to do so was the product of the advantages provided by the city's modern designs (Frank Lloyd Wright's Ennis House) and landmarks such as the Bradbury Building in downtown.[49] Moreover, Paull notes that Ridley Scott did much of the concept drawings with Syd Mead, a self-described "visual futurist." At first this approach to *Blade Runner* appears to affirm Klein's view that the film (as well as its sequel,

Blade Runner: 2049) has "achieved something rare in the history" of cinema by becoming "a paradigm for future cities [and] for artists across the disciplines."[50] Yet *Blade Runner* and *Blade Runner: 2049* can also be read as part of a longer history of the Los Angeles region as the site of place substitution. With these films, the place substitution is any city and any dystopian future ravaged by climate change and late capitalism rather than, say, the shores of France (provided by the Pacific Coast) in Francis Boggs's *Count of Monte Cristo*. Sunshine modernism, in this regard, serves as a fitting epilogue to the story of how California photography, *Ramona* myths, film tourism and attractions, and California painting imagined a space for an American film industry and its host city to take shape during the early twentieth century.

ANTI-TOURS

Screenwriter Robert Towne read the work of Carey McWilliams while writing *Chinatown* (1974): "McWilliams wrote about Southern California with sensibilities my eye, ear, and nose recognized."[51] The book he was referring to was *Southern California: An Island on Land*, in which McWilliams provides an early portrait of the region as a land of contradictions, a "sub-tropical paradise" that "might someday be severed from a continent to which it has always been capriciously attached."[52] The work of McWilliams and other early twentieth-century chroniclers of Los Angeles and regional history, both nonfiction and historical fiction, provides a literary basis for what Robert Burgoyne describes as the metahistorical film: one that "starts by questioning the dominant understanding of a particular event, and that challenges the way that the history of that event has been written and disseminated."[53] *Chinatown*, while telling a fictional story, argues that any history of L.A. written by the booster class is immediately suspect and that the real history of the city's creation can be better understood through a familiarity with noir narrative conventions, as the style and genre is one of L.A.'s most endearing and prolific. *Who Framed Roger Rabbit?* can be seen as an ideological companion piece to *Chinatown*—it reveals a hidden L.A. history by an ironic happy ending through which the wrongs of L.A.'s past are made right; this cartoon version of *Chinatown*, as Thom Andersen describes it, offers a "counter-historical happy ending" in which the victory is allowed to be celebrated privately.[54]

This imagined community provides John Schlesinger's period drama *Day of the Locust* (1975) a state of mind and place setting. Based on Nathaniel West's 1939 novel of the same name (and set in the same year as the novel's release), *Day of the Locust* centers on the lives of set painter and concept artist Tod Hacket (William Atherton) and aspiring actress Faye (Karen Black). Early in the film, the two spend an afternoon outing around Los Angeles—posing for photographs in front of celebrity homes in Beverly Hills, journeying to the Hollywood sign for ice cream from a nearby tourist stand, and taking in a screening of a film featuring Faye in a minor role (though most of her scenes were cut from the final picture). As Tod, Faye, and Earle (a cowboy actor whom Faye is dating) leave the cinema, a newsreel highlighting growing tensions in Europe flashes on the screen. What is notable about this moment is that their backs are turned to Hitler, who appears on-screen as they walk out of the theater, as if the three of them exist only in their insular Hollywood world, their "island on land" apart from the grim realities of the rest of the world. Perhaps the characters of *The Day of the Locust* are trapped within this world because, at the time the story takes place, Hollywood had entrenched itself as an imagined community by writing its own history as well as generating a common culture.

The overlap between Hollywood history and Los Angeles history has provided Los Angeles cinema with key works that resonate across a variety of scholarly perspectives, whether they are films chronicling the lives of real filmmakers—*Man of a Thousand Faces* (Joseph Pevney, 1957), *Chaplin* (Richard Attenborough, 1992), and *Ed Wood* (Tim Burton, 1994)—or imagined ones—*Singing in the Rain* (Gene Kelly and Stanley Donen, 1952), *Mulholland Drive* (David Lynch, 2001), and *Map to the Stars* (David Cronenberg, 2014). As a complex work with one foot in neo-boosterism and one in debunking, Quentin Tarantino's *Once upon a Time in Hollywood* (2019) performs a cinematic recovery of a pivotal moment in Los Angeles history. The story of washed-up Hollywood actor Rick Dalton (Leonardo DiCaprio), his student double Cliff Booth (Brad Pitt), and actress Sharon Tate (Margot Robbie), Tarantino's film evokes Hollywood in a transition period in the year 1969. The Tate-LaBianca murders at the hands of Charles Manson's followers in that summer provide what scholars describe as an "impact event": a traumatic historical event that alters public discourse and ushers in new subjectivities.[55] This shift in perception of the counterculture is best described in a passage from Thomas Pynchon's novel *Inherent Vice*, in which the story's hippie hero, detective Doc Sportello, summarizes the impact of Manson to flat-topped, conservative detective Bigfoot Bjornsen: "Well, what I've been noticing since Charlie Manson got popped is a lot less eye contact from the straight world. You folks used to be like a crowd at the zoo—'Oh, look, the male one is carrying the baby and the female one is paying for the groceries' sort of thing, but now it's like, 'pretend they're not even there, 'cause maybe they'll mass murder your ass.'"[56]

Yes, Tarantino's ninth film is *Once upon a Time in Hollywood*, not *Once upon a Time in Los Angeles*—except that the histories of both are so intertwined that the film suggests they are indistinguishable, an overlap that serves as an example of what Edward Soja describes as a a city's third space. *Once upon a Time in Hollywood* casts Los Angeles as a place between "reality and folklore," where "so many fantasies of the frontier have been conceptualized, financed, and played out."[57] Even the film's title, a tip of the hat to Sergio Leone's *Once upon a Time in the West*, alludes to the frontier-like qualities that Los Angeles held in the cultural imagination even in 1969 (and perhaps even fifty years later).

In a city rooted in contradictions—in filmic depictions, antecedent visual forms, and varied expressions of modern-day Angeleno identity—Los Angeles cinema and Los Angeles cinema scholarship offer a corrective in the form of what Norman Klein refers to as "anti-tours": showcasing locations where there had once been something in order to reveal more about the process of preservation and erasure.[58] I would like to end with an anti-tour of my own. One anti-tour stop that exists at a convergence point between Los Angeles film history and pre-cinema Southern California visual culture can be found at the site of Charles Chaplin's first film for Keystone Studios. On Glendale Boulevard in Echo Park, close to where the Glendale Freeway (CA-2) connects to I-5, one passes through the historic region of Edendale: the location of the earliest Los Angeles film studios during the 1910s. At 1728 Glendale Boulevard, at the time of this writing, is Mugshot Coffee Roasters, currently next to a Jack in the Box and across the street from a U-Haul dealer. This was the site of Charlie Chaplin's first on-screen performance: *Making a Living* (Mack

Sennett's Keystone Studios, released early February 1914). He did not appear as his iconic Tramp character in this film, instead playing a wily con artist named Edgar English. Following this performance, Chaplin donned a pair of baggy trousers, bowler hat, cane, and a small mustache for every role until *The Great Dictator* (1940), starting first with *Mabel's Strange Predicament* (1914) and then *Kid Auto Races at Venice* (1914). *Making a Living* was largely shot on a residential street around the corner from Keystone Studios, and as was the case with so many other Sennett slapstick films, this one allowed audiences to explore "unfamiliar territory that was rapidly evolving before their eyes."[59] The Keystone comedies coincided with a period of rapid growth in Los Angeles, and these films, with their car chase scenes around the city, "provided revealing descriptions of the shape of Los Angeles" from "multiple ground-level perspectives" even for those who had never set foot in the city.[60] This cinematic mapping of the city through film is linked to what Mark Shiel identifies as the relationship between visual narration and urban expansion through the increased speed of travel, rooted in a fundamental relationship between Southern California photographers and the railroad companies that facilitated Los Angeles's construction during the Progressive Era.

The early years of cinema were marked by technological advances in established practices of pre-cinema visual culture during the twentieth century—visual spectacle forms that are linked to industrialization, a reconfiguration of notions about spatial relationships (including, as we have seen with Los Angeles's development, urban planning), and advancements in aesthetic and narrative strategies for the stories that we tell about ourselves. Yet even as films became more advanced (and eventually started to speak), nineteenth-century visual culture continued to provide a well from which filmmakers and exhibitors could draw to be even more revolutionary: matte paintings that combined artistic styles with the principles of optical illusions and camera lenses and technology to accommodate the panoramic form, for example. What is interesting about this relationship between film and pre-cinema visual culture is that it flourished in Los Angeles in explicit connection to the symbiotic growth between the city and its movie industry. As multimedia organizations, the early Los Angeles studios employed thousands and created a multitude of businesses designed to cater to the needs of the studios. Los Angeles served as an experimental space for innovations in marketing, distribution, and exhibition. Architecture movements such as modernism and California eclectic took their cue from motion pictures' principles of art design, similarly to how Craftsman bungalows and other turn-of-the-century Southern California dwellings are wedded, in varying degrees, to notions of healthy living promoted visually and viscerally through pre-Hollywood visual culture. It is no accident then that the design of Los Angeles during the period of its burgeoning film industry from roughly 1907 to 1920 was based around movement rather than monumentality—a distinguishing characteristic that would, as scholars have observed, set the tone for urban development during the postwar years.

While the early filmmakers may have been "sun seekers" in varying degrees, they relocated to Lummis's "Land of Sunshine" and McGroarty's "Land of Heart's Desire" in response to a visual culture that had already demonstrated the economic opportunities afforded through narrative visual mythmaking. In response, Southern California hosted a reinvention of the studio form that began in places like New Jersey and Paris during the late 1890s, and Los Angeles grew to meet the new industry's demands. By the end of the Progressive Era, the economic role that cinema played in Los Angeles directly impacted most of the other components of the city's social and cultural aspects—a relationship that not only continues today but also provides a privileged site for the retrieval of cultural and historical memory.

Historical Timeline

1781

El Pueblo de Nuestra Señora la Reina de Los Angeles is founded by a party led by explorer Gaspar de Portolá during a period of Spanish colonization.

1786

Jean-Louis-Robert Prevost produces one of California's first known nature drawings.

1816

Louis (Ludwig) Choris paints *Indian of California*, an early California example of art as an ethnographic study.

1818

Mikhail T. Tikhanov paints *Balthazar*—a depiction of California's Miwok Indians.

1821

Louis Daguerre designs the diorama theater with Charles Marie Bouton. This would serve as the prototype for painted panorama exhibition halls through the century.

1846

John Banvard debuts his *Mississippi from the Mouth of the Missouri to New Orleans* panorama, which would go on to tour nationally and internationally.

1850

California achieves statehood.

1851

Land Act is passed in California, raising property taxes on Southern California ranchos (such as San Pedro, La Brea, Los Feliz, and Santa Monica), a form of disenfranchisement of the state's Mexican population, leading to a decline of Hispanic cultural heritage sites.

Daguerreotypes of the San Francisco Bay produced, inaugurating photography in California.

Robert Vance's *Views of California* exhibited, featuring three hundred full-plate daguerreotypes of San Francisco and California gold country.

Carleton Watkins arrives in California.

1852

John Wesley Jones's *Pantoscope of California* exhibited, drawing upon fifteen hundred daguerreotypes in its creation.

1864

Carleton Watkins's first continuous panorama photography—*San Francisco from Nob Hill*—produced.

1866

First attempts by the Southern Pacific Railroad Company to construct a line through the Tehachapi Mountains.

1871

Timothy O'Sullivan joins the Army Corp of Engineers on an expedition through the American Southwest (the Wheeler Expedition).

1872

Exposition Park established in Los Angeles, originally named Agricultural Park.

1873

Charles Nordhoff publishes *California for Health, Pleasure, and Residence*.

1876

H. T. Payne's *Semi-Tropical California* and *Southern California Scenery* published.

A set of 180 photographs of O'Sullivan's Southwest photography displayed at the Philadelphia Centennial Exposition.

1877

Carleton Watkins documents the Southern Pacific's Tehachapi Loop using panoramic photography.

1878

Eadweard Muybridge produces the second of his series of San Francisco panoramas.

Archduke of Austria Ludwig Salvator publishes *Eine Blume aus dem Goldenen Lande oder Los Angeles/A Flower from the Golden Land, or Los Angeles*.

1880

Population of Los Angeles reaches 11,183.

1882

Thomas A. Gary's *Orange Culture* in California is published.

1884

Helen Hunt Jackson's novel *Ramona* is published.

Charles Fletcher Lummis arrives in Southern California.

1885

The Southern Pacific Railroad Company reduces its fares from the East Coast to Southern California by two-thirds.

William Andrew Spalding publishes *The Orange: Its Culture in California*.

1887

The Los Angeles Panorama Company opens a diorama building on South Main Street with its debut spectacle, *The Siege of Paris* (Felix Phillippoteaux, 1870–71).

Another panorama exhibition hall is constructed in Washington Gardens (South Main and Washington Boulevard) incorporating the park's natural setting into the artist's spectacle.

Transfer of real estate in Los Angeles County rises to $95 million (up from $28 million the previous year).

1888

Bryon Martin Lelong publishes *A Treatise on Citrus Culture in California*.

Southern Pacific Railroad Company partners with the California State Board of
   Trade to send promotional railcars ("California on Wheels") to cities east
   of the Rocky Mountains.
Charles Fletcher Lummis and Company publishes *The Home of Ramona*.

1890
Population of Los Angeles reaches 50,395.
First Tournament of Roses Parade held in Pasadena.

1891
Burbank Theater Building opens in downtown Los Angeles and starts publishing
   the *Weekly Los Angeles Theatrical and Amusement Guide*.

1893
Columbia Exposition held in Chicago.

1894
Land of Sunshine magazine founded.
First permanent display of paintings by the Los Angeles Chamber of Commerce.

1895
Society of Fine Arts in California formed.

1896
T. L. Tally opens a film exhibition parlor on Spring Street in downtown Los
   Angeles.

1898
Edison short film *South Spring Street, Los Angeles, California* shot in the down-
   town area. This actuality film is believed to be the first motion picture shot in
   Los Angeles.
Henry E. Huntington and Isais Hellman form the Los Angeles Railways.

1900
Population of Los Angeles reaches nearly 102,000.
Lou V. Chapin's *Artwork in Southern California* photographic box set released.

1902

T. L. Tally opens the Electric Theater (later renamed the Lyric Theater) on Third and Main.

First photographic salon in Southern California established.

Land of Sunshine renamed *Out West* magazine.

1903

The Historical Society of Southern California releases the *Los Angeles and Southern California Photo Album.*

Rafu Shimpo launched in the Little Tokyo District of downtown Los Angeles, reporting on film exhibition and film culture to Los Angeles's Japanese American population.

1904

J. L. Berthon architecture company releases *Our Architecture* photo album.

1906

Tally's Broadway Theater opens on Broadway and Spring.

California Art Club formed in Pasadena by painter William Wendt.

The Painters Club formed.

Views and Films Index established.

Los Angeles Stereopticon and Film Exchange begins operations in downtown Los Angeles.

1907

The Count of Monte Cristo filmed in Southern California and released the following year by Selig Polyscope, directed by Francis Boggs and starring Hobart Bosworth as Edmond Dantes.

Moving Picture World established.

1908

Motion Picture Patent Company agreement signed by Edison, Biograph, Vitagraph, Essanay, Selig Polyscope, Lubin Manufacturing, Kalem Company, Star Film Paris, and American Pathé.

1909

Selig Polyscope shoots *The Heart of a Race Tout* using the drying yards of Sing
  Lee's Chinese Laundry (751 South Olive Street between Seventh and Eighth
  Streets).
Selig Polyscope's Pacific Coast Studio established in Edendale, Los Angeles.
Charles Fletcher Lummis leaves the editorial board of *Out West*, and the maga-
  zine becomes a promotional arm of the Los Angeles Chamber of Commerce.
Tally's Electric Theater begins operating as *Teatro Electrico* in order to attract
  Spanish-speaking audiences.

1910

D. W. Griffith directs the first film adaptation of *Ramona*.
F. H. Richardson's *Motion Picture Handbook: A Guide for Managers and Operators
  of Motion Picture Theaters* published.

1911

Nestor Film Studios established at the Blondeau Tavern at Sunset and Gower
  in Hollywood.
John S. McGroarty writes *The Mission Play*. Between its first performance in
  1912 and its final performance in 1929, the three-hour play was seen by an
  estimated 2.5 million people.

1912

Mack Sennett establishes the Keystone Studios in Edendale, Los Angeles.
Biograph, Kalem, Bison, and American Pathé establish studios in Los Angeles.
Teatro Metropolitan established in downtown Los Angeles.

1913

Selig Zoo opens in Lincoln Heights.
The Los Angeles Museum created in Exposition Park (later renamed the Natural
  History Museum of Los Angeles County).
Photoplayers Club of Los Angeles founded.

1914

Moving Picture Stars Art Stamp Album published.
The Hearst-Selig News Pictorial premieres.

1915

Selig Polyscope runs *The Movie Special* train from Chicago to California and
back again.

Panama Pacific International Exposition held in San Francisco from February 20
to December 4.

Theodore Payne plants a wild garden in Exposition Park, drawing on the California horticulture techniques of Francesco Franceschi.

1916

Robert E. Welsh publishes *A-B-C of Motion Pictures*.

The Christie Studios Film produced, one of the earliest examples of studio tour
films.

1917

The Los Angeles–based motion picture industry consolidates and becomes the
most effective marketing tool for California real estate and land development.

First National establishes a Spanish adobe–inspired studio in Los Angeles.

The Mexican Revolution ends, though sporadic violence associated with the conflict continues into the 1920s.

Behind the Scenes, Mack Sennett Studios produced.

1920

First National releases its city symphony *Los Angeles, ca. 1920*.

The Romance of Motion Picture Production by Lee Royal published.

Thomas H. Ince Studios film produced.

75–80 percent of American films are made in Los Angeles.

1921

The California Water Color Society formed in Los Angeles.

Chouinard Art Institute founded by Nelbert Murphy Chouinard near present-
day McArthur Park.

The use of "Hollywood" as a stand-in for the movie industry at large is used for
the first time in an edition of *Photoplay*.

Spandena House of Beverly Hills built by art director Harry Oliver.

1922

The "Los Angeles Plan" created, sponsored by the City of Los Angeles with the
    advertised aim of historical conservation.
Frank Lloyd Wright finishes construction on the Barnsdale Park Hollyhock
    House.
Rudolph Schindler completes the King's Road House.

1923

Exhibition from the Group of Independent Artists of Los Angeles—a "united
    front for the new forms," including cubism, dynamism, and expressionism.

1924

Guz Aguila, a revista librettist, exiled to Los Angeles.
Frank Lloyd Wright completes the Ennis House in the Hollywood Hills.

1925

5 million daily movie admissions on average.

1926

Rudolph Valentino: His Romantic Life and Death by Ben Allah published.
A Million and One Nights: A History of the Motion Picture by Terry Ramsaye
    published.
Art director Cedric Gibbons constructs Louis B. Mayer's Santa Monica home in
    the Spanish Colonial style.

1929

The All-Year-Round Club of California, a marketing arm of the Los Angeles
    Chamber of Commerce (renamed the Greater Los Angeles Visitors Bureau
    in 1958), publishes *Southern California through the Camera*, with international
    distribution.
Teatro Capitol, formerly the Casino Theater, established in downtown Los
    Angeles.
Richard Neutra's Lovell Health House in the Hollywood Hills is completed.

1930

Population of Los Angeles rises to 1.2 million.

Hollywood studios employ over fifteen thousand people, paying $72.1 million in annual salaries.

Hollywood studios report $129.3 million in ticket sales.

1932

David Alfaro Siqueros completes La América Tropical near Olvera Street, downtown Los Angeles.

Construction on Carl Lammle's Universal Pictures Building at Hollywood and Vine, designed by Richard Nuetra, is completed.

1937

William M. Pizor produces *A Street of Memory*, a vericolor film of historical Olvera Street in downtown Los Angeles.

Notes

Introduction

1 Davis, *City of Quartz*, 25.

2 Though there is little evidence to support this view, it features notably in Carey McWilliam's influential book *Southern California: An Island on Land* (1946), in which he describes the "movie camps" as being regarded as a "troublesome, harum-scarum lot" and an "unmitigated nuisance."

3 McWilliams, *Southern California*, 330.

4 Also known as the Edison Trust, this trust of major film companies (including Edison, Biograph, Essanay, Selig Polyscope, and Kalem), film distributors, and film stock suppliers was created in 1908 and disbanded in 1915.

5 The exceptional work of Mark Shiel, Andrew A. Erish, and Eileen Bowser in particular has debunked the "escape from patent agents" explanation.

6 Davis, *Ecology of Fear*, 12.

7 As early as 1910, publications like *Moving Picture World* described Southern California's shooting conditions in these terms. For further reading, see Hallett, *Go West, Young Women!* and Shiel, *Hollywood Cinema and the Real Los Angeles*.

8 Jacobson, *Studios Before the System*, 169.

9 Shiel, *Hollywood Cinema and the Real Los Angeles*, 20.

10 Keil, *Early American Cinema in Transition*, 6.

11 Scott, *On Hollywood*, 3.

12 Karlstrom, "Los Angeles in the 1940s," 302.

13 Davis, *City of Quartz*, 20.

14 Ibid., 34.

15 Brook, *Land of Smoke and Mirrors*, 11.

16 Klein, *The History of Forgetting*, 10.
17 Banham, *Los Angeles*, 19–20.
18 Ibid., 83.
19 Ibid., 143.
20 Ibid., 203.
21 For further reading, see Starr, *Inventing the Dream*.
22 Ivakhiv, *Ecologies of the Moving Image*, 35.
23 Ibid., 32.
24 For recent explorations, see Harrison, *From Steam to Stream*.
25 Bruno, *Atlas of Emotion*, 178.
26 McManus, "A Focus on Light," 11.
27 Gunning, "The Cinema of Attractions," 384.
28 For further reading, see Anderson, *Imagined Communities*.
29 Fine, *Imagining Los Angeles*, 19.

Chapter 1

1 The All-Year-Round Club, founded in 1921 by real estate mogul and general manager of the *Los Angeles Times* Harry Chandler and managed by the Los Angeles Chamber of Commerce, aimed at promoting tourism in the region. The organization was later renamed the Greater Los Angeles Visitors and Convention Bureau. All-Year-Round Club, *Southern California through the Camera*.
2 Hise, *Magnetic Los Angeles*, 9.
3 Wolfe, "California Landscapes," 212.
4 Scott, *On Hollywood*, 16.
5 Rositzka, *Cinematic Corpographies*, 5.
6 Conley, *Cartographic Cinema*, 22.
7 Bruno, *Atlas of Emotion*, 178.
8 For further reading, see Rositzka, *Cinematic Corpographies*.
9 The cinematic cartography performed in *The Searchers* was effectively rendered in Douglas Gordon's 1995 art installation *Five Year Drive By*, in which the film was projected on a screen amid the landscape of the American Southwest, at one frame per forty-five minutes. The result was a film journey that spanned the five-year length of the film's events.
10 Sandweiss, *Print the Legend*, 54.
11 Sometimes referred to as "American Eden" painting, the Hudson River School of the early nineteenth century infused American landscapes with

mythic and celestial metaphors. Influenced by European Romanticism, Hudson River School artists like Albert Bierstadt and Frederic Edwin Church drew inspiration from the writings of Emerson and Thoreau and presented American landscapes layered with a language of emotion and rooted in concepts of American destiny.

12 Tyler Green's *Carleton Watkins: Making the West America* has been a welcome contribution to the exploration of Watkins's Southern California photography and work with the Southern Pacific.

13 Marshall, "Negative Appeal with Vincent Brook."

14 Shiel, *Hollywood Cinema and the Real Los Angeles*, 23.

15 Hornby, *Still Modernism*, 14.

16 McCarroll, *California Dreaming*, 11.

17 Fine, *Imagining Los Angeles*, 5.

18 Sandweiss, *Print the Legend*, 20.

19 Comment, *The Panorama*, 18.

20 Oettermann, *The Panorama*, 66.

21 Olsson, *Los Angeles Before Hollywood*, 102.

22 Washington Gardens was later renamed Chutes Park and then Luna Park at the corner of South Main and Washington Boulevard in downtown Los Angeles.

23 Olsson, *Los Angeles Before Hollywood*, 16.

24 Sandweiss, *Print the Legend*, 54.

25 Shiel, *Hollywood Cinema and the Real Los Angeles*, 23.

26 Novak, *Realism, Photography, and Nineteenth-Century Fiction*, 14.

27 Nickel, *Carleton Watkins*, 26.

28 Green, *Carleton Watkins*, 84.

29 Additionally, Watkins would shoot panorama photographs of Portland, Oregon and Salt Lake City, Utah around this time, as single images and with connected large plates.

30 Nickel, *Carleton Watkins*, 26.

31 Ibid., 22.

32 Brevern, "Two or Three Things Photography Did to Painting," 105.

33 Bronfen, *Specters of War*, 20.

34 Virilio, *War and Cinema*, 69.

35 Stam, Burgoyne, and Flitterman-Lewis, *New Vocabularies in Film Semiotics*, 12.

36 Latsis, "The City View(ed)," 204.

37 Gunning, "The Cinema of Attractions," 225.

38 Latsis, "The City View(ed)," 203.

39 Ibid., 204.

40 McWilliams, *Southern California*, 5.

41 Sandweiss, *Print the Legend*, 92.

42 Ibid., 166.

43 Green, *Carleton Watkins*, 327.

44 Ibid., 332.

45 Quoted in Shiel, *Hollywood Cinema and the Real Los Angeles*, 23.

46 Green, *Carleton Watkins*, 334

47 Rubin, *Impressionism and the Modern Landscape*, 17.

48 Green, *Carleton Watkins*, 328.

49 Fogelson, *The Fragmented Metropolis*, 67.

50 Shiel, *Hollywood Cinema and the Real Los Angeles*, 20.

51 Davis, *Timothy H. O'Sullivan*, 83.

52 Huntington Library Special Collections, Pasadena, CA.

53 Davis, *Timothy H. O'Sullivan*, 89.

54 Braddock and Kusserow, *Nature's Nation*, 20.

55 Quoted in ibid.

56 For further reading, see Sandweiss, *Print the Legend*.

57 For further reading, see Hariman and Lucaites, *No Caption Needed*.

58 Quoted in McKinney, "Nordhoff Peak Is Challenge."

59 Huntington Library Special Collections, Pasadena, CA.

60 *Scientific American*, November 25, 1876, 337.

61 Warner, *Our Italy*, 12.

62 Mission San Fernando Rey de España is presently Mission San Fernando in Mission Hills, San Fernando Valley. Mission San Gabriel Arcángel is presently Mission San Gabriel, situated near the incorporated cities of Alhambra, Monterey Park, and San Marino in the San Gabriel Valley near Pasadena.

63 McWilliams, *Southern California*, 49.

64 Ibid., 65.

65 Verhoeff, "Virtual Museums."

66 For further reading, see Crary, *Techniques of the Observer*.

67 Shiel, *Hollywood Cinema and the Real Los Angeles*, 23.

68 Ibid.

69 Actuality films were short, nonfiction films that depicted real, and often unstaged, events, places, and people. This form of filmmaking is considered a predecessor to documentary filmmaking.

70 Watts, "Photography in the Land of Sunshine," 343.

71 Ibid., 345.

72 Ibid.

73 Ibid., 350.

74 See Benjamin, "A Short History of Photography."

75 McCarroll, *California Dreaming*, 12.

76 Pollack, *Edward Weston Papers*, 4.

77 Weston, *Seeing California*, 56.

78 Shiel, *Hollywood Cinema and the Real Los Angeles*, 24.

79 Gray, *Ansel Adams*, 34.

80 Hornby, *Still Modernism*, 14.

81 Shiel, *Hollywood Cinema and the Real Los Angeles*, 24.

82 James, *The Most Typical Avant-Garde*, 10.

83 For further reading, see Brewster and Jacobs, *Theater to Cinema*.

84 McCarroll, *California Dreaming*, 26.

85 Described in Clarke, *Early Film Making in Los Angeles*, 17, available through UCLA Film and Television Archive, Los Angeles.

86 Edison Actualities archived by the Library of Congress, Washington, DC. Accessed as part of the UCLA Film and Television Archive, Los Angeles.

87 Chute's Park, often described as a "a forerunner to Disneyland," is on Washington Boulevard between Main and Figueroa Streets.

88 Keil, *Early American Cinema in Transition*, 6.

89 Shiel, *Hollywood Cinema and the Real Los Angeles*, 70.

90 Bengstrom, *Silent Traces*, 259.

91 Olsson, *Los Angeles Before Hollywood*, 71.

92 The Kinema Theatre would also host the West Coast premiere of *The Jazz Singer* in 1927.

93 Fine, *Imagining Los Angeles*, 53.

94 *Southern California Holiday*.

Chapter 2

 1 Cinemagraphic Division curriculum and course information pack (1967), Special Collections Archive, California Arts Institute, Valencia, CA.

 2 William Hurtz (1919–2000) was trained at Chouinard Art Institute from 1932 to 1938. He would later work as an animator for Disney (notably on *Pinocchio* and *Fantasia*) and for the U.S. military during World War II. He is also notable for his work with Saul Bass on title sequences, including

Anatomy of a Murder, Psycho, Ocean's Eleven, and *Around the World in 80 Days*.

3 Mary Blair (1911–78) was a Disney animator known primarily for her work on *Alice in Wonderland, Peter Pan, The Three Caballeros*, and *Lady and the Tramp*. Additionally, Blair was the lead character designer for Disneyland's It's a Small World ride. Maurice Noble (1911–2001) was an animator, production designer, and background artist for Disney and for Warner Bros., known primarily for her work with Chuck Jones on characters like Bugs Bunny, Daffy Duck, Road Runner, and Wile E. Coyote.

4 McManus, "A Focus on Light," 11.

5 Here, it is important to note that the term "watercolor" will be used to apply to the art form and technique, whereas the separated "Water Color" will be used to describe this society.

6 James, *The Most Typical Avant-Garde*.

7 Luminist style refers to landscape painting of the mid-nineteenth century that considered the impact of light on natural settings.

8 Jones, *Twilight and Reverie*, 1.

9 The term *tonalism* originated with Wanda Corn's 1972 *The Color of Mood*.

10 Jones, *Twilight and Reverie*, 2.

11 Landauer, *California Impressionists*, 12.

12 Stern and Siple, *California Light*, 21.

13 Landauer, *California Impressionists*, 11.

14 Stern, "The California Impressionist Style in Perspective," 74.

15 Starr, *Inventing the Dream*, 120.

16 Ibid., 121.

17 Ibid., 122.

18 *The Land of Sunshine: The Magazine of California and the West*, November 1898.

19 Watts, "Photography in the Land of Sunshine," 341.

20 Klein, *The History of Forgetting*, 10.

21 Payne, *Composition of Outdoor Painting*, 16.

22 The lid of the box was the easel itself, and in the box were the palette, brushes, and paint tubes. Fastened to the bottom of the box were the easel's legs, which were collapsible.

23 See Bazin, "The Ontology of the Photographic Image."

24 Starr, *Inventing the Dream*, 120.

25 Browne, "Some Recent Landscapes by William Wendt," 257.

26 For further reading, see McWilliams, *Southern California*.

27 Landauer, *California Impressionists*, 29.

28 Riley, *Color Codes*, 72.

29 Street and Yumibe, *Chromatic Modernity*, 25.

30 Alton, *Painting with Light*, 119.

31 Gordon T. McClelland and Jay T. Last, for example, have published studies and printed collections of California-based fruit box labels dating from the 1880s to the 1950s, not only providing valuable insight into California cultural history but also illustrating the prominence of these colors in the visual marketing of California life during this time period—with over fourteen hundred labels presented in these collections. See *Fruit Box Labels* (1995) and *California Orange Box Labels: An Illustrated History* (1985). Additionally, see Davidson, *Fruit Crate Art*.

32 Landauer, *California Impressionists*, 29.

33 Farmer, *Trees in Paradise*, 129.

34 Quoted in ibid., 135.

35 Ibid., 133.

36 Brook, *Land of Smoke and Mirrors*, 10.

37 Sandberg, "Location, Location," 28.

38 Brook, *Land of Smoke and Mirrors*, 12.

39 Boym, *The Future of Nostalgia*, 14.

40 Moure, "The Struggle for a Los Angeles Art Museum," 247.

41 Ibid., 248.

42 Ibid., 249.

43 Out West 1, no. 1 (1911): 222, archive.org.

44 Schad, "An Art-Hungry People," 21.

45 Ibid., 328.

46 Seares, "William Wendt," 232.

47 Terry, "Moving Pictures and the Deaf," 154.

48 *A Tour of the Thomas H. Ince Studios*.

49 Courtesy of the Hobart Bosworth Collection, Margaret Herrick Library, Beverly Hills, CA.

50 Landauer, *California Impressionists*, 16.

51 *Los Angeles Times*, October 11, 1908, 3.

52 Ibid.

53 *Los Angeles Times*, October 1914.

54 Keyes, "From Giverny to Laguna Beach," 51.

55 Ibid.
56 Stern, "The California Impressionist Style," 78.
57 Irvine Art Museum (imca.uci.edu).
58 Hernendez, Cone, and Calahan, "How *Plein Air* Painting Influences the Movie Industry."
59 Stern, *Windows in Time*, 45.
60 Ibid.
61 Chouinard Art Institute course catalogue (1935–36), Special Collections Archive, California Institute of Arts, Valencia, CA.
62 Chouinard Art Institute course catalogue (1939), Special Collections Archive, California Institute of Arts, Valencia, CA.
63 McClelland and Last, *The California Style*, 27.
64 Ibid., 7.
65 Ibid., 10.
66 Ibid., 11.
67 Keil, *Early American Cinema in Transition*, 6.
68 For further reading, see McClelland and Last, *The California Style*; McClelland, *Emil Kosa Jr.*
69 McClelland, *Emil Kosa Jr.*, 43.
70 Stern, *Windows in Time*, 162.
71 Tweedie, "The Painted Backing and Its Afterlives."
72 Tweedie, *Moving Pictures, Still Lives*, 1.
73 Rothman, "Film, Modernity, Cavell," 316.
74 Karlstrom, "Los Angeles in the 1940s," 306.
75 Ibid., 314.
76 Ibid., 315.
77 Ibid., 314.
78 Wendt letter to McCrea, May 5, 1901, available from the Laguna Beach Art Museum archives.
79 Davis, *City of Quartz*, 33.
80 Hackman, *Out of Sight*, 20.
81 Ibid.
82 For further reading, see Bahr, *Weimar on the Pacific*.
83 Russeth, "The Los Angeles Home that Defined Modern Art."
84 Hackman, *Out of Sight*, 3.
85 Quoted in Levin, *Synchromism and American Color Abstraction*, 14.
86 Quoted in ibid., 47.

87 Davis, *City of Quartz*, 33.
88 Wright, *Modern Painting*.
89 Alton, *Painting with Light*, 156.
90 Anderson, *Modern Spirit*.
91 Ibid.

Chapter 3

1 Lent, "The Dark Side of the Dream," 337.
2 Davis, *Ecology of Fear*, 205.
3 Stanley, "In the Country of the Dream."
4 Wolfe, "California Landscapes," 213.
5 Starr, *Inventing the Dream*, 143.
6 Afra, "Seventeen Happy Days in Hollywood," 201.
7 Gunning, "The Cinema of Attractions," 386.
8 All-Year-Round Club of California, *Southern California through the Camera*.
9 Sandberg, "Location, Location," 28.
10 Ibid.
11 Kirk, "Picturing California," 358.
12 Ibid., 361.
13 Farmer, *Trees in Paradise*, 335.
14 Ibid., 230.
15 Adamson, *Eichler*, 154.
16 Spaulding and Hope quoted in Starr, *Inventing the Dream*, 142.
17 Farmer, *Trees in Paradise*, 357.
18 Klein, *The History of Forgetting*, 28.
19 Starr, *Inventing the Dream*, 26.
20 Nordhoff, *California*, 56, 22, 249, 194.
21 See McWilliams, *Southern California*, 142.
22 Salvator, *Eine Blume aus dem Goldenen Lande oder Los Angeles*, 61.
23 Lummis, *A Tramp across the Continent*, 269.
24 Starr, *Inventing the Dream*, 92.
25 Kilston, *Sun Seekers*, 46.
26 Bingham, *Charles F. Lummis*; Starr, *Inventing the Dream*, 125.
27 Klein, *The History of Forgetting*, 29.
28 Fine, *Imagining Los Angeles*, 5.
29 *Land of Sunshine*, June 1895, 164.
30 *Land of Sunshine*, November 1895, 254.

31 Ibid., 262.

32 Davis, "Landscapes of Imagination," 173.

33 Klein, *The History of Forgetting*, 28.

34 Camp, "From Nuisance to Nostalgia," 82.

35 For further reading, see Hendricks, *Albert Bierstadt*.

36 Farmer, *Trees in Paradise*, 357.

37 Ibid., 374.

38 Davis, *Ecology of Fear*, 203.

39 Camp, "From Nuisance to Nostalgia," 86.

40 Ibid., 84.

41 Ibid., 81.

42 Ibid., 92.

43 Ibid., 86.

44 Farmer, *Trees in Paradise*, 386.

45 Duncan, King, and Kirkpatrick, "Romance without Responsibilities," 123.

46 Verheoff, "Virtual Museums," 346.

47 For further reading on Aby Warburg's notion of pathos formula, see Bronfen, *Specters of War*.

48 Camp, "From Nuisance to Nostalgia," 86.

49 Ibid.

50 Davis, "Landscapes of Imagination," 178.

51 Erish, *Col. William N. Selig*, 80.

52 Ibid.; Hallett, *Go West, Young Women!*, 7.

53 Francis Boggs to W. N. Selig, August 16, 1909, from the collections of the Margaret Herrick Library, Academy of Motion Picture Arts and Sciences, Beverly Hills, CA.

54 Erish, *Col. William N. Selig*, 5.

55 Ibid., 10.

56 Ibid., 82.

57 Ibid., 87.

58 Ibid.

59 Jacobson, "Fantastic Functionality," 54.

60 Erish, *Col. William N. Selig*, 56.

61 Quoted in ibid.

62 Quoted in ibid., 88.

63 Ibid., 140.

64 Afra, "Seventeen Happy Days in Hollywood," 201.

65 Shiel, *Hollywood Cinema and the Real Los Angeles*, 36.

66 Bean, "The Imagination of Early Hollywood."

67 Scott, *On Hollywood*, 138.

Chapter 4

1 All-Year-Round Club of California, *Southern California through the Camera*, 2.

2 Ibid., 43.

3 *Los Angeles Times*, February 21, 1926, B7.

4 Gunckel, Horak, and Jarvinen, *Cinema between Latin America and Los Angeles*, 1.

5 McWilliams, *Southern California*, 65.

6 DeLyser, "Ramona Memories," 886.

7 Fine, *Imagining Los Angeles*, 17.

8 DeLyser, "Ramona Memories," 903.

9 Fine, *Imagining Los Angeles*, 5.

10 DeLyser, "Ramona Memories," 888.

11 McWilliams, *Southern California*, 73.

12 DeLyser, "Ramona Memories," 895.

13 Ibid., 894.

14 Ibid., 902.

15 Brook, *Land of Smoke and Mirrors*, 48.

16 DeLyser, "Ramona Memories," 889.

17 Ibid., 889.

18 Ibid., 888.

19 Fine, *Imagining Los Angeles*, 36.

20 Quoted in Shiel, *Hollywood Cinema and the Real Los Angeles*, 52.

21 Starr, *Inventing the Dream*, 292; Brook, *Land of Smoke and Mirrors*, 44.

22 Quoted in Brook, *Land of Smoke and Mirrors*, 54.

23 Shiel, *Hollywood Cinema and the Real Los Angeles*, 51.

24 Brook, *Land of Smoke and Mirrors*, 52.

25 Ibid., 53.

26 Ibid., 54.

27 Fine, *Imagining Los Angeles*, 34.

28 Shiel, *Hollywood Cinema and the Real Los Angeles*, 37.

29 Quoted in Garcia, "Ramona in the City," 51; Lent, "The Dark Side of the Dream," 329.

30 Garcia, "Ramona in the City," 51.

31 Ibid., 52.
32 Curtis, "The First Theater in California," 479.
33 Starr, *Inventing the Dream*, 86.
34 Ibid., 88.
35 Quoted in McWilliams, *Southern California*, 78.
36 Ovnick, "The Mark of Zorro," 47.
37 Fine, *Imagining Los Angeles*, 17; Venis, "L.A. Novels and the Hollywood Dream Factory," 349.
38 Lent, "The Dark Side of the Dream," 337.
39 Theisen, "Meet Screen Show's Granddaddy," 27.
40 *Moving Picture World*, December 4, 1915.
41 Schumach, "T. L. Tally."
42 Gunckel, *Mexico on Main Street*, 17.
43 Ibid.
44 Ibid., 29.
45 Ibid., 35.
46 Ibid., 15.
47 Ibid., 42.
48 Avila, "El Espectáculo," 31.
49 Ibid., 35.
50 Quoted in Brook, *Land of Smoke and Mirrors*, 12.
51 Williams, "The Bridges of Los Angeles County," 62.

Chapter 5
1 For further reading, see Anderson, *Imagined Communities*.
2 Quoted in Scott, *On Hollywood*, 188.
3 Olsson, *Los Angeles Before Hollywood*, 65.
4 Hallett, *Go West, Young Women!*, 13.
5 Quoted in Brook, *Land of Smoke and Mirrors*, 5.
6 McWilliams, *Southern California*, 13.
7 Fearing, "Outside the Studio Gates," 102.
8 McWilliams, *Southern California*, 330.
9 Ibid., 345.
10 Klein, *The History of Forgetting*, 27.
11 Brook *Land of Smoke and Mirrors*, 19.
12 Quoted in Olsson, *Los Angeles Before Hollywood*, 76.
13 Ibid., 94.

14 *Moving Picture World*, August 14, 1915.

15 *Los Angeles Theatrical and Amusement Guide*, 2.

16 Olsson, *Los Angeles Before Hollywood*, 116.

17 Los Angeles Stereopticon and Film Exchange distribution contract, Selig Polyscope Collection, Margaret Herrick Library, Academy of Motion Picture Arts and Sciences, Beverly Hills, CA.

18 Kosmik Film Service contracton, Selig Polyscope Collection, Margaret Herrick Library, Academy of Motion Picture Arts and Sciences, Beverly Hills, CA.

19 Motion Picture Archives, Seaver Center, Natural History Museum of Los Angeles County, Los Angeles.

20 Hallett *Go West, Young Women!*, 115.

21 Ibid., 15.

22 Ibid., 48.

23 Ibid., 144.

24 Ibid., 13.

25 Quoted in ibid., 151.

26 Motion Picture Archives, Seaver Center, Natural History Museum of Los Angeles County, Los Angeles.

27 Gunckel, *Mexico on Main Street*, 31.

28 Kanellos, "A Brief History of Hispanic Periodicals," 37.

29 Avila, "El Espectáculo," 35. The newspaper is still in publication today

30 Ogihara, "The Exhibition of Films for Japanese Americans," 81.

31 Ibid., 82.

32 *Rafu Shimpo*, July 1, 1917–April 30, 1935, available on microfilm through the Los Angeles County Library.

33 Ogihara, "The Exhibition of Films for Japanese Americans," 87.

34 Welsh, *A-B-C of Motion Pictures*, 12.

35 Royal, *The Romance of Motion Picture Production*, 8–10.

36 Ramsaye's book is available at the Margaret Herrick Library, Academy of Motion Picture Arts and Sciences, Beverly Hills, CA.

37 Famous Players–Lasky Corporation, *The Story of Famous Players Lasky*, 22.

38 Clarke, *Early Film Making*, 29.

39 Knutson, "Reviewed Works," 534.

40 Clarke, *Early Film Making in Los Angeles*, 29.

41 The Zamorano Club, advertised as one of the oldest organizations of "bibliophiles and manuscript collectors" in Southern California, was founded

in 1928. It sponsors public lectures and publications on a variety of topics. Founded in 1946, the Corral of Westerners hosts events and sponsors publications to promote the study and understanding of American western history.

42 Hall, "Oh Pioneers!" 188.
43 Clarke, *Early Film Making in Los Angeles*, 53.
44 Scott, *On Hollywood*, 11.
45 Motion Picture Archives. Seaver Center, Natural History Museum of Los Angeles County, Los Angeles.
46 Fogelson, *The Fragmented Metropolis*, 127.
47 Motion Picture Archives, Seaver Center, Natural History Museum of Los Angeles County, Los Angeles.
48 Afra, "Seventeen Happy Days in Hollywood," 200.
49 Gray, *Show Sold Separately*, 81.
50 Afra, "Seventeen Happy Days in Hollywood," 199.
51 Ibid., 200.
52 Erish, *Col. William N. Selig*, 153.
53 Ibid., 155.
54 Ibid., 156.
55 Shiel, *Hollywood Cinema and the Real Los Angeles*, 65.
56 Gray, *Show Sold Separately*, 81.
57 Klinger, *Beyond the Multiplex*, 100.
58 Sandberg, "Location, Location," 52.
59 Ibid., 24.
60 Banham, *Los Angeles*, 109.

Chapter 6

1 Albrecht, *Designing Dreams*, xii.
2 James, *The Most Typical Avant-Garde*, 9.
3 Fine, *Imagining Los Angeles*, 19.
4 Quoted in ibid.
5 Karlstrom, "Los Angeles in the 1940s," 302.
6 West, *The Day of the Locust*, 9.
7 Banham, *Los Angeles*, 43.
8 Quoted in Adamson, *Eichler*, 74.
9 Jacobson, "Fantastic Functionality," 53.
10 Ibid., 52

11 Ibid., 53.

12 Ovnick, "The Mark of Zorro," 32.

13 Adamson, *Eichler*, 154.

14 Ibid., 74.

15 Ovnick, "The Mark of Zorro," 28.

16 Ibid., 34.

17 Ibid., 35.

18 Shiel, *Hollywood Cinema and the Real Los Angeles*, 70.

19 Carr, Los Angeles, 271.

20 Ovnick, "The Mark of Zorro," 29.

21 Banham, *Los Angeles*, 95.

22 Hobart, "Life within a Fairy Tale."

23 Berg, "Louis B. Mayer," 144–45.

24 Shiel, *Hollywood Cinema and the Real Los Angeles*, 170.

25 Famous Players–Lasky Corporation, *The Story of Famous Players Lasky*, 2.

26 Albrecht, *Designing Dreams*, 89.

27 Ibid., 90.

28 Ibid., 92.

29 Banham, *Los Angeles*, 93–95.

30 Ibid., 107.

31 Ibid., 39.

32 Albrecht, *Designing Dreams*, xii.

33 Ibid.

34 Andersen, *Los Angeles Plays Itself*.

35 Banham, *Los Angeles*, 42.

36 For further reading on Rancière, see Steinberg, Walter Benjamin and the Demands of History.

37 Tweedie, "The Painted Backing and Its Afterlives," 25.

38 Ainsworth, "Effort Speeded to Save Mansion"; Meyer, "At the Edge of Her Time," 17.

39 Shiel, *Hollywood Cinema and the Real Los Angeles*, 91.

40 Ibid., 163.

41 Jacobson, *Studios Before the System*, 89.

42 Ibid., 119.

43 Ibid., 198.

44 Karlstrom, "Los Angeles in the 1940s," 303. The Ennis House is significant for its role in Los Angeles film history, appearing in films such as *House*

on *Haunted Hill* (1959), *The Day of the Locust* (1975), *Blade Runner* (1982), *The Rocketeer* (1991), and the television series *Buffy the Vampire Slayer* (1997–2003).

45 Ibid.
46 Rudolph Schindler, "Moderne Architektur: Ein Programm" (1912), cited in Sweeney and Sheine, *Schindler*, 10.
47 Noever, *Schindler by MAK*, 10.
48 Ibid., 12.
49 Rudolph Schindler, "Moderne Architektur: Ein Programm" (1912), cited in Sweeney and Sheine, *Schindler*.
50 Quoted in Klein, *The History of Forgetting*, 45.
51 Lavin, "Richard Neutra and the Psychology of the American Spectator," 47.
52 Albrecht, *Designing Dreams*, 13.
53 Shiel, *Hollywood Cinema and the Real Los Angeles*, 204.
54 Banham, *Los Angeles*, 83.
55 Smith, *Case Study Houses*.
56 Ibid., 18
57 Ibid., 13.
58 Ibid., 39, 61.
59 Ibid., 76.
60 Albrecth, *Designing Dreams: Modern Architecture in the Movies*, 78.
61 Ibid.
62 Quoted in LoBrotto, "Lawrence G. Paull," 9.
63 Ibid., 12.

Chapter 7

1 Andersen, *Los Angeles Plays Itself*.
2 James, *The Most Typical Avant-Garde*, 9.
3 Latsis, "The City View(ed)," 205.
4 Davis, *City of Quartz*, 24.
5 Hise, *Magnetic Los Angeles*, 9.
6 Lent, "The Dark Side of the Dream," 331.
7 Quoted in ibid., 129.
8 Banham, *Los Angeles*, 195.
9 Rocchi, "Interview."
10 Bryant, *Onto-Cartography*, 124.
11 Shiel, *Hollywood Cinema and the Real Los Angeles*, 70.

12 Though not shown in Anderson's film, the films of John Garfield (1946's *The Postman Always Rings Twice* in particular) are referenced throughout the novel in a manner that reveals a clash between the old and the new that was mirrored in Hollywood politics at the time.

13 Glick, *Los Angeles Documentary*, 42.

14 Ibid., 50. Paul Rotha was a British film theorist and documentary filmmaker operating largely during the 1920s and 1930s.

15 *Collateral*, DVD, "Making of" featurette: Michael Mann explains why he shot most of the film on digital.

16 Quoted in Brook, *Land of Smoke and Mirrors*, 127. For further reading, see Holm, *Film Soleil*.

17 Batchelor, *Chromophobia*, 22.

18 Polanski, *Roman by Polanski*, 348.

19 Landauer, *California Impressionists*, 29.

20 It is interesting to note that the original music video for the Doors' song "L.A. Woman" (directed by the band's keyboard player, Ray Manzarek) features visuals that are strikingly similar to this sequence from *L.A. Takedown*.

21 Rocchi, "Interview."

22 Karlstrom, "Los Angeles in the 1940s," 306.

23 Ibid., 314.

24 Ibid., 315.

25 Ibid., 314.

26 For further reading, see Hackman's *Out of Sight*.

27 Banham, *Los Angeles*, 19–20.

28 Newman, *Nightmare Movies*, 24.

29 Quoted in Cooper, *Reyner Banham Loves Los Angeles*.

30 Allan, "Ed Ruscha, Pop Art, and Spectatorship," 231.

31 Ibid., 232.

32 For further reading, see also Martin-Jones, "Globalization's Action Crystals."

33 Davis, *Ecology of Fear*, 277.

34 For further reading, see Jameson, "On Magic Realism in Film."

35 Davis, *Ecology of Fear*, 291.

36 Ibid.

37 McWilliams, *Southern California*, 21–48.

38 Banham, *Los Angeles*, 154.

39 Quoted in McRoy, "Italian Neo-realist Influences," 40.

40 Massood, *Black City Cinema*, 107.

41 Masilela, "The Los Angeles School of Black Filmmakers," 103.

42 Banham, *Los Angeles*, 155.

43 Ibid.

44 Davis, *Ecology of Fear*, 359.

45 Brook, *Land of Smoke and Mirrors*, 142.

46 Klein, *The History of Forgetting*, 94.

47 Quoted in LoBrutto, "Lawrence G. Paull," 171.

48 Ibid., 169.

49 Ibid., 171.

50 Klein, *The History of Forgetting*, 95.

51 Towne, "It's Only L.A. Jake."

52 McWilliams, *Southern California*, 204.

53 Burgoyne, *The Hollywood Historical Film*, 125.

54 Andersen, *Los Angeles Plays Itself*.

55 For further reading, see Kaplan, *Trauma Culture*.

56 Pynchon, *Inherent Vice*.

57 Stanley, "In the Country of the Dream."

58 Klein, *The History of Forgetting*, 3.

59 Shiel, *Hollywood Cinema and the Real Los Angeles*, 70.

60 Ibid., 69.

Bibliography

Adamson, Paul. *Eichler: Modernism Rebuilds the American Dream*. Salt Lake City: Gibbs Smith, 2002.

Afra, Kia. "Seventeen Happy Days in Hollywood: Selig Polyscope's Promotional Campaign for *The Movie Special* of July 1915." *Film History* 22, no. 2 (2010): 199–218.

Ainsworth, Ed. "Effort Speeded to Save Mansion." *Los Angeles Times*, September 29, 1963.

Albrecht, Donald. *Designing Dreams: Modern Architecture in the Movies*. Santa Monica: Hennessey and Ingalls, 1986.

Allan, Ken D. "Ed Ruscha, Pop Art, and Spectatorship in 1960s Los Angeles." *Art Bulletin* 92, no. 3 (September 2010): 231–49.

All-Year-Round Club of California. *Southern California through the Camera* (1929). Huntington Library Special Collections, Pasadena, CA.

Andersen, Thom. *Los Angeles Plays Itself*. 2003. Released by Cinema Guild, 2014.

Alton, John. *Painting with Light*. Los Angeles: University of California Press, 2013. (Originally published in 1949.)

Anderson, Benedict. *Imagined Communities: Reflections on the Origin and Spread of Nationalism*. New York: Verso, 1983.

Anderson, Susan M. *Modern Spirit: The Group of Eight and Los Angeles Art of the 1920s*. Laguna Art Museum Exhibition, June 2021. Laguna Art Museum Exhibition Archives.

Avila, Jacqueline. "El Espectáculo: The Culture of the Revistas in Mexico City and Los Angeles, 1900–1940." In *Cinema between Latin America and Los Angeles: Origins to 1960*, edited by Colin Gunckel, Jan-Christopher Horak, and Lisa Jarvinen. New Brunswick: Rutgers University Press, 2019.

Bahr, Ehrhard. Weimar *Weimar on the Pacific: German Exile Culture in Los Angeles and the Crisis of Modernism*. Berkeley: University of California Press, 2007.

Banham, Reyner. *Los Angeles: The Architecture of Four Ecologies*. Los Angeles: University of California Press, 2009.

Batchelor, David. *Chromophobia*. London: Reaktion Books, 2000.

Bazin, André. "The Ontology of the Photographic Image." Translated by Hugh Gray. In *What Is Cinema?* Vol. 1. Berkeley: University of California Press, 2004. (Originally published in 1967.)

Bean, Jennifer. "The Imagination of Early Hollywood: Movie-land and the Magic Cities, 1914–1916." In *Early Cinema and the National*, edited by Richard Abel, Giorgio Bertellini, and Rob King. Bloomington: Indiana University Press, 2016.

Bengstrom, John. *Silent Traces: Discovering Early Hollywood through the Films of Charlie Chaplin*. Santa Monica: Santa Monica Press, 2006.

Benjamin, Walter. "A Short History of Photography." In *Walter Benjamin: An Introduction to his Work and Thought*, by Uew Steiner. Translated by Michael Winkler. Chicago: University of Chicago Press, 2010.

Berg, A. Scott. "Louis B. Mayer: MGM's Archetypical Studio Head at Home." *Architectural Digest*, April 1990, 144–45.

Bingham, Edwin R. *Charles F. Lummis: Editor of the Southwest*. Pasadena: Huntington Library Press, 2006. (Originally published in 1955.)

Bowser, Eileen. *The Transformations of Cinema, 1907–1915*. Berkeley: University of California Press, 1994.

Boym, Svetlana. *The Future of Nostalgia*. New York: Basic, 2001.

Braddock, Alan, and Karl Kusserow. *Nature's Nation: American Art and Environment*. Princeton: Princeton University Press, 2018.

Brevern, Jan Von. "Two or Three Things Photography Did to Painting." In *Photography and Other Media in the Nineteenth Century*, edited by Nicoletta Leonardi and Simon Natale. University Park: Pennsylvania State University Press, 2018.

Brewster, Ben, and Lea Jacobs. *Theater to Cinema: Stage Pictorialism and the Early Feature Film*. Oxford: Oxford University Press, 1997.

Bronfen, Elisabeth. *Specters of War: Hollywood's Engagement with Military Conflict*. New Brunswick: Rutgers University Press, 2012.

Brook, Vincent. *Land of Smoke and Mirrors: A Cultural History of Los Angeles*. New Brunswick: Rutgers University Press, 2013.

Browne, Charles Francis. "Some Recent Landscapes by William Wendt." *Brush and Pencil* 6 (1900).

Bruno, Giuliana. *Atlas of Emotion: Journeys in Art, Architecture, and Film*. New York: Verso, 2002.

Bryant, Levi R. *Onto-Cartography: An Ontology of Machines and Media*. Edinburgh: Edinburgh University Press, 2014.

Burgoyne, Robert. *The Hollywood Historical Film*. Oxford: Blackwell, 2008.

Camp, Stacey Lynn. "From Nuisance to Nostalgia: The Historical Archaeology of Nature Tourism in Southern California, 1890–1940." *Historical Archaeology* 47, no. 3 (2013): 81–96.

Carr, Harry. Los Angeles: *City of Dreams*. New York: D. Appelton-Century, 1935.

Clarke, Charles G. *Early Film Making in Los Angeles*. Los Angeles: Dawson's Bookshop, 1976.

Comment, Bernard. *The Panorama*. London: Reaktion Books, 1999.

Conley, Tom. *Cartographic Cinema*. Minneapolis: University of Minnesota Press, 2007.

Cooper, Julian, dir. *Reyner Banham Loves Los Angeles*. One Pair of Eyes Series. BBC Production, 1972.

Corn, Wanda M. *The Color of Mood: American Tonalism, 1880–1910*. San Francisco: M. H. de Young Memorial Museum, 1972.

Crary, Jonathan. *Techniques of the Observer: On Vision and Modernism in the Nineteenth Century*. Boston: MIT Press, 1992.

Curtis, William Albert. "The First Theater in California." *Out West* 28 (1908).

Danks, Adrian. "A Man out of Time: John Boorman and Lee Marvin's *Point Blank*." *Senses of Cinema* 45 (November 2007).

Davidson, Joe. *Fruit Crate Art*. Cape Cod: Wellfleet, 1990.

Davis, Mike. *City of Quartz: Excavating the Future in Los Angeles*. New York: Verso, 1990.

———. *Ecology of Fear: Los Angeles and the Imagination of Disaster*. New York: Vintage Books, 1998.

Davis, Keith. *Timothy H. O'Sullivan: The King of Survey Photographs*. New Haven: Yale University Press, 2011.

Davis, Susan G. "Landscapes of Imagination: Tourism in Southern California." *Pacific Historical Review* 68, no. 2 (May 1999): 173–91.

DeLyser, Dydia. "Ramona Memories: Tourist Practices, and Placing the Past in Southern California." *Annals of the Association of American Geographers* 93, no. 4 (2003): 886–908.

Diaz, David R. *Barrio Urbanism: Chicanos, Planning, and American Cities*. New York: Routledge, 2005.

Duncan, Calvin L., Julie L. King, and Jay F. Kirkpatrick. "Romance without Responsibilities: The Use of lmunocontraceptive Porcine Zona Pellicida to Manage Free-Ranging Bison on Catalina Island." *Journal of Zoo and Wildlife Medicine* 44, no. 4 (December 2013): 123–31.

Erish, Andrew A. *Col. William N. Selig: The Man Who Invented Hollywood*. Austin: University of Texas Press, 2012.

Famous Players–Lasky Corporation. *The Story of Famous Players Lasky* (1919). Behrendt Manuscript Collection, Seaver Center Archives, Los Angeles, CA.

Farmer, Jared. *Trees in Paradise: The Botanical Conquest of California*. Berkeley: Heydey, 2017.

Fearing, Franklin. "Outside the Studio Gates." *Hollywood Quarterly*. 2, no. 1 (October 1946): 102–4.

Fine, David M. *Imagining Los Angeles: A City in Fiction*. Las Vegas: University of Nevada Press, 2000.

Fogelson, Robert M. *The Fragmented Metropolis: Los Angeles, 1850–1930*. Los Angeles: University of California Press, 1993.

Garcia, Desirée. "Ramona in the City: Mexican Los Angeles, Dolores del Rio, and the Making of a Mythic Story." In *Cinema between Latin America and Los Angeles: Origins to 1960*, edited by Colin Gunckel, Jan-Christopher Horak, and Lisa Jarvinen. New Brunswick: Rutgers University Press, 2019.

Glick, Joshua. *Los Angeles Documentary and the Production of Public History, 1958–1977*. Oakland: University of California Press, 2018.

Gray, Andrea. *Ansel Adams: An American Place, 1936*. Tucson: Center for Creative Photography, 1983.

Gray, Jonathan. *Show Sold Separately: Promos, Spoilers, and Other Media Paratexts*. New York: NYU Press, 2010.

Green, Tyler. *Carleton Watkins: Making the West America*. Oakland: University of California Press, 2018.

Gunckel, Colin. *Mexico on Main Street: Transnational Film Culture in Los Angeles Before World War II*. New Brunswick: Rutgers University Press, 2015.

Gunckel, Colin, Jan-Christopher Horak, and Lisa Jarvinen, eds. *Cinema between Latin America and Los Angeles: Origins to 1960*. New Brunswick: Rutgers University Press, 2019.

Gunning, Tom. "The Cinema of Attractions: Early Film, Its Spectator, and the Avant-Garde." In *The Cinema of Attractions Reloaded*. Amsterdam: Amsterdam University Press, 2006.

Hackman, William. *Out of Sight: The Los Angeles Art Scene of the Sixties*. New York: Other Press, 2015.

Hall, Barbara. "Oh Pioneers! The Academy's Embrace of Early Film History, 1945–51." *Moving Image: The Journal of the Associated Moving Image Archivists* 13, no. 1 (Spring 2013): 185–93.

Hallett, Hillary A. *Go West, Young Women! The Rise of Early Hollywood*. Los Angeles: University of California Press, 2013.

Hariman, Robert, and John Luis Lucaites. *No Caption Needed: Iconic Photographs, Public Culture, and Liberal Democracy*. Chicago: University of Chicago Press, 2007.

Harrison, Rebecca. *From Steam to Stream: Cinema, Railways, and Modernity*. London: Bloomsbury, 2018.

Hendricks, Gordon. *Albert Bierstadt: Painter of the American West*. New York: Crescent, 1988.

Hernendez, Mike, Bill Cone, and Sharon Calahan. "How *Plein Air* Painting Influences the Movie Industry." *Plein Air podcast*, May 13, 2019.

Hines, Thomas S. *Richard Neutra and the Search for Modern Architecture*. New York: Oxford University Press, 1982.

Hise, Greg. *Magnetic Los Angeles: Planning the Twentieth Century Metropolis*. Baltimore: Johns Hopkins University Press, 1997.

Hobart, Christy. "Life within a Fairy Tale." *Los Angeles Times*, January 13, 2005.

Holm, D. K. *Film Soleil*. Harpenden: Oldcastle Books, 2005.

Hornby, Louise. *Still Modernism: Photography, Literature, Film*. New York: Oxford University Press, 2017.

Huddleston, John. *Killing Ground: Photographs of the Civil War and the Changing American Landscape*. Baltimore: Johns Hopkins University Press, 2004.

Ivakhiv, Adrian J. *Ecologies of the Moving Image: Cinema, Affect, Nature*. Waterloo: Wilfrid Laurier University Press, 2013.

Jackson, Helen Hunt. *Ramona*. Boston: Little, Brown, 1884.

Jacobson, Brian R. "Fantastic Functionality: Studio Architecture and the Visual Rhetoric of Early Hollywood." *Film History: An International Journal* 26, no. 2 (2014).

———. *Studios Before the System: Architecture, Technology, and the Emergence of Cinematic Space.* New York: Columbia University Press, 2015.

James, David E. *The Most Typical Avant-Garde: History and Geography of Minor Cinemas in Los Angeles.* Los Angeles: University of California Press, 2005.

Jameson, Frederic. "On Magic Realism in Film." *Critical Inquiry* 12, no. 2 (Winter 1986): 301–25.

Jones, Harvey L. *Twilight and Reverie: California Tonalist Painting.* Oakland: Oakland Museum, 1995.

Kanellos, Nicolas. "A Brief History of Hispanic Periodicals in the United States." In *Hispanic Periodicals in the United States, Origins to 1960: A Brief History and Comprehensive Bibliography,* edited by Nicholas Kanellos and Helvetia Martell. Houston: Arte Publico, 2000.

Kaplan, E. Ann. *Trauma Culture: The Politics of Terror and Loss in Media and Literature.* New Brunswick: Rutgers University Press, 2005.

Karlstrom, Paul J. "Los Angeles in the 1940s: Post-modernism and the Visual Arts." *Southern California Quarterly,* Winter 1987, 301–28.

Keil, Charlie. *Early American Cinema in Transition: Story, Style, and Filmmaking, 1907–1913.* Madison: University of Wisconsin Press, 2002.

Keyes, Donald D. "From Giverny to Laguna Beach." In *California Impressionists.* Irvine: Irvine Museum, 1996.

Kilston, Lyra. *Sun Seekers: The Cure of California.* Los Angeles: Atelier, 2019.

Kirk, Anthony. "Picturing California." *California History* 76, nos. 2/3 (Summer/ Fall 1997): 357–74.

Klein, Norman M. *The History of Forgetting: Los Angeles and the Erasure of Memory.* New York: Verso, 2008.

Klinger, Barbara. *Beyond the Multiplex: Cinema, New Technologies, and the Home.* Berkeley: University of California Press, 2006.

Knutson, Robert. "Reviewed Works: Early Filmmaking in Southern California." *Southern California Quarterly* 58, no. 4 (Winter 1976): 534–35.

Landauer, Susan. *California Impressionists.* Irvine: Irvine Museum, 1996.

Latsis, Dimitrios. "The City View(ed): Muybridge's Panoramas of San Francisco and Their Afterlives in Early Cinema." In *The Image in Early Cinema: Form and Material,* edited by Scott Curtis, Phillipe Gauthier, Tom Gunning, and Joshua Yumibe. Bloomington: Indiana University Press, 2018.

Lavin, Sylvia. "Richard Neutra and the Psychology of the American Spectator." *Grey Room,* no. 1 (Autumn 2000): 42–63.

Lent, Tina Olson. "The Dark Side of the Dream: The Image of Los Angeles in Film Noir." *Southern California Quarterly* 69, no. 4 (Winter 1987): 329–48.

Levin, Gail. *Synchromism and American Color Abstraction, 1910–1925*. New York: Whitney Museum of American Art, 1978.

LoBrutto, Vincent. "Lawrence G. Paull." In *By Design*. Westport, CT: Praeger, 1992.

Los Angeles Theatrical and Amusement Guide (1906). Motion Picture Archives, Seaver Center, Natural History Museum of Los Angeles County, Los Angeles.

Lummis, Charles Fletcher. *A Tramp across the Continent*. New York: C. Scribner and Sons, 1892.

Mack, Mark. Introduction to *Schindler, Kings Road, and Southern California Modernism*, edited by Robert Sweeney and Judith Sheine. Berkeley: University of California Press, 2012.

Marshall, Colin. "Negative Appeal with Vincent Brook." *Notebook on Cities and Culture* podcast, February 28, 2013. Available on iTunes.

Martin-Jones, David. "Globalization's Action Crystals: Los Angeles in Michael Mann's Blockbusters." In *Delueze in World Cinemas*. New York: Continuum, 2011.

Masilela, Ntongela. "The Los Angeles School of Black Filmmakers." In *Black American Cinema*, edited by Manthia Diawara. New York: Routledge, 1993.

Massood, Paula. *Black City Cinema: African American Urban Experiences in Film*. Philadelphia: Temple University Press, 2003.

McCarroll, Stacey. *California Dreaming: Camera Clubs and the Pictorial Photography Tradition*. Boston: Boston University Art Gallery, 2004.

McClelland, Gordon T. *Emil Kosa Jr*. Beverly Hills: Hillcrest, 1990.

McClelland, Gordon T., and Jay T. Last. *The California Style: California Watercolor Artists, 1925–1955*. Beverly Hills: Hillcrest, 2002.

———. *California Watercolors: 1850–1970*. Beverly Hills: Hillcrest 2002.

McGroarty, John S. *California: Its History and Romance*. Los Angeles: Grafton, 1911.

McKinney, John. "Nordhoff Peak Is Challenge." *Los Angeles Times*, December 30, 1989.

McManus, Michael P. "A Focus on Light." In *California Light, 1900–1930*, edited by Patricia Trenton and William H. Gerdts. Laguna Beach: Laguna Beach Art Museum, 1990.

McRoy, Jay. "Italian Neo-realist Influences." In *New Punk Cinema*, edited by
   Nicholas Rombes. Edinburgh: Edinburgh University Press, 2005.

McWilliams, Carey. *Southern California: An Island on Land*. Santa Barbara:
   Peregrine Smith, 1973. (Originally published in 1946.)

Meyer, Kimberli. "At the Edge of Her Time." In *Sympathetic Seeing: Esther
   McCoy and the Heart of American Modernist Architecture and Design*. Los
   Angeles: MAK Center for Art and Architecture, 2011.

Moure, Nancy. "The Struggle for a Los Angeles Art Museum, 1890–1940."
   Southern California Quarterly 74, no. 3 (Fall 1992): 247–75.

Neutra, Richard. *Survival through Design*. New York: Oxford University Press,
   1954.

Newman, Kim. *Nightmare Movies: Horror on Screen since the 1960s*. London:
   Bloomsbury, 2011.

Nickel, Douglas R. *Carleton Watkins: The Art of Perception*. New York: Henry
   Abrams, 1999.

Noever, Peter, ed. *Schindler by MAK*. Los Angeles: MAK Prestel, 2005.

Nordhoff, Charles. *California for Health, Pleasure, and Residence*. New York:
   Harper Brothers, 1873.

Novak, Daniel A. *Realism, Photography, and Nineteenth-Century Fiction*. Cambridge: Cambridge University Press, 2012.

Oettermann, Stephan. *The Panorama: History of a Mass Medium*. Princeton:
   Princeton University Press/Zone Books, 1997.

Ogihara, Junko. "The Exhibition of Films for Japanese Americans in Los Angeles during the Silent Film Era." *Film History* 4 (1990): 81–87.

Olsson, Jan. *Los Angeles Before Hollywood: Journalism and American Film Culture,
   1905–1915*. Stockholm: Kristianstads Boktryckeri, 2008.

Ovnick, Merry. "The Mark of Zorro: Silent Film's Impact on 1920s Architecture in Los Angeles." *California History* 86, no. 1 (2008): 28–64.

Payne, Edgar. *Composition of Outdoor Painting*, Los Angeles: Payne Studios/
   Derus Fine Art Books, 1941.

Polanski, Roman. *Roman by Polanski*. New York: William and Morrow, 1984.

Pollack, Peter. *Edward Weston Papers*. Compiled by Amy Stark. Tucson: Center
   for Creative Photography, 1956.

Pynchon, Thomas. *Inherent Vice*. London: Penguin, 2009.

Richardson, F. H. *Motion Picture Handbook: A Guide for Managers and Operators
   of Motion Picture Theaters*. 3rd ed. New York: Moving Picture World, 1916.

Riley, Charles A. *Color Codes: Modern Theories of Color in Philosophy, Painting and Architecture, Literature, Music, and Psychology*. Hanover: University of New England Press, 1995.

Rocchi, James. "Interview: 'Nightcrawler' Director Dan Gilroy Talks Jake Gyllenhaal, Robert Elswit, and Sociopaths." *IndieWire*, October 29, 2014.

Rositzka, Eileen. *Cinematic Corpographies: Remapping the War Film through the Body*. Berlin: De Gruyter, 2018.

Rothman, William. "Film, Modernity, Cavell." In *Cinema and Modernity*, edited by Murray Pomerance. New Brunswick: Rutgers University Press, 2006.

Royal, Lee. *The Romance of Motion Picture Production*. Los Angeles: Royal, 1920.

Rubin, James H. *Impressionism and the Modern Landscape: Productivity, Technology, and Urbanization from Manet to Van Gogh*. Los Angeles: University of California Press, 2008.

Russeth, Andrew. "The Los Angeles Home That Defined Modern Art." *Architectural Digest*, September 2020.

Salvator, Ludwig. *Eine Blume aus dem Goldenen Lande oder Los Angeles*. Los Angeles: Jake Zeitlin, 1929. (Originally published in 1878.)

Sandberg, Mark B. "Location, Location: On the Plausibility of Place Substitution." In *Silent Cinema and the Politics of Space*, edited by Jennifer Bean, Anupama Kapse, and Lauren Horak. Bloomington: Indiana University Press, 2014.

Sandweiss, Martha A. *Print the Legend: Photography and the American West*. New Haven: Yale University Press, 2002.

Schad, Jaspar. "An Art-Hungry People: The Impact of Progressivism, World War I, and the Panama Pacific International Exposition on Art in Los Angeles, 1915–1930." *Southern California Quarterly* 97, no. 4 (Winter 2015).

Schumach, Murray. "First Film House is the Victim of Time." *New York Times*, April 17, 1962.

Scott, Allen J. *On Hollywood: The Place, the Industry*. Princeton: Princeton University Press, 2005.

Seares, Mabey Urmy. "William Wendt." *American Magazine of Art* 7, no. 6 (April 1916): 232–35.

Shiel, Mark. *Hollywood Cinema and the Real Los Angeles*. London: Reaktion Books, 2012.

Smith, Christina M. "Representations of Class from a 'Grunt's-Eye View' in Soldier-filmed Iraq War Documentaries." Paper presented at American War

Cinema since Vietnam: Politics, Ideology, and Class, Society for Cinema and Media Studies conference, Chicago, March 6, 2013.

Smith, Elizabeth A. T. *Case Study Houses*. Koln: Taschen, 2006.

Soja, Edward. *Thirdspace: Journeys to Los Angeles and Other Real-and-Imagined Places*. Oxford: Blackwell, 1996.

Southern California Holiday (1953). Atchison, Topeka, and Santa Fe Railway Film Collection. Kansas State Historical Society, Topeka.

Stam, Robert, Robert Burgoyne, and Sandy Flitterman-Lewis. *New Vocabularies in Film Semiotics: Structuralism, Post-Structuralism, and Beyond*. New York: Routledge, 1992.

Stanley, Ben. "In the Country of the Dream: On Cliff Booth, John Wayne, and Joan Didion." *Bright Lights Film Journal*, July 21, 2021.

Starr, Kevin. *Inventing the Dream: California through the Progressive Era*. New York: Oxford University Press, 1986.

Steinberg, Michael P., ed. *Walter Benjamin and the Demands of History*. Ithaca: Cornell University Press, 1996.

Stern, Jean. "The California Impressionist Style in Perspective." In *California Impressionists*. Irvine: Irvine Museum, 1996.

———. *Windows in Time: California Scene Paintings from the Hilbert Collection*. Orange: California Scene, 2015.

Stern, Jean, and Molly Siple. *California Light: A Century of Landscapes*. New York: Rizzoli, 2011.

Street, Sarah, and Joshua Yumibe. *Chromatic Modernity: Color, Cinema, and Media of the 1920s*. New York: Columbia University Press, 2019.

Sweeney, Robert, and Judith Sheine. *Schindler, Kings Road, and Southern California Modernism*. Berkeley: University of California Press, 2012.

Terry, Alice T. "Moving Pictures and the Deaf." *Silent Worker* 30 (June 1918): 154.

Theisen, Earl. "Meet Screen Show's Granddaddy." *International Photographer*, August 1932, 27.

Tichenor, Brian. "The Landscape Designs of Ralph Cornell." *California and the West Series* podcast, November 17, 2017. Huntington Library, Pasadena, CA.

A Tour of the Thomas H. Ince Studios (1920). UCLA Film and Television archive, Los Angeles.

Towne, Robert. "It's Only L.A. Jake." *Los Angeles Times*, May 29, 1994.

Tweedie, James. *Moving Pictures, Still Lives: Film, New Media, and the Late Twentieth Century*. New York: Oxford University Press, 2018.

———. "The Painted Backing and Its Afterlives." Paper presented at the Society for Cinema and Media Studies conference, Seattle, March 15, 2019.

Venis, Linda. "L.A. Novels and the Hollywood Dream Factory: Popular Art's Impact on Los Angeles Literature in the 1940s." *Southern California Quarterly* 69, no. 4 (Winter 1987): 349–69.

Verheoff, Nanna. "Virtual Museums." In *The West in Early Cinema*. Amsterdam: Amsterdam University Press, 2006.

Virilio, Paul. *War and Cinema: The Logistics of Perception*. London: Verso, 1989.

Warner, Charles Dudley. *Our Italy*. New York: Harper Brothers, 1891.

Watts, Jennifer. "Photography in the Land of Sunshine: Photography and the Regional Ideal." *Southern California Quarterly* 87, no. 4 (Winter 2005–6): 339–76.

Welsh, Robert E. *A-B-C of Motion Pictures*. New York: Harper Brothers, 1916.

West, Nathaniel. *The Day of the Locust*. New York: New Directions, 2009. (Originally published in 1939.)

Weston, Edward. *Seeing California with Edward Weston*. Los Angeles: Westways, Automobile Club of Southern California, 1939.

Williams, Bruce. "The Bridges of Los Angeles County: Marketing Language in the Chicano Cinema of Gregory Nava." *Canadian Journal of Film Studies* 14, no. 2 (Fall 2005): 54–70.

Wolfe, Charles. "California Landscapes: John Divola and the Cine-Geography of Serial Photography." In *The Image in Early Cinema: Form and Material*, edited by Scott Curtis, Phillipe Gauthier, Tom Gunning, and Joshua Yumibe. Bloomington: Indiana University Press, 2018.

Wright, William Huntington. *Modern Painting: Its Tendency and Meaning*. New York: Dodd, Mead, 1927.

Yumibe, Joshua. "The Color Image." In *The Image in Early Cinema: Form and Material*, edited by Scott Curtis, Phillipe Gauthier, Tom Gunning, and Joshua Yumibe. Bloomington: Indiana University Press, 2018.

Index

Note: Page numbers appearing in italics refer to photographs.